Terrorism has no Religion

TERRORISM HAS NO RELIGION

Dr. R.N. Trivedi

MD PUBLICATIONS PVT LTD
NEW DELHI
www.mdppl.com

Published by :

MD Publications Pvt Ltd
"MD House", 11, Darya Ganj,
New Delhi - 110 002
Phone : +91-11-41563325 (Customer Service)
+91-11-41562846 (Editorial)
E-mail (orders): order@mdppl.com
Website: www.mdppl.com

ISBN: 978-81-7533-206-5

Published and Printed by Mr. Pranav Gupta on behalf of **MD Publications Pvt Ltd** at Times Press, New Delhi.

PREFACE

Holy war, suicide bombings, fighting for faith, and killing in the name of God — from Crusaders to terrorists, from sacred shrines to New York City, history is tainted by a grave disease afflicting humankind. All the known religions of the world call for love, peace, tolerance and freedom of belief and mutual understanding and many of the terrorists' acts are committed by people who call themselves religious, and attribute their horrendous and evil acts to the religion. However, God condemns their acts in the scripture. There is no religious scripture that does not condemn terrorism. Every righteous person in any religion would condemn such actions regardless of terrorist's race, country or religious background.

All known religions has its own beliefs, rules, regulations, faiths, and they accept "atheism" as a part of human life. Atheism is a part of every religion and by accepting atheism, those religions preach tolerance. When community living is the way of life, tolerance makes such coexistence easier. But the only religion which does not accept atheism is Islam. It preaches Jihad or holy war. When a Muslim kills another human being who doesn't belong to Islam it is not considered as a sin by Islam. Quran preaches it's readers to wage a war against those who act against their religion. The talk of war is itself an evil thing. When combined with religious poison, it becomes a lethal weapon.

Islam is very intense in its preaching and its way of life is tough and the only religion which doesn't allow or tolerate any criticism. Of course Hindu fanatics and Christian fanatics are there. But Hindu fanatics believe in direct attacks both verbal and physical and they retaliate only under intense provocation. Christian fanatics get their religious feelings soothed by converting people to Christianity.

Thus, the love of God is not reserved for people of religious sects or denominations that cling to an exclusive belief of guaranteed "salvation." God's infinite love flows to the charitable, righteous, benevolent, equitable, and the just. Those who recognize their accountability and work towards being good. There are Submitters to the Creator in every faith. They are those who place no limits on their belief in the unseen and impose no judgments on the different forms of striving towards attaining God's mercy. This common striving encourages unity within a diverse group of people who advance their personal strides by learning from one another.

I am very grateful to Mr. Pranav Gupta, Director of MD Publications Pvt Ltd, New Delhi, for his cooperation and support for this book.

Dr. R.N. Trivedi

Contents

	Preface	*v*
1.	Terrorism has no Religion: An Introduction	1
2.	Terrorism and the Irrelevance of Religion	13
3.	Movement against Terrorism	21
4.	Terrorism and Organized Crime	35
5.	Post-Modern Terrorism	79
6.	Religious Foundations of Suicide Bombings	135
7.	Origins of Suicidal Terrorism	167
8.	Religion of Terror	209
9.	Spiritual Jihad against Terrorism	227
10.	Source of Terrorism and Violence	259
	Bibliography	293
	Index	299

1

Terrorism has no Religion

An Introduction

"Terrorism has no religion..."

This is the new slogan spreading fast. Well, this is the proper, much needed secularist approach at this time of crisis...otherwise the already angry mob will go ballistic!

But...I think the time has come to drop our pseudo-secularism and really, really face the harsh truth and take some stern actions. Whenever and wherever there is a terror attack happens, the people who execute such gory attacks are Muslims. Some may be cooked up by a foreign nation for a geographical hold or gain...Some may be cooked up by local politicians for the power gain...Some maybe cooked up by religious fanatics. Whether it's an international conspiracy...or local political conspiracy or religion based one...whatever be the reason, the people who fall prey to this and execute such crusades are Muslims. Can any one of you refuse that? The barbarism known as terrorism, that is so preoccupying the world at present, is the work of ignorant and fanatical people, completely estranged from Qur'anic morality, and who have absolutely nothing to do with religion. The solution to these people and groups who try to carry out their savagery under the mask of religion is the teaching of true Qur'anic morality.

Our responsibility is to be objective and fair handed when examining the issue of terrorism. To be recognize that the overwhelming majority of Muslims around the world are peace-loving and harmonious by their nature. In fact Muslims have suffered too at the hand of terrorists. Over 5,0000 civilians have been murdered by terrorist in Iraq *alone* since 2003.The biased picture painted by the media that terrorism and Islam go together hand in hand is simply not true. The Message Society encourages you to learn about Islam from its original sources the Holy Qur'an and the biography of the Prophet Mohammed and his disciples.

'Mankind! We created you from a man and woman, and made you into families and nations so that you can be acquainted with each other; the noblest of you, in the sight of God, is the best in conduct. When studying any religion it is very essential to examine the original sources of the religion rather than making conclusions on the actions of the followers of that religion. This is because the followers, who are after all humans, will no doubt commit acts that are contrary to the teachings of that religion. Therefore it's very unfair to blame Islam for the crimes and the evil acts that have been carried out by dictators in this day and age in the name of Islam or indeed other religions.

The Religion of Peace

Terror, in its broadest sense, is violence committed against non-military targets for political purposes. To put it another way, targets of terror are entirely innocent civilians whose only crime, in the eyes of terrorists, is to represent "the other side". The word "Islam" is derived from the word meaning "peace" in Arabic. Islam is a religion revealed to mankind with the intention of presenting a peaceable life through which the infinite compassion and mercy of God manifest on earth.

Islam's divine sources are the Qur'an, which is based on concepts of morality, love, compassion, humility, sacrifice, tolerance and peace and the sayings of the Prophet of Islam Mohammed and his Household – peace and blessings be upon them – Any Muslim who lives by those precepts in its true sense will be most polite, careful of thought, modest, just, trustworthy. He will spread love, respect, harmony and the joy of living all around him.

The Values of the Qur'an

The values of the Qur'an hold a Muslim responsible for treating all people, whether Muslim or non-Muslim, kindly and justly, protecting the needy and the innocent and "preventing the dissemination of mischief". Mischief comprises all forms of anarchy and terror that remove security, comfort and peace. As God says in a verse, "God does not love corruption".

Those who think that they will be successful by causing wickedness, upheaval and oppression, and by killing innocent people are committing a great error. God has forbidden all acts of wickedness involving terrorism and violence, condemned those who engage in such acts and said, "God does not uphold the works of those who cause mischief." in one of His verses.

Forcing people to believe in a religion or to adopt its forms of belief is completely contrary to the essence and spirit of Islam. According to Islam, true faith is only possible with free will and freedom of conscience. Of course, Muslims can advise and encourage each other about the features of Qur'anic morality. All believers are charged with explaining Qur'anic morality to people in the nicest manner possible. They will explain the beauties of religion in the light of the verse, "Call to the way of your Lord with wisdom and fair admonition..." .

Carrying out suicide attacks on innocent civilians in the name of Islam is a total violation of the true Islamic doctrine. The only people who do such acts are those who have a very mistaken perception of Islam, have no idea of true Qur'anic morality, fail to use their reason and conscience, are under the influence of evil ideologies, and who have been brainwashed with feelings of hatred and revenge. Everybody must oppose such actions.

What is with us Indians? Why are we so blasé' about terror? Why do terrorists always get the better of us? And continue to rip-off the all-wise smug look of our intelligence set-up? As for our polity, their opinion or vacuous outpourings of grief are just that Vacuous. Why are we so hypocritical and helpless? It would be easy to reiterate Prime Minister Manmohan Singh's words, "Terrorism is the biggest threat ....terrorists doesn't know borders..... We must act with determination to fight terrorism. We cannot lose the battle against ideologies of hatred." Brave words worthy of applause.

How? By endless tough talk on ongoing proactive and crushing terrorism. And if that doesn't sell with the *aam aadmi* cleverly save their skin and deflect criticism by appointing a committee to probe the causes of failure or by promptly initiating a blame game. Enough to satisfy everyone's conscience that each has done his bit for the nation. Remember, we still have to hear the last word on Kargil and Kandhaar. The tragedy of it all is that all this tough talk has so far been no more than so much of hype and hot air.

Especially in an era of symbolic action and manipulative politics right from Kandhaar to Ahmedabad via Kargil, Jaipur, Kabul and Bangalore it's the same words. Only the terminology has changed. So it does not sound like the ad nauseum repeated broken record. Each Government points an accusing finger at its predecessor or its successor. The pot calling the kettle black. It really does not matter. Only the chehra differs. If the Vajpayee-led NDA government has to come to terms with its Kandhaar and Kargil ghosts, the UPA's record is no better.

In the last four-and-half-years not one terrorist has been arrested and no case has been solved. Yet, statistics continue to be reeled out to assure the nation how well the Government is fighting terror. Never mind that nearly 300 of the 670 districts are in the terrorist tentacles. Of these, 70 districts have already been ravaged by terrorists. Is this how we fight terror? The Kandhaar and Kargil have been replaced by Kabul and Bangalore.

What makes matters worse is that sitting in Delhi; the Central Government suffers from the disease or reflex action of out of site, out of mind. The terror is happening in somebody else's backyard. Forgetting that Jharkhand, Bihar, UP, Maharashtra, Karnataka, Gujarat and other States are part of the country called India. Terror has already cost us more than 72,000 civilians and 12,000 security personnel. In the last three years alone, Islamic terrorists have killed 5,617 people. And all the dead and injured are mere statistics lost in the files. Who cares?

Worse, for reasons best known we have communalised terrorism. Borne out by the fact that Afzal Guru, the perpetrator of the attack on India's temple of democracy, Parliament, languishes in jail despite the Supreme Court's order to hang him. Why? Because he is a Muslim and it would send a wrong message to the minority vote bank! Only in India will be seen the strange site of a State (Kashmir) rising in defence of Afzal Guru and wanting his release. The Government watches helplessly and the police told not to unduly question or harass anyone from the minorities.

Clearly the Government does not want to do anything which may even remotely hurt the Muslim sentiment. Or be misconstrued as 'deliberately' singling out a person who belongs to a minority community especially with elections to many State Assemblies later this year. Terrorism or no terrorism. Ignoring the fact that the Muslim clergy too has condemned the terrorists for bringing a bad name to the community.

Forgetting that a terrorist has neither religion nor a caste and the only the religion he knows is to kill. Be it a Hindu militant or a Muslim jehadi. He is faceless. His only belief is to create a psychological fear in the enemies' mind whatever it takes. So how do we get the better of him? By issuing warnings of to act against this heinous crime against humanity. How? One Government dumped TADA with POTA. Its successors dumped POTA as a bad law and instead talked of applying the "healing touch" to the wounds of the misguided youths and bring them around.

Importantly, if anyone should be held guilty for terrorism, which is increasingly reigning havoc in our country, it should be our self-obsessed polity. So long as they are personally secure from the terrorists the rest can go to hell. See how worried are all about getting Z-plus security with it paraphernalia of gun-toting commandos, bullet-proof car, escort car and a sub-inspector to guard one round-the-clock. What to speak of highly securitized homes.

Have they shed even one tear for the innocent thousands killed over the years in terrorist blasts? Or for the valiant security forces and personnel who have laid down their lives so that India can live. No, a big no. What is there to know about terrorism that we haven't suffered over the agonizing years? Just comprehend the widows, orphans and aging parents left in their bloody trail.

The crux of the problem is that the Centre continues to grope in the dark about how to deal with terrorism. What is the end we seek? Sadly, New Delhi is not clear about our policy and strategy. We persist in wallowing in *ad hocism* and live for the moment. Treating the country like a sanitized State, a piece of chocolate that can be relished by a diabetic. In this milieu, India should be declared a disturbed country to counter the *jehadis*. For how long will the Government merely react? Is it not time to think and act?

Even as the UPA Government showcases the Indo-US nuclear deal as its biggest achievement has Manmohan

Singh ever bothered to ask President Bush why is it that no terrorist attack has taken place in the US post 9/11, 2001. What were the ingredients of his war on terror? Or for that matter, UK's Gordon Brown about why no terrorist has dared to blow up the London tube again post 7/7/2005. How did they both create fear in the terrorist mind? Notwithstanding the fact that Osama bin Laden and other extremist organizations supported by him have vowed to seek revenge. Did this deter them from ensuring that their country is free from terrorists?

No country can ever be free of suicide bombers. Who are willing to die for their cause? But unlike the Americans and Britons, who will die for their nation, the tragedy of India is that while our soldiers are willing to die for their country, our political tribe are only interested in somehow living. In fact, the *netagan* care a damn for India. Only about I, me and myself. Statesmanship is only in the memory of a distant past. The common man is caught in the crossfire between blasts and more blast and the *aam aadmis'* cries of anguish gagged by the inane political gibberish.

The sad truth is that terrorist like wanton prostitutes continue to repeatedly rape us. Day after day and month after month. We yell blue murder from the rooftops and pledge to take revenge. Nothing more, nothing less. The tragedy of it all is that the terrorists know that these are the just words. Empty words. After all, what can one expect of 'impotent' leaders? Leaving one with a sinking feeling. We enjoy being raped.

Islam on Terrorism

One of the distinctive characteristics of the times we live in is the overwhelming presence of violence in our societies. Whether it is a bomb going off in a market place, or the hijacking of an aircraft where innocent people are held at ransom to achieve political ends, we live in an age, where the manipulation and loss of innocent lives has become commonplace. Such is the all-pervasive nature of indiscriminate violence, that "terrorism" is considered as one of the prime threats to peace and security in our societies.

The word terrorism came into wide usage only a few decades ago. One of the unfortunate results of this new terminology is that it limits the definition of terrorism to that perpetrated by small groups or individuals. Terrorism, in fact, spans the entire world, and manifests itself in various forms. Its perpetrators do not fit any stereotype. Those who hold human lives cheap, and have the power to expend human lives, appear at different levels in our societies. The frustrated employee who kills his colleagues in cold-blood or the oppressed citizen of an occupied land who vents his anger by blowing up a school bus are terrorists who provoke our anger and revulsion. Ironically however, the politician who uses age-old ethnic animosities between peoples to consolidate his position, the head of state who orders "carpet bombing" of entire cities, the exalted councils that choke millions of civilians to death by wielding the insidious weapon of sanctions, are rarely punished for their crimes against humanity.

It is this narrow definition of terrorism that implicates only individuals and groups, that has caused Muslims to be associated with acts of destruction and terror, and as a result, to become victims of hate violence and terror themselves. Sometimes the religion of Islam is held responsible for the acts of a handful of Muslims, and often for the acts of non-Muslims!

Could it be possible that Islam, whose light ended the Dark Ages in Europe, now propound the advent of an age of terror? Could a faith that has over 1.2 billion followers the world over, and over 7 million in America, actually advocate the killing and maiming of innocent people? Could Islam, whose name itself stands for "peace" and "submission to God", encourage its adherents to work for death and destruction? For too long, have we relied on popular images in the media and in Hollywood films, for answers to these pertinent questions? It is now time to look at the sources of Islam, and its history to determine whether Islam does indeed advocate violence.

Sancity of Human Life

The Glorious Qur'an says:

"...take not life, which God hath made sacred, except by way of justice and law: thus doth He command you, that ye may learn wisdom."

Islam considers all life forms as sacred. However, the sanctity of human life is accorded a special place. The first and the foremost basic right of a human being is the right to live. The Glorious Qur'an says:

"...if any one slew a person - unless it be for murder or for spreading mischief in the land - it would be as if he slew the whole people: and if any one saved a life, it would be as if he saved the life of the whole people."

Such is the value of a single human life, that the Qur'an equates the taking of even one human life unjustly, with killing all of humanity. Thus, the Qur'an prohibits homicide in clear terms. The taking of a criminal's life by the state in order to administer justice is required to uphold the rule of law, and the peace and security of the society. Only a proper and competent court can decide whether an individual has forfeited his right to life by disregarding the right to life and peace of other human beings.

Ethics of War

Even in a state of war, Islam enjoins that one deals with the enemy nobly on the battlefield. Islam has drawn a clear line of distinction between the combatants and the non-combatants of the enemy country. As far as the non-combatant population is concerned such as women, children, the old and the infirm, etc., the instructions of the Prophet are as follows: "Do not kill any old person, any child or any woman". "Do not kill the monks in monasteries" or "Do not kill the people who are sitting in places of worship." During a war, the Prophet saw the corpse of a woman lying on the ground and observed, "She was not fighting. How then she came to be killed?" Thus non-combatants are guaranteed security of life even if their state is at war with an Islamic state.

Jihad

While Islam in general is misunderstood in the western world, perhaps no other Islamic term evokes such strong reactions as the word 'jihad'. The term 'jihad' has been much abused, to conjure up bizarre images of violent Muslims, forcing people to submit at the point of the sword. This myth was perpetuated throughout the centuries of mistrust during and after the Crusades. Unfortunately, it survives to this day.

The word Jihad comes from the root word jahada, which means to struggle. So jihad is literally an act of struggling. The Prophet Muhammad (peace be upon him) said that the greatest jihad is to struggle with the insidious suggestions of one's own soul. Thus jihad primarily refers to the inner struggle of being a person of virtue and submission to God in all aspects of life.

Secondarily, jihad refers to struggle against injustice. Islam, like many other religions, allows for armed self-defense, or retribution against tyranny, exploitation, and oppression. The Glorious Qur'an says:

"And why should ye not fight in the cause of God and of those who, being weak, are ill-treated (and oppressed)? Men, women, and children, whose cry is, "Our Lord! Rescue us from this town, whose people are oppressors; and raise for us from thee one who will protect; and raise for us from thee one who will help!"

Thus Islam enjoins upon its believers to strive utmost, in purifying themselves, as well as in establishing peace and justice in the society. A Muslim can never be at rest when she sees injustice and oppression around her. As Martin Luther King Jr. said:

"We will have to repent in this generation not merely for the hateful words and actions of the bad people but for the appalling silence of the good people."

Islam enjoins upon all Muslims to work actively to maintain the balance in which God created everything. However, regardless of how legitimate the cause may be, the Glorious Qur'an never condones the killing of innocent people. Terrorizing the civilian population can never be termed as jihad and can never be reconciled with the teachings of Islam.

Even Western scholars have repudiated the myth of Muslims coercing others to convert. The great historian De Lacy O'Leary wrote:

"History makes it clear, however, that the legend of fanatical Muslims, sweeping through the world and forcing Islam at the point of sword upon conquered races is one of the most fantastically absurd myths that historians have ever repeated."

Muslims ruled Spain for roughly 800 years. During this time, and up until they were finally forced out, the non-Muslims there were alive and flourishing. Additionally, Christian and Jewish minorities have survived in the Muslim lands of the Middle East for centuries. Countries such as Egypt, Morocco, Palestine, Lebanon, Syria, and Jordan all have significant Christian and/or Jewish populations.

This is not surprising to a Muslim, for his faith prohibits him from forcing others to see his point of view. The Glorious Qur'an says:

"Let there be no compulsion in religion, Truth stands out clear from Error, whoever rejects evil and believes in

God hath grasped the most trustworthy hand-hold that never breaks. And God heareth and knoweth all things."

The Great Unifier

Far from being a militant dogma, Islam is a way of life that transcends race and ethnicity. The Glorious Qur'an repeatedly reminds us of our common origin:

"O mankind! We created you from a single (pair) of a male and a female, and made you into nations and tribes, that ye may know each other (not that ye may despise (each other). Verily the most honored of you in the sight of God is (he who is) the most righteous of you. And God has full knowledge and is well acquainted (with all things)."

Thus, it is the universality of its teachings that makes Islam the fastest growing religion in the world. In a world full of conflicts and deep schisms between human beings, a world that is threatened with terrorism, perpetrated by individuals and states, Islam is a beacon of light that offers hope for the future.

2

Terrorism and the Irrelevance of Religion

What is wrong with the world today? One of the root causes of terrorism in the world today is the ruthlessness of capitalism as it is being practised in the world today. The main issue for corporates the world over is to maximise profits at any cost. The main ruse of capitalism is to keep on becoming bigger and bigger so that eventually when there is a global meltdown as is presently happening the governments of the respective countries are forced to bail them out with huge infusion of tax payers money. The second issue for corporates the world over is to maximise profits at any cost.

The most tragic effect of this is the human cost of downsizing the workforce. In the recession currently going on in the world, the primary aim of every business to reduce loses is to cut jobs. How come nobody thinks that a more equitable solution would be to lower the salaries of the top brass which I am sure would more than cover the salaries of the employees due to be sacked. Businesses have reached the stage today that the material assets if the company are more important than the human assets. What happens when jobs are cut? The remaining employees are loaded with extra work. Eventually both the employed and the jobless are stressed out due to overwork or no pay. However the guys who are the promoters and CEOs of publicly traded companies the world over rarely get affected because the promoters liability is limited to the assets of the company and the CEOs get a handsome severance package never mind if they have made the company totally bankrupt!

The joblessness in the developed world now adds to the joblessness in the developing world. Joblessness means no money to live that is where religion comes in:

When a person is jobless and consequently hungry in desperation he will resort to any means to survive. This is when the god men of the major religions of the world come in and brainwash these poor people into believing that religion will solve their problems. The religious leaders of the religions to which they belong, exploit their vulnerability and convince them to do something in the name of their religion so that they can be assured at least of a better life after death (e.g. Heaven, Plenty of Virgins, etc.). They are provided monetary benefits and assured lifetime support for their families.

Furthermore, religion was and is meant to help the human individual spiritually and should never enter the material domain. Unfortunately, the world over, religion has entered politics and business. Common sense tells me that, if the gods of the respective religions are as intelligent and powerful and miraculous as they claim him to be, then we do not need to go through religion to gain access to god but can talk to him directly.

This is precisely what results in:

Most of the elite and page 3 people are totally ignorant when they state that terrorism has no religion. Just look at history. Most of the major wars and terrorist attacks have been waged in the name of religion. Most religions propagate the view that the present life is only a step to life after death, but none have been able to furnish the incontrovertible proof of life after neither death nor any guarantee that life after death will be full of everlasting happiness if you follow the tenets of their respective religions in the present life. What makes it even worse today is that politics and religion are being made dependent on each other, for the simple reason that religion constitutes a substantial vote bank.

Terrorist go on suicide mission in the mistaken belief that if they die for their respective god then they will have everlasting happiness after death. The suicide bombers should wonder why the religious leaders who encourage this really believed this then they would have gone on suicide missions themselves. But then the terror recruits are never allowed to think rationally. Throughout history you can see that more people have been killed in the name of religion then for any other causes, because religious leaders have misled their followers in the reward of a fantastic life after death which, to date, has never been proven beyond reasonable doubt.

So, in conclusion, will terrorism ever be eradicated? Certainly not! Why not? Only if:

1. Capitalism has a more equitable sharing of wages from the top to the bottom rung.
2. Democracy makes way for appointment of professionals on merit.
3. Politics is abolished and governance is on the basis of merit.
4. All religions should tell the real truth that they do not know about life after death and agree to delete the offending chapters in their books about nonbelievers of their respective religion.
5. The fact is accepted that terrorism has everything to do with religion.

I do not see the possibility of any of the above happening in remaining part of my lifespan because there is no longer any rational way of doing things. None of the leaders in the religious, corporate and the government today have the stature and ability to stand up to the irrationality of the way the human race is behaving lest they lose their cozy positions. The only way out is to pray to god directly to make sure that "change is gonna come!"

Money can buy people. If the lure is huge, people can be made to do all kind of anti social activities... even murders. But does poverty alone really have the power to turn a man into a human bomb? Definitely not. Illiteracy is the reason?? Often terrorists are found to be well-educated ones! Sometimes their brilliance even surpasses all others. Even some terrorists are illiterate ones; illiteracy alone doesn't have the power to turn a man into a human bomb.

Decades long exploitation of these Muslim countries' wealth and their geographical importance by the West is the root cause of Muslims' anger. But the times have changed. Some Muslim countries are filthy rich! Many Muslims excel in their academics. Rich Muslim countries can help those poor ones who are struggling and thus avoid falling prey to western domination. So...why they are not channeling all these opportunities and their academic brilliance into uplifting their own people, their own countries, instead of using it to plot terror attacks???

Religion is a faith. It's a way of life. It's a discipline. Almost a personal thing. Only because it's followed by millions and billions, religion turns into a huge thing. Though every religion has its own beliefs, rules, regulations, faiths, they also accept "atheism" as a part of it. It's a part of human life. Atheism is a part of every religion. Why atheism is important? Why even religions accept this? Because by accepting atheism, those religions preach tolerance. When community living is the way of life, tolerance makes such co-existence easier.

But the only religion which does NOT accept atheism is Islam. It preaches Jihad. Jihad means holy war! When a

Muslim kills another human being who doesn't belong to Islam, It's not considered as a sin by Islam! Quran preaches it's readers to wage a war against those who act against their religion!! The talk of war is itself an evil thing. When combined with religious poison, it becomes a lethal weapon. What could be 'holy' in this so called war...I wonder? Islam doesn't teach or preach its followers "Tolerance". What kind of religion is this? Quran may have so many other goody goody things in it. But here I recall the old saying a whole barrel of milk can kill hundreds with a mere drop of poison in it.

If 'terrorism has no religion' is true...why every terrorists happens to be a Muslim? What makes these young, handsome, well educated guys turn into a human bombs...make them sacrifice their life itself...all to cause destruction, total destruction...cruel killings of innocent people? Only religion has this kind of psychological power over human mind. By practicing Islath's intense religious rituals with the combination of preaching about one's moral duty turns a religious minded Muslim into a fanatic... and he turns into a human bomb...willingly sacrifice his precious life to do evil things like mass killings, spreading panic and terror among innocent humans. In short, destruction in every form! All in the name of religion!

Islam is very intense in its preaching. Its way of life is tough. The only religion to make it followers prays 5 times a day! The only religion which doesn't allow or tolerate any criticism! Writers who have the audacity to criticize get fatwa! Result? Life long exile and fear for life forever. Why this level of intolerance towards criticism? What could be the better way to teach these writers a lesson and thus by sending out a warning to the rest of the world 'Don't mess with our religion"! This is what I call religious fanaticism!

Tell them not to wear head scarf to school because of the school's rules, and what we see next? A huge turn out on the streets condemning the school for its audacity, it's insensitivity towards their religion. What religion has anything to do with an educational institution? Do any other people who belong to other religions make such silly demands? This is what I call religious fanaticism.

Ask them to restrict their childbirth...again a huge turn out on streets crying hoarse! This is what I call religious fanaticism. Of course Hindu fanatics and Christian fanatics are there. But Hindu fanatics believe in direct attacks both verbal and physical and they retaliate only under intense provocation. Christian fanatics get their religious feelings soothed by converting people to Christianity.

In India…where Hindus live in majority, Media…both electronic and print media, movies can make fun of their religion…that is Hinduism. No one makes a big thing out of it. But Muslims don't even allow a harmless joke... They treat it very seriously...get royally upset, pass resolutions in their madhrassa's meetings, phewwww... real fanatics!

Burka Dutt, a well known journo, asked a Muslim gentleman [who was among the crowd near the Taj to voice their protest over terror attacks] to voice his opinion. He said the main reason for coming there was to stop people from maligning his religion that is Islam... that Islam talks about eternal peace and nothing else! He didn't condemn the attacks all his thoughts were solely on how to save his religion!

But this is not new to us. Whenever there is a terror attack happens, Muslim community come out in huge numbers to talk about unity. They ask the rest of the people to practice unity, practice patriotism, to stay calm, to keep cool, etc. Ok nothing wrong in that and Indians are always ready to practice unity at the time of crisis. With such a diversified population, nothing is better than unity to life as a wholesome and peaceful life. But why no Muslims condemn these terrorists strongly? Why there is no 'Fatwa' passed on these terrorists? Why there is an obvious lack of intensity in voicing their protests or condemnation? Why there are no huge turn outs on streets, protesting against terrorism in the name of Islam? If they can still mourn of December 6th...why not this? Why not even a single Muslim protest against the delay in hanging Afzal Guru?

Rani Khan [a fellow blogger] says that Mumbai attack in an international conspiracy cooked up by Israel and US. Ok...even if it's such, who executed it? A Pak Muslim with lots of help from local Indian Muslims! Had it not been a religious fanatic available to execute such evil attacks, the entire plan would still be in shelf! Muslims need to act fast. The rest of the world is not interested in hearing about the goodness of Islam. We all know every religion has equal dose of good and bad in it. But comparatively, the only religion which breeds hundreds of terrorists and happens to be the breeding ground of all kind of evil things seems to be Islam. High time we quit avoiding this issue. High time we catch the bull by its horn! All we need is peace. Live and let live.

3

Movement against Terrorism

The seminal declaration by the Darul Uloom, one of the most revered Islamic seminaries in the world, denouncing terrorists and rejecting terrorism as being 'un Islamic have far-reaching implications and profound consequences for the Indian polity. Over 4,000 Ulema from across the country representing over 6,000 *madarasas* attended the All India Anti-Terrorism conference at Deoband, near Saharanpur in west Uttar Pradesh.

The Darul Uloom started soon after the national revolt of 1857 as an Arabic school in the Jama Masjid of Deoband. This was converted into an institution of higher learning in 1866. Continuing the anti-British spirit of 1857, the Deobandis, as they are usually called, played an important role in collaboration with Mahatma Gandhi and other leaders in the Indian freedom struggle. Opposing the two-nation theory, they propagated Indian nationalism. Maulana Madani had said, we, the inhabitants of India have one thing in common, and that is our Indian ness in spite of our religious and cultural differences?

At this conference, a fatwa was issued against terrorism. The chief rector of Darul Uloom announced? We don't have any link or association with terrorism, terrorists, whatsoever. The fatwa pointed out that terrorism completely negated the teaching of Islam?, which is the faith of love and peace.

This Deoband declaration should go a long way in removing confusion from the minds of those misguided people who interpret Islamic teachings to suit their fundamentalist positions and motives. The Ulema at Deoband have issued their rejection and renunciation of terrorism on the basis of the same Islam and the Holi Quran which some militants use to justify their unjustifiable and unpardonable acts. The Darul Uloom, which has been known to be a hard line puritanical brand of Islam, was alleged to have inspired the Taliban. Though those at Deoband had always denied any connection or links with the Taliban, the present declaration of jihad against terrorism has emphatically clarified their position.

This has, indeed, come at an important time in the context of the global war against terrorism launched US imperialism. This so-called war had, as its ideological underpinning, theories such as Samuel Huntington's 'Clash of Civilisations or the latter 'The Age of Horrorism' by Martin Amis. This Deoband declaration has reiterated the simple truth that terrorism has no religion. A small band of people genuinely misguided or tempted by mercenary gains often hijack religious sanction as authority.

In the Indian context, the communal forces have often sought political benefit by citing the so-called silence of the Muslim clergy over terrorist violence. This, in the first place, is not true. Muslim organisations and Islamic institutions have often been as alert as anyone else in condemning terrorist violence. In this context, the Darul Uloom, by unequivocally declaring all kinds of terrorism is anti-national and anti-Islamic has made it clear that Muslims reject violence and love peace as much as any other, belonging to other religious affiliations.

India has its own experience with its own varied groups of extremists claiming allegiance to various religions/castes/ regions that have indulged and continue to indulge in violent terrorist activities. These have to be isolated and rejected from our body politic by a determined and united effort that goes beyond the boundaries of any one religion, caste or region. This, however, may not suit the objectives of the communal forces that thrive on generating communal animosity by misusing religious affiliations of the people. This became clear when Advani characterised the 2008-09 budget as being 'communal because it made some measly allocations for improving the welfare of the religious minorities.

The RSS/BJP's opposition to the Sachar Committee recommendations also stem from the same mindset that tends to categorise Indian Muslims as being anti-national. It is the spread of such communal hatred, for the sake of consolidating the majority vote bank to further their political destinies that continue to plague our country and society and divert our attention and energies away from addressing and resolving the more important pressing problems of our people.

This Deoband declaration should, in this context, be of immense value in strengthening the forces of secular democracy in the country and the unity of our multi-religious, multi-lingual, multi-cultural, plural society. Mankind has unequivocally and universally condemned the terrorist attack on the USA on 11 September, 2001 as a crime against humanity, as an outrage against conscience, and expressed its unreserved sympathy for the victims, irrespective of their nationality or religion.

Practically all states have offered, in principle, all possible cooperation to the USA in its resolve to root out terrorism in all its forms and manifestations, from all parts of the globe. Some have joined the USA-led alliance and are privy to its war plans. But while preparing to 'smoke out' Osama bin Laden from his shelter in Afghanistan by all possible means, the USA and its allies have wisely taken note of the criticism of USA goals, immediate and long-term, and of the legality and effectiveness of the methods contemplated.

The USA is now making a distinction between Osama bin Laden, the Afghan people and the Taliban regime, which is still in control of the Afghan territory and commands the allegiance of a majority of the Afghan people, though it is now recognized only by Pakistan. The stated goal of the US military action now no longer mentions bombing Afghanistan 'back to the Stone Age', which would have implied killing of hundreds of thousands of innocent Afghans. It has even disavowed the goal of toppling the Taliban regime, so long as it does not impede the capture of Osama, leaving it to the continuing civil war, which appears to have gathered momentum since 11 September and to the emergence of the ex-King Zahir Shah as the head of an interim national Government.

By delaying military action, the USA is not only trying to ensure the success of its pin-pointed intervention when it comes but also to reduce loss of life and property to the minimum. It has created the impression that it is not acting hastily, in anger or revenge, but executing a well-considered plan to achieve an objective which generally enjoys the overall support of the people of the world. Yet, critical questions remain to be answered. While the USA may have showed the evidence it has to link Osama bin Laden or the Taliban with the terrorist outrage, to its close allies, it is yet to place them before such staunch supporters like Saudi Arabia, Egypt and Pakistan which were to play key role in the USA strategy, and before the people of the world who remain skeptical about the world outreach of an individual, or his terrorist network.

Secondly, the UN Security Council has reiterated no doubt its condemnation of terrorism but has not sanctioned unilateral use of force by the USA. The USA may not care but the world would have been more satisfied if the military operations against Afghanistan were not taken unilaterally but under the UN flag. The basic dilemma is whether US undertakes this operation as right of self-defence under

Article 51, or as the head of a UN collective operation to eliminate a threat to world peace. Self-defence plea by a superpower against an individual looks ridiculous to many people. It is doubtful whether the UN Charter when it was adopted envisaged aggression against sovereign states by individuals or private groups in the form of terrorist strikes.

The UN system is an inter-state system and is designed to deal with the relationship of states with each other which are held accountable for their action and inaction, in the larger interest of world peace and stability. The Charter cannot envisage chasing shadows but responsible and accountable states. What the world needs is a comprehensive UN Convention against Terrorism which obliges states to cooperate politically, economically and militarily, to fight terrorist networks across the globe and defines terrorism to take in acts of terrorism, internal or international, by individuals, groups or states, directed against states or their people, or a section thereof, to overawe them, in order to promote or gain a political objective.

Thirdly, Osama bin Laden has repeatedly linked his hostility to the USA and even his 'Islamic' zeal to the USA military presence in the Arab Peninsula, of which Saudi Arabia occupies nearly 75%, and to the USA policy towards Palestine. While the first factor is not widely known nor does it evoke much reaction, being limited in scope, the second, indeed, is the basic source of the widely prevalent antipathy, nay, hostility, towards the USA throughout the world particularly in the Arab and Muslim world. One hoped that the USA would, at this tragic moment, engage in introspection as to why, despite its unquestionable greatness as the most powerful State in human history, and, its unparalleled contribution to the progress and welfare of mankind in many fields and its generous sharing of its wealth with the stricken people everywhere, it does not command love.

Perhaps, the powerful do not need nor care for love. But the USA must try to understand the genesis of the condensed anger and frozen hatred which motivates fanatics to hurt it, at the cost of their own lives. There is no sign yet that the US has undertaken any review of its long-term policy towards Israel which exists only because of continuous flow of US aid, military and financial, and more so, towards the Palestinian people who have been defrauded at every turn and robbed of their homeland, and today live at the mercy of Israel, like animals in cages! It has even made no attempt to restrain Israel from committing ever-expanding punitive acts against the civil population, which have reached new levels of savagery since 11 September, with anti-Muslim and anti-Arab waves which have surged in the West and even reached our shores. This is an unfortunate development as terrorism has no religion and no habitation. In India, we recognize the many features of terrorism which are not limited to any particular religion or ethnicity or locale.

Also there is no doubt, considerable resentment in many parts of the world towards the hypocrisy implicit in the USA consistently chanting democracy and supporting dictators, evoking freedom and repressing people! USA also comes in for criticism for adopting double standards even in humanitarian situations. But such criticism presupposes the hope and trust the people of the world repose in the capacity of the USA to set things right, to put the world on the right course.

The USA has so far failed to show full consciousness of its moral responsibility as the only superpower today. Terrorism arising out of a deep sense of national grievance or ethnic humiliation or religious persecution cannot be eradicated from the face of the earth through military means but only through political means. People of the world, above all, want peace and justice. They all believe that no cause, howsoever just, can justify the cold-blooded massacre of innocent human beings; they are all prepared to engage the scourge of terrorism in a global campaign but not selectively.

Finally, by focusing so far on Osama bin Laden in the first phase and by arousing but not fulfilling the expectations of other States and peoples which have been targets of terrorism, indigenous as well as imported, for decades, the USA has failed to harness, in full measure, mankind's profound revulsion in the wake of 11 September tragedy. The least that could be done by the US policy planners, by themselves or through the UN system, is to take the initiative to build an international structure against terrorism in all its forms and manifestation and at the same time revive and reinforce the UN machinery to tackle the political roots of terrorism.

Law Relating to Terrorism

The world has witnessed Freedom movements through centuries, but the one that made a mark on history is the Americans war of independence against British initiated during the year 1770 by throwing tea chests off-board the ships in sea at the Boston harbor, resulting in violence, political resistance and war between the British and the American colonists, finally; getting America its independence from the British occupation. Since then and particularly after the first and second world wars number of freedom movements took place in various parts of the world, resulting in creation of number of independent States, in Africa, Middle East and South East Asia from occupation by British, Dutch, Portuguese and Spanish Empires. Similarly, after the fall of Soviet Empire again through freedom movements' number of countries have emerged as independent countries in Eastern Europe and Central Asia, but none of these freedom movements was classified as terrorism. The Northern Ireland violent freedom movement from Britain both within Northern Ireland and also in Britain has been going on for almost half a century. Those responsible for freedom movement adopted militant and guerilla action wherever possible, yet at no point of time the movements or actions on the part of IRA classified as terrorism, nor did the British Government declare a war or take military action against Northern Ireland.

There does not appear to be any specific law relating to freedom movements. However, the United Nation Charter states one of its purposes is to promote and encourage respect for human rights and for fundamental freedom for all. To my mind, this should include freedom struggle against colonial occupation of people, or racist or repressive regimes violating human rights on the basis of race, language or religion.

In this respect one can rely on the United Nation General Assembly agreement of 1973 on the legal status of combatants struggling against colonial and racist regimes for the right to self-determination. The principles agreed are:-

i. Such struggles are legitimate and in full accord with the principles of international law;

ii. Attempts to suppress struggle against colonial and racist regimes are incompatible with United Nation Charter, the Universal Declaration of Human Rights and the Declaration on the Granting of Independence to colonial countries and people as well as with the principles of international law concerning friendly cooperation amongst States.

The 1948 United Nation Assembly's adoption and proclamation of universal declaration of human rights can also be relied upon, which recognizes inalienable rights of freedom to all human beings. The world has witnessed a change since the 11th September attack on World Trade Center and Pentagon and freedom movements are likely to suffer being labeled and dealt with as terrorism.

Terrorism is older than the word itself, which has roots in the "Reign of Terror" during the French Revolution. The practice of threatening, injuring or killing innocent people for political, religious or other ideological reasons goes back to at least Biblical times. *Zeal* (Greek for "jealous") is the basis of *zealot* – the name given to a Jewish sect that led a bloody uprising against Roman occupation 2,000 years ago. And *thug* (Hindu for "thief" based on Sanskrit "sthagati" for "concealed person") originally referred to a member of a band of killers in India who waylaid and strangled travellers as part of a religious ritual.

Would "zealots" and "thugs" be considered "terrorists" today? There is disagreement over what the word means. Richard Baxter, a judge on the International Court of Justice, once said: "We have cause to regret that a legal concept of 'terrorism' was never inflicted upon us. The term is imprecise; it is ambiguous; and above all, it serves no operative legal purpose." Similarly some people have reacted to a different famous comment, in 1964 by U.S. Supreme Court Justice Potter Stewart who admitted it might be impossible to "intelligibly" define obscenity, but quickly added "I know it when I see it."

The world awoke to the word "terrorism" only after the 11th September 2001 when civilian planes hit the World Trade Center and the Pentagon. Prior to this, the Middle East, Philippine, throughout Africa, Indonesia, India and several countries have witnessed violent movements against the government in power or the occupation forces, but none of these was ever termed as terrorism. The latest example is East Timor, where the United Nation even brokered peace and independence from Indonesia.

The word "terrorism" has many approximate meanings and it evades exactitude. It is like many abstract words which different people understand differently. The meaning is usually given to an idea or thing by classification and generalization by finding its purpose, goals and functions. Often the opposite clarifies the meaning more sharply such as the meaning of light is the absence of darkness. It, therefore, relates something to something else to appreciate similarities and differences.

The interesting thing about human language is that it defies logical build-up that meanings change with the change of time. It always keeps pace with the user's social development. Meanings are always not those found in the dictionary or lexicon. For example, the pitch of the voice, phonetic distortion and facial expressions can easily give a twist to the established meaning. Language is not simply patterns of noise. No matter how systematic noise is. It cannot be a language until it has been given a meaning and it derives the meaning largely from its use in real-life situations.

Now take the word "terror". It can be as harmless as to say "It is terrible weather", or "I am terribly sorry" or "I am sorry I am terribly late". But at the same time, terrorism has come to mean many horrendous things. It seems to have become a word incorporating all such words as fear, horror, intimidation, breaking of the law, madness, oppression, panic, repression, savagery, scare-mongering, shock, threats, turmoil, war of nerves, etc. From this collection of words, it crashes down to nefarious deeds such as random shooting in public places and bomb blasts.

The word terrorism came for discussion before the United Nations during the conference in Durban, South Africa, when the organization was sharply criticized for deep divisions over racism. The world today is certainly not united over the definition of "terrorism". During the past few decades, the United Nations has adopted a dozen protocols and conventions that condemn global terrorism, which urge countries to fight and banish it from the face of earth, as said by its Secretary General Kofi Annan. But the members of the United Nations have not been able to sit down and agree on exactly what they are talking about.

As far back as 1937, the League of Nations tried to settle the matter. It defined "terrorism" as "all criminal acts directed against a State and intended or calculated to create a state of terror in the minds of particular persons or a group of persons or the general public". But the draft proposal was never ratified. A 1999 United Nation resolution reiterates that criminal acts intended or calculated to provoke a state of terror in the general public, a group of persons or particular persons for political purposes are in any circumstance unjustifiable, whatever the considerations of a political, philosophical, ideological, racial, ethnic, religious or other nature that may be invoked to justify them.

After the 11th September attacks and a 5-day debate at the United Nations, the General Assembly once again declared that terrorism is a threat to worldwide peace, but during discussion it was clear that many members did not consider what they call "legitimate attempts by people to resist foreign occupation" as terrorism. When a suicide bomber kills a crowd of shoppers in Israel is it "terrorism" or merely tragic violence in a war over territory? Or when Kashmir Freedom Fighters hurl a bomb at Indian Security Forces is it terrorism? What if only soldiers are killed? If troops end up shooting unarmed civilians is it State terrorism? And how should the world see governments that help foreign militia overthrow existing regimes and governments, as has been practiced by the intelligence agencies of the West throughout the last century.

Since the United Nation has failed to come up to a universally acceptable definition of terrorism, some of the western countries have gone alone in defining terrorism to suit their own purpose.

i. The Canadian government tabled a legislation expected to pass soon which states, "Terrorist activity is an action within or outside Canada that is taken or threatened for political, religious or ideological purposes and threatens the public or national security by killing, seriously harming or endangering a person causing substantial damage that is likely to seriously harm people, or by interfering with or disrupting an essential service, facility or system".

The Canadian Security Intelligence Service (CSIS) Act compels its members to investigate activities "directed toward or in support of the threat or use of acts of serious violence against persons or property for the purpose of achieving a political objective within Canada or a foreign state."

According to a CSIS report last year, "this distillation of terrorism into its basic elements makes no effort to ascribe value to the motives of the actors, and gives equal weight to terrorist acts directed toward foreign states and to persons who provide support for such acts. Terrorist violence and activities in support of such violence may be carried out in the name of independence, freedom, or religious belief, but Canada has chosen through its legislation to give first consideration to the act of serious violence, not the nature of the cause."

ii. The US State Department relies on its own guideline in Title 22 of the US Code, Section 2656f(d), "The term ` terrorism' means premeditated, politically motivated violence perpetrated against noncombatant targets by subnational groups or clandestine agents, usually intended to influence an audience". The use of the word "noncombatant" implies civilian and unarmed military support staff. The word "subnational" excludes the possibility that a country's own national government could be directly guilty of terrorism.

iii. Last year, Britain introduced a similar law that prohibits threats or actions "designed to influence (any) government or to intimidate the public (in any country) ... for the purpose of advancing a political, religious or ideological cause." Critics also think that the illegal "actions" referred to in this legislation are far too broad. They argue that vandals damaging property or disrupting phone lines might be considered terrorists, and that the phrase "serious risk to health" could include a union going on strike at a hospital.

In addition to outlining what constitutes terrorism, some countries have also drafted lists of groups that fall into the category. Critics view the practice as arbitrary, especially since the evidence collected is sometimes not made public on grounds of national security. It's worth noting that the entries are regularly updated. Washington, for instance, recently revised its Federal Register. The Japanese Red Army and the Peruvian group Tupac Amaru were dropped. The Real IRA, accused of the 1998 bombing of Omagh in Northern Ireland, was added.

The original IRA, whose political wing, Sinn Fein, is involved in peace negotiations, remains off London's list. But Hezbollah, which holds seats in Lebanon's parliament, is considered a terrorist outfit. Skeptics question the criteria used for classifying some organizations as terrorists. For instance, until the early 1980s Iraq had a prominent spot on the U.S. list of countries supporting terrorism. When Baghdad went to war with Iran, one of America's bitter enemies, it was removed from the scroll. After the fighting stopped, Iraq was put back on.

Over the time, some of the decisions made by governments have become conspicuous reminders of how subjective the process can be. For example, former South African president Nelson Mandela, who won the Nobel Peace Prize for his struggle against apartheid, was once branded a terrorist. Scholars like Noam Chomsky , an American linguist well known for his criticism of Washington foreign policy, in his book "Necessary Illusions" contends that the meaning of the term "terrorism" is not seriously in dispute, because it has been laid out in so many government documents, including the official U.S. Code.

He then cites a U.S. Army Manual's definition, which states, "the calculated use of violence or threat of violence to attain goals that are political, religious or ideological in nature. This is done through intimidation, coercion, or instilling fear". Based on these words, Chomsky goes on to argue that the United States itself actively supports international terrorism on a scale in many countries that puts its rivals to shame.

It appears, therefore, the western countries are laying their own definition of terrorism to suit their individual purpose, the world having not come up with a universally acceptable definition. However, recently in Istanbul at a conference of European Union and OIC the participants have unanimously come to a conclusion and given a slogan, "terrorism has no religion". I think this in itself is an achievement because otherwise after the event of 11th September the world was moving towards the conflict of civilization. It is an irony that terrorism has been going in Ireland both within and outside Ireland but those responsible for violent attacks are being called loyalists, nationalists, separatists and were never labeled as terrorists.

In Sri Lanka terrorism has claimed thousand of lives since quarter of century and those responsible are called Tamil tigers or Tamil separatists but not terrorists. Recently, in Nepal there have been terrorist attacks killing hundreds of policemen and civilians but those have been termed as Mao separatists and not terrorists, whereas in Palestine and Kashmir, the people are struggling against illegal occupation of their homeland and are being labeled as terrorists. It is unfortunate that wherever Muslims are fighting for their survival/independence, the term terrorism is commonly used both by the western countries as well as western electronic and print media. It is, therefore, imperative, the West in particular and the United Nation should find a universally acceptable definition of terrorism to avoid freedom movements by Muslims in particular and generally by others, being labeled as terrorism.

4

Terrorism and Organized Crime

Last October, Italian investigators confirmed a disturbing trend in the War on Terrorism, the growing link between terrorism and organized crime. The investigators revealed that al Queda was using the Naples-based Camorra mafia, with its extensive network and expertise in forging documents, to move its operatives through Europe to safe houses in such cities ás Paris, London, Berlin and Madrid. According to DIGOS, Italy's political crime unit, the number of al Queda operatives passing through Naples may have exceeded a thousand. Il Mattino, Naple's major daily newspaper described the arrangement, should any trouble arise at any time, the Camorra's alliances will send them (al Queda operatives) off on one of the many trains leaving the city's main station, or via speed-boat - the same vessels the Camorra uses to traffic cigarettes, drugs and other contraband."

The Comorra-al Queda alliance is another example of a growing global security challenge that is both disturbing and complex. The once distinct line between organized crime and terrorism is blurring rapidly, and this development is creating new challenges for the U.S. and its allies in the War on Terrorism. It may seem like a marriage of strange bed fellows. After all, the business of organized crime is business, and the style of the mafia is to keep a low a profile as possible as they build their illicit business. Terrorists, on the other hand, seek a high profile so they can instill fear and insecurity in pursuit of their objectives.

The Age of Globalization has created the conditions allowing terrorists and organized crime groups to join forces. With the Cold War's end in the early 1990s, terrorist and insurgent groups, which the Soviet Union financed, had to become more self sufficient. The FARC (Revolutionary Armed Forces of Colombia), Colombia's largest guerrilla group, is a graphic example. Since the early 1990s, FARC has become increasingly involved in Colombia's drug trade, mainly in protecting drug crops, processing labs and airfields for a fee and in taxing peasants who grow crops in areas under their control. By 2000, U.S. authorities estimated that FARC annual take from the drug trade to be as high as $400 million annually.

The guerrillas have helped fill the void created by the take down of Colombia's Cali and Medellin cartels. "The guerrillas have taken a direct role in the drug trade because the vacuum could easily be filled," explained Bruce Bagley, an expert on the Latin American drug trade at Miami University in Miami, Florida. "The money they are making from the drug trade has given them the degree of autonomy they need to pursue their agenda."

The Colombian guerrillas are suspected of exchanging drugs for arms with international terror groups such as the IRA. Meanwhile, intelligence agencies in Latin America report that at least one organized crime group, the Chechen mafia; have been using Argentina as a transit country for shipments of Colombian cocaine to Europe. In return, the Chechens sell arms to criminal syndicates in Brazil and Colombia.

The terrorism-organized crime alliance has affected other South American countries as well. In Ecuador, for instance, police broke up an international drug trafficking ring run by

Rady Zaiter, a Lebanese restaurant owner residing in Quito Zaiter was sending up to 70 percent of his illicit profits to Hezbollah. In Brazil, 19 members of Zaiter's ring were arrested and $65 million worth of cocaine confiscated.

The terrorist-drug trade connection in Latin America poses serious challenges for the U.S. government as it strives to protect the homeland. Reports in 2003 indicated that al Quaeda may be working with Mexican drug trafficking and organized crime groups in an attempt to sneak into the U.S. If true, this development is ominous, given the American problems with border security.

Drug trafficking, however, is not the only criminal activity in which terrorists and criminals collaborate. Kidnapping, human and contraband smuggling, counterfeiting money and CDs, fraud (credit card, cell phone cloning and identity theft) and even extortion and armed robbery have also been lucrative ways of making money. For example, until their arrest in 2002 a Hezbollah cell based in Charlotte, North Carolina, raised money from credit card fraud and cigarette smuggling to help finance the Lebanon-based group, which the U.S. government has designated a terrorist group.

Meanwhile, India's most wanted criminal, Dawood Ibrahim, is believed to have worked out a deal with al Qeda and other terrorist groups to share his smuggling routes, which extend from India to Europe. Ibrahim is accused of the 1993 terrorist bombing in Mumbai, India that killed 257 people.

"The most profitable form if human smuggling for the terror-organized crime alliance is sex slavery," according to Arnaud de Borchgrave, head of the Center for Strategic and International Studies Transnational Threat Initiative. "Each year, 7000,000 women disappear," Borchgrave told Investor's Business Daily. "They come from the Soviet Republic and from as far as China and Burma. Go to Liege

(Belgium) and Mons and Antwerp (the Netherlands). You find them everywhere. And the profits kick back."

Champions of globalization contend that the economic trend has provided legitimate benefits— free trade, economic integration and the spread of advanced technology, for example. But, no doubt, it is also creating the conditions in which terrorists and criminals can move and interact more easily. As Kimberly L. Thachuk, Deputy Director of the Globalization Project at the Institute for National Strategic Studies, National Defense University, Washington DC, explained, "Criminal organizations and terrorist groups are flourishing as a result of the conditions for heightened worldwide interdependence, increased global commerce and rapid communications and transportation."

The growing connection terrorism-organized crime connection, security experts say, has changed the nature of the War on Terrorism, exacerbated the threat to the global community and created the need for a new paradigm in strategic thinking. At the 2004 forum titled "Deadly Networks: The Nexus between Organized Crime and Terrorism," held at George Washington University in Washington DC, experts urged the U.S., and its allies to adopt variety of strategies to combat the threat. They included focusing on the financial links between the two groups, learning to use the Internet as well as the bad guys and having intelligence communities investigate better the cross over points between the groups.

Perhaps equally important is strengthening the legal, social and political institutions in the counties corrupted by the terror-organized crime nexus. As Frank Cilluffo, a former special assistant to the president in the U.S. Homeland Security office, explained in testimony before the U.S. House Committee on the Judiciary's Subcommittee on Crime in December 2000, The United States cannot solve the problem itself. "It must provide them (other counties) with the tools to help themselves."

Roots of Islamic Terrorism

This article traces the roots of Islamic terrorism, with special focus on Afghanistan. Notes are added on practical and philosophical problems of world media in finding the right track. From systematic errors in revealing little details, to serious misconceptions about basic facts and principles, we can relatively easily learn how much of "common knowledge" rests actually on superficial research and popular myths. Instead of becoming critical and aware of the traps laid around the issue, both Islamists and Islamophobes fail to recognize how they are manipulated.

Terrorism is Real

Terrorism is not as difficult a concept as some claim. It is a political ideology (-ism) on the use of terror, which is arbitrary, unrestricted and unspecified fear. This excludes traditional warfare against regular armies and police forces, and individual assassinations of public figures. Neither separatism nor criminal violence as such is necessarily terrorism. To call act terrorism, we should always ask, Does this really spread blind terror among the general populace? A bomb blown in a market place, or in a civilian airplane, intends to create common fear among customers and bystanders alike, because just about anybody could become a victim.

The victims are typically anonymous, and the very idea of the act was to cause damage or a credible threat. The assassination of a political leader, throwing stones on occupation troops, or bombing of enemy positions during a declared war or after an order to surrender has been given, may be repulsive and kill innocent people, but there is no terror, if no average "man of the street" needs to feel uneasy about his security the next day. No women or children should need to fear that they could be mistaken as presidents, soldiers, or military installations.

Somebody may have bad luck and be targeted accidentally, but if it is terrorism, we will find ourselves asking: Why? What is the object? Terrorism is rarely the ultimate end itself, as anarchy or communism is thought to be, but merely a method to promote some politics. That is why terrorists represent a political ideology. Even when they are in fact nothing but common criminals or psychopaths, terrorists make efforts to find a political excuse for their acts.

We know that not every political movement has created a terrorist splinter group, or served as an excuse for terrorism. Actually, terrorism has been the favourite method of extreme socialists only - both of the (left-wing) international, and the (right-wing) national varieties. Since the Jacobins of the French revolution held a "Reign of Terror" in 1794, the international socialists (communists) and national socialists (fascists) have shared a common tendency to use terrorism. A clear definition of terrorism helps to identify and trace it through history. It can be dated and located. This makes it very real - and thus also possible to be exterminated.

Socialists became Islamic Terrorists

Modern terrorism was born within a year, 1967-1968. International socialists (communists) started the fashion all over the world simultaneously, which should make us suspicious about the common roots. National socialists followed suit, turning Marxists of Muslim origin into Islamists of Marxist origin. In May 18th, 1967, Yuri Andropov took over the leadership of the KGB. The Russian security services evolved into a state within the Soviet state, as it became clear when Andropov became the communist party's general secretary after Leonid Brezhnev's death, in 1982.

During Andropov's era, which was far longer than that of any other KGB chief, the Soviet secret services supported international terrorism through satellite states and Marxist "liberation fronts". "On becoming chairman of the KGB in

1967, Andropov immediately announced his intention to revive KGB 'special actions' as an essential tool of Soviet policy during the Cold War."

The man who became Andropov's deputy was former Azerbaijani KGB chief Semyon Tsvigun, who committed suicide on January 19th, 1982. His wife was the sister of Brezhnev. Eduard Topol wrote a spy novel about the case, titled "Red Square". In the novel, Tsvigun's widow accuses Andropov for being an anti-Semite, organizing international terrorism, and having his subordinate assassinated. Reality, however, does not corroborate any rift within the KGB. Tsvigun's son became a KGB officer too, and was appointed as a Soviet diplomat in Cairo from August 1984. Tsvigun's son-in-law became the main supplier of arms to Islamist terrorists in Afghanistan, by 1995.

On June 2nd, 1967, violent student demonstrators met the Shah of Iran in West Germany. All of free Europe was plagued by student demonstrations in May 1968, causing a nearly revolutionary situation in France. Numerous left-wing terrorist cells were formed in Germany, Italy, and other western countries. Their activities peaked in 1977, after which the West German terrorists retired in communist East Germany.

The (North Irish) IRA and (Basque) ETA started their terrorism in 1968, with peaks around 1976. Andropov considered an IRA request for arms delivery for three years until subscribing it in 1972.

German and Italian left-wing terrorists cooperated by summer 1969, and in October 1971, altogether 16 terrorist groups held a meeting in Florence, Italy. Beside the IRA and ETA, many Palestinian and Latin American (ERP, ELN, MLN, and MIR) groups joined to the international terror network by 1973. In the USA, Soviet agents incited racial tension by writings in the name of the Ku Klux Klan, and by a bomb explosion in New York City, in summer 1971.

The same year, Soviet agents made contacts to a Quebecois separatist group, the FLQ.

In Latin America, communist Cuba was the source of revolutionary activities in many countries, although the KGB kept its own agents there too. In October 1967, "Che Guevara", whose girl-friend was an East German, was executed in Bolivia, becoming a romantic idol for teenage girls. Thirty-four years later, his picture could be seen on the T-shirts of young Palestinian brawlers. In Mexico, the KGB was involved in student riots from July to October 1968, prior to the Olympic Games.

Uruguay experienced urban guerrilla activities by the MLN, peaking between 1968 and 1972. Argentine followed between 1970 and 1975. Communists had big hopes on Chile, but were bitterly disappointed by the military coup in 1973. By the end of the 1970s, communist optimism was definitely on the decline everywhere in the world. At that point, the KGB desperately needed any kind of a boost of revolutionary spirits. Surprisingly, the Middle East came to rescue.

In December 1967, a Lebanese Christian, George Habash, who had been a Pan-Arabic national socialist, had broadened his field by founding the PFLP, a Palestinian organization. Although it split already by the next year, the PFLP remained the most pro-Soviet Palestinian terrorist group, with widest global ties. It caused the Central Committee of the Soviet Communist Party to adopt the Palestinian cause in 1968. In July 1970, Andropov allowed the first direct Soviet arms delivery to the PFLP. From that on, both the KGB and - perhaps even more so - the Russian military intelligence, GRU, provided Palestinian terrorists with arms and training. From 1972 on, this was coordinated by Habash, who had close connections to Japanese and Latin American terrorist groups.

The man chiefly responsible for exporting Palestinian terrorism was Wadi Haddad, deputy leader of the PFLP, recruited as agent "Nationalist" by the KGB in 1970. Andropov revealed his aims in a report to Brezhnev himself, "The nature of our relations with W. Haddad enables us to control the external operations of the PFLP to a certain degree, to exert influence in a manner favorable to the Soviet Union and also to carry out active measures in support of our interests through the organization's assets while observing the necessary conspirational secrecy."

The once fashionable airplane hijackings had been begun by the PFLP in July 23rd, 1968. At that time, the Soviet Union, having supported the establishment of Israel and armed its forces 20 years earlier, had already invested a lot of resources into the Palestinian cause and Arab Socialism. Arms had been initially smuggled through Egypt.

"By the summer of 1968, the Soviet Union had progressed far toward converting Egypt into its principal base of subversion against the Arab world." Thirty-three years later, Egypt was the principal base of Islamic terrorists. Soviet Union, however, failed in Egypt. In May 1971, Anwar Sadat wiped out most of KGB agents. In July 1972, Soviet advisors were expelled from Egypt. Eight years later, Sadat paid for this with his life, being assassinated by members of an Islamist group. Sadat's peace policy toward Israel made it easy for the remnants of the KGB network to ally with the right-wing Muslim Brotherhood. This is the background of Ayman az-Zawahiri, the second man of Al-Queda.

Yasser Arafat's al-Fatah organization received its first Soviet arms shipment in September 1972. Palestinians were, however, split into pro-Iraqi and pro-Syrian parties and factions. Although both Iraq and Syria were ruled by an Arab Socialist Baath party, and extremely friendly toward the Soviet Union after the end of 1950s, the deepening friction between these two Arab states cut through the Palestinians, and frustrated Soviet efforts to unite Arabs against Israel and the western world.

The Yom Kippur War of 1973, and the subsequent oil embargo from October 1973 to March 1974, which was aimed against the USA, taught the KGB two lessons, that the traditional, orthodox Arab Socialist partners and their Palestinian proxies could not be trusted and achieved little through military endeavours and terrorism; but that the future was economic, and lay with the oil-fields in Saudi Arabia and Gulf emirates. Thus Political Islam, or Islamism, replaced Socialism as the most promising basis for winning Arab hearts and hurting western interests in the Middle East. After the debacle in Egypt, the KGB turned toward Saudi Arabia, where King Faysal had been assassinated in May 1975, and King Khalid ruled until 1982. Here, the KGB could find most valuable connections through the Muslim Brotherhood.

The key link may have been Muhammad Maruf ad-Dawalibi, former Prime Minister of Syria, and founder of the Islamic Socialist Front in autumn 1949. He had declared already in April 1950, that Arabs would prefer "thousands time more to become a Soviet Republic than to be spoils of Jews". Dawalibi's preference for Soviet rule had not been shaken by Soviet support for Israel as late as September 1951. Instead, he recommended Arab leaders to seek even harder for Soviet support. Dawalibi was exiled from Syria, but he became a councellor of King Khalid, and the chairman of the Islamic Conference that convened in Pakistan in 1976.

Saudi Arabia became after 1974 the main financier of international terrorism, regardless of the professed Atheism of Palestinian Marxist groups. For example, only in the year 1989, the PLO received 85 million US$ and Hamas 72 million US$ Saudi payments. At the same time, Kuwait too financed Hamas with 60 million US$.

This policy, explained as payoffs to keep terrorists away from Saudi targets, was supervised by the Saudi intelligence chief, the king's nephew, Prince Turki, from 1977 until his unexplained sacking at the end of August, 2001.

Another Saudi god-father of Islamism was the senile Mufti Abdulaziz Bin Baz, who declared that the sun revolved around the earth (1966), and that the earth was flat (1969), among other equally "Islamic" doctrines. With Saudi money, such ideas where transmitted through the Islamic Conference, and its organizer, the Muslim World League, all over Muslim world.

Iraq was in mid-1970s Russia's most trusted ally in the Muslim world (except for South Yemen, which was already officially a Soviet satellite), and the only nominally non-communistic state, where the KGB ceased its activities, because there appeared to be no need for any supervision. When Saddam Hussein had some Iraqi communists executed, in May 1978, the KGB became worried, but the outbreak of Iraqi-Iranian war in 1980, came as a surprise to Soviet diplomacy. For a while, Soviet Union wavered in whom to support, but when the USA, Egypt, and Saudi Arabia had made their choice for Iraq, the Soviet Union switched sides. Following this, many Soviet-sponsored terrorists had to move from Iraq to Iran, Syria, or Lebanon.

Iran became Russia's most loyal ally after the Islamic revolution in 1979. This relationship has lasted over two decades, and is still cherished by the Islamists among Shi'ite clergy and security services. When Soviet troops invaded Afghanistan later the same year, there was only one spontaneous demonstration in Tehran, after which Iran has tamely followed Russia's actions against neighbouring Muslim people.

The Iranian revolution took the KGB by surprise, but it was a pleasant surprise, and the Soviet Union chooses to side with the Islamist revolutionaries already by November 1978. Azerbaijan's contemporary president, former party leader and KGB chief (a successor and friend of Tsvigun), Hayder Aliyev, was the expert on Middle East, who had soon convinced the Politburo, that Ayatollah Khomeini should be supported by the Soviet Union. This assessment caused a permanent division within the Iranian communist

(Tudeh) party, because it was instructed to support Khomeini despite the doubts of the party's own general secretary. He was replaced by a relative of Khomeini.

Among the closest associates of Khomeini, there were many Communists who had conveniently grown beards. Mustafa Ali Chamran had studied in California and Egypt before he founded a Red Shi'ite secret society. His pupils included later foreign minister Ibrahim Yazdi, oil minister Mohammed Gharazi, and a Lebanese fellow student in Berkeley University, Hussein Shaikh al-Islam, who led the occupation of the US Embassy in Tehran. This occupation, shortly before the Soviet invasion of Afghanistan, focused Iranian radicalism into anti-Americanism. Mohammed Beheshti, whose death at a bombing on June 28th, 1981, remained a mystery, had resided in East Germany.

Khomeini's early companion and foreign minister, Sadegh Ghotbzadeh, was a link to Syria. Most left-wing radicals were repressed only after summer 1981, by which time many former Communists had successfully accommodated with the new regime. Both Ghotbzadeh and Chamran had received Palestinian terrorist training. As a student in the USA, Ghotbzadeh had been recruited by the GRU.

"It is significant that anti-Americanism was first propagated as a major theme of Muslim fundamentalism by young men and women from Islamic countries who had spent time in the United States as students or workers." These included the founding father of the Muslim Brotherhood in Egypt, Said Qutb, who had lived in the USA for two years around 1949/1950. The four pilots of September 11th, 2001, included one native German citizen, whose Moroccan father was no Islamist at all, a Lebanese of liberal background, and a United Arab Emirates' subject, both of whom had spent five years in Germany, and the Egyptian-born terrorist leader Muhammad Atta, who had immigrated into Germany nine years earlier.

Daniel Pipes' article "The Western Mind of Radical Islam" describes well, how so many Islamic terrorists actually adopted more ideas from contacts to western society than from their own traditions, "Fundamentalist leaders tend to be well acquainted with the West, having lived there, learned its languages, and studied its cultures. ... Indeed, the experience of living in the West often turns indifferent Muslims into fundamentalists. ... In contrast to this ostentatious familiarity with Western ways, fundamentalists are distant from their own culture. ... Having found Islam on their own as adults, many fundamentalists are ignorant of their own history and traditions."

This became very obvious through the biographies of those who committed the suicide attacks of September 2001, and who were typically from wealthy families, liberally educated, and had lived many years in Hamburg, London, and America. Pipes takes notice of the fact that "fundamentalist Muslims" (or rather, "Islamists", as they care little of traditions and their true fundaments), have introduced distinctly Christian notions into their religion. He presents plenty of detailed examples, among others that "fundamentalists have turned Fridays into a Sabbath, something it had not previously been. ... Ignorant of the spirit underlying the Shari'a, fundamentalists enforce it along territorial, not personal lines..."

While original Islamic law had complex separate provisions for Jews and Christians, Islamists tend to regard them as intolerantly as non-Christians used to be regarded in pre-19th century Europe. Islamists also tend to confuse Islamic concepts (f. ex. regarding ritual purity, food prescriptions, etc.) with similar but not identical Christian concepts. A visible example is the uniform-like "Islamic head-scarf", which could be derived rather from prescriptions in the Epistle of St. Paul than from interpretations of the Koran, or from traditional customs.

There is also a curious tendency to threat apostates with death sentence (while the Koran forbids the use of force in matters of religion), and to prevent female followers from marrying Christian men, while men have always been allowed to marry Christian women, and the Koran explicitly orders the same marriage restrictions or exemptions equally for both sexes. Actually, it was the Christian Canon and laws (for example in Russia until the beginning of 20th century), that threatened an apostate with death penalty and prevented mixed marriages.

When Christian societies found out that such laws had no base in religion, Islamists took them over, although they had even less base in Islam. For example, in the Malaysian state of Sabah, Muslim women were banned from mixed marriages only after the 1970s, when Islamism became a global fashion. Fundamentally anti-Islamic fashions and interpretations of religion were exported from Saudi Arabia globally since the 1970s, with heavy financial backing.

Pipes describe the way Islamists "have set up church-like structures. The trend began in Saudi Arabia, where the authorities built a raft of new institutions..., for example, the Secretary of the Muslim World League, the Secretary General of the Islamic Conference... The Islamic Republic of Iran soon followed the Saudi model and went beyond it..."

Anti-Americanism became a strong common denominator for not only Muslims, but also Christians and Atheists in the Middle East. This was not so surprising, since not only Habash, but also another Marxist Palestinian party leader, Nayef Hawatmeh of the DFLP, was a Christian. The PLO included many Christian Arabs, but since 1985, it too adopted an "Islamic" policy. Arafat's own Al-Fatah organization together with the Communist Party of Jordan allied with the Muslim Brotherhood.

In the Karabakh conflict, Khomeini supported Christian Armenians, whose terrorist movement ASALA had been originally established by a former Iraqi member of the PFLP, "Hagop Hagopian", and had shared common training camps in Lebanon with the PFLP, from 1977 to 1982.

After July 1983, ASALA disappeared in the same Lebanese valley, where another anti-Turkish organization, the PKK, emerged next summer. This was no novelty, since pro-Soviet Armenians had participated in the founding of an anti-Turkish Kurdish party already in 1927 - also in Lebanon. Both ASALA and PKK were rumoured to have been brainchildren of a Soviet Armenian KGB officer Karen Brutents.

Another Armenian terrorist faction, renamed ARA, moved from Iraqi and PFLP protection to Iranian and Lebanese (actually Syrian) custody by the end of 1984. This coincided with the swift of Soviet sympathy from Iraq to Iran during the Iraqi-Iranian war. They were activated against Azerbaijani Muslims in 1987.

The "Islamic revolution" in Iran inspired also frustrated left-wing Arabs. The Arab world had been demoralized by the 1973 war, by failure to gain enough from the oil crisis, and by the Lebanese civil war in 1975-1976. Even a Christian Marxist like Jérôme Shahin came to the conclusion, that neither Arab Socialism nor Pan-Arabic unity, but only Islam could inspire Arab "masses". Another Marxist, Anwar Abdulmalek, advocated "Political Islam", and described Khomeini as "progressive by definition" because of the innate anti-Americanism of Islamic heritage. The "Abdelmalek-Shahin syndrome" gave suddenly hope to alienated left-wing intellectuals.

Islamism became the new ideology for Algerian independence champion Ahmad Ben Bella (1984), who had been decorated with a Lenin medal twenty-one years earlier. In Morocco, Socialists turned into Islamists included Abdulkarim Moti and Abdussalam Yassine. The latter published an open letter to the king in 1974, was imprisoned, and lives still under house arrest as the leader of Adl wa Ihsane (Justice and Well-fare) Party.

This conversion from Marxism to Islam was no worse a spiritual problem than the conversion of traditionally deeply Roman Catholic nationalist organizations like the IRA and ETA, into Marxist terrorist groups in the 1960s. German right-wing terrorists of the Wehrsportgruppe felt no problems either, in being trained in 1981 by left-wing Palestinians in Lebanon.

Despite possible ideological objections, those communists and other extremists, who remained loyal to Russia's strategic mission in the Middle East, were ready to serve it under a new ideological disguise. This was noticed by some researchers by mid-1980s, "The most significant new factor is the Soviet realization that two movements - radical-revivalist Islam (commonly but misleadingly called 'fundamentalist') and traditionalist Islam - have become the most decisive trends in the Muslim world, and that if Moscow is to have any influence there, it must find a way to exploit and manipulate them - particularly the radical-revivalists, who are most useful to them. ... They know that their hopes for success lie in persuading the radical-revivalist Muslims to see the Soviets as an instrument to be used against a common enemy, the West."

Soviet Islamists in Afghanistan

Russia has long traditions in the political art of provocation, dating back to the imperial age, when the secret police finally lost track of its own web of "agents provocateurs", who successfully infiltrated and compromised opposition parties by committing themselves to so serious crimes, that they could just as well be considered revolutionaries in police disguise. Provocations were adopted by the Soviet secret services, and widely used in the "ethnic conflicts" that appeared suddenly in Central Asia and the Caucasus, between 1987 and 1993.

Provocations were exercised already during the invasion of Afghanistan, as has been recently (in February 2002) revealed by Vasili Mitrokhin, a KGB officer from 1956 to 1984, who prepared a secret report in 1987 and defected to Britain in 1992. He describes "false flag" operations, where "Soviet-trained Afghan guerrilla units posed as CIA-supported, anti-Soviet mujahidin rebels [Islamic freedom-fighters] to create confusion and flush out genuine rebels".

In January 1983, there were 86 such "false bands", trained by KGB officer V. Kikot of the 8th Department of the "Directorate S". Kikot was transferred from Cuba, and was acquainted with training Palestinian terrorists. There were also over 110 agents infiltrated in Iran and over 200 agents in Pakistan, including Murtaza Bhutto, son of the former president and brother of the future prime minister.

Former KGB general Oleg Kalugin assured correctly on a BBC World News TV discussion on September 23rd, 2001, that there were more terrorists of Al-Queda who had been trained by the KGB than by the CIA, but his words were not taken seriously by other debaters, who preferred to blame the prevailing poverty in Palestinian refugee camps, American non-involvement there, American involvement in assisting Afghan freedom-fighters in the 1980s, and global inequality, as breeding-grounds for terrorism. For some reason, logically inconsistent and practically unfounded theories remain far more popular in western media than the simple facts confessed by top-ranking ex-Soviet officials.

Afghan freedom fighters recognized Gulbuddin Hikmatyar as a KGB provocateur already by 1985. Two-thirds of the conflicts between Afghan guerrilla factions were caused by KGB provocation. This should have been no surprise, since Hikmatyar is told to have spent four years in the Afghan communist party (PDPA) before becoming a "devout" Muslim. Even an Afghan left-wing feminist group accuses Hikmatyar for participation in an assassination carried out by the KGB in 1985.

"The Soviets manipulated and exploited Gulbaddin Hekmatiyar's Hizbi-i Islami [Islamic Party] primarily through the numerous agents in his military council, which included representatives not only from the Muslim Brotherhood but also from Libya, Iran, and the PLO. In the mid-1980s, Gulbaddin Hekmatiyar was known to have visited Libya and Iran and was rumored to have visited the PDRY [communist South Yemen]."

As CNN's reporter Richard Mackenzie has said, Hikmatyar "gained notoriety in Afghanistan for killing more fellow Mujahideen than he did communists."

Many observers predicted early enough, what would be the alternative to communist power in Kabul. "Since 1978 the Communist regimes in Kabul have consistently identified Gulbuddin Hekmatyar, the most radical figure, as the primary or even the sole leader of the entire Resistance... In the event that the Communist regimes in Kabul were ever to be replaced or joined by the most radical elements in the Resistance and these elements attempted to implement their extremist programs, it appears certain that they would meet with massive public opposition, setting off disorders which would provide the Soviets with an opportunity to return in the guise of providing stability.

In such a case, an international community convinced that the Afghans are 'incapable' of self-government would hardly protest." This was very much what happened indeed, and within 15 years from this prophesy, the time seemed ripe for Russia to make it happen.

Although Hikmatyar was (like the Taliban leaders later) a Sunni Muslim, he regarded Iran as his model, and took refugee in Iran, where he sympathized the Taliban until he was forced to disappear from Tehran in February 2002. A great mystery, wondered by many western researchers and journalists who had observed the Afghan war, was how notoriously anti-American Hikmatyar, despite his bad reputation and terrorist sympathies, became a favourite of the Pakistani ISI (until 1993), and thus a main recipient of US military aid for Afghan guerrillas in the mid-1980s. Several explanations, including KGB infiltration of the CIA (or rather ISI), have been provided.

The most probable explanation is simply that the CIA possessed more money than wisdom. A former CIA agent, Reuel Marc Gerecht, described in his article "The Counterterrorist Myth", how throughout the Afghan war, the Directorate of Operations never developed a team of Afghan experts. The first case officer to have some proficiency in an Afghan language did not arrive until 1987. After 1989, the CIA abandoned Afghanistan, in the firm belief that the Cold War was over, and for the following ten years, no CIA official paid a visit to the legendary commander Ahmadshah Masud in Afghanistan, to learn that the war was far from over yet.

Although American contribution to the Afghan war has been exaggerated, it remains a dark cloud over the CIA's credibility. The British were critical about CIA's policy and far more efficient by providing Stinger missiles to Masud, who used them to expel the Russians. Hikmatyar sold his Stingers to Iran in 1987.

Russia's aid for the communist army exceeded all foreign aid to the guerrillas. From 1986 to 1990, the USA sent weapons worth of 2, 5 to 3, 2 billion US$ and Saudi Arabia for the same amount, while the Soviet Union provided an arsenal worth an estimated 5, 7 billion US$, according to moderate estimates. Saudi Arabia may have continued financing its own proxies in the years 1991-1992. But this was certainly more than equalled by Russia's shipments, estimated as high as worth of 4 billion US$ annually (20-30 daily flights), continuing at least until 1991.

There are discrepancies between the numbers presented in different sources, but whatever reasons the USA may have had for spending money on Hikmatyar, Russia's legacy prolonged the most destructive civil war beyond the official disintegration of the Soviet Union and the fall of Kabul. Afghan communists have a broad history of "turning coats", or to be more accurate, of growing beards and adopting the title "Mullah" attached to a pseudonym. Prior to the Soviet invasion, the communists had been divided into three factions:

Maoist radicals of the Khalq faction led by Hafizullah Amin (1979), who was deposed by the Soviets. These included army officer Turan Abdurrahman, who joined the guerrilla already in 1979, and reappeared as "Mullah Borjan", the supreme commander of the Taliban military in 1996, before he was killed under unknown circumstances;

Moderates of the Khalq faction, led by Nurmuhammad Taraki (1978-1979), who was deposed by Amin. These included defence minister Shahnawaz Tanai, and several other generals, who joined Hikmatyar between 1990 and 1992, but defected to the Taliban by 1996, organizing their air force, air defence (Muhammad Gilani), artillery (Shah Sawar), communications units, military intelligence, and security services (Muhammad Akbar);

Kremlin loyalists of the Parcham faction led by Babrak Karmal (1979-1986), Najibullah (1986-1992), and Abdurrashid Dostum, who is an ethnic Uzbek general. Dostum's air force bombed Kabul to ruins before it too defected to the Taliban in May 1997. Dostum himself joined the "Northern Alliance" with the legal government only when he was reduced to military marginality, and although he generously received an office in Kabul, he would still like to challenge the interim government, and remains a trouble-maker in the Northern provinces, with support from Uzbekistan.

Taliban commandants were identified in an excellent article by Stéphane Allix in Le Monde diplomatique, January 1997. They all had a past in the communist Khalq faction. The KGB was not supposed to recruit agents among them, but concentrated on the Parcham faction, but the GRU must have been interested specially in recruiting Khalq officers.

The founder of the Taliban, "Mullah" (without much of clerical education) Omar, was a comrade-in-arms of "Mullah Borjan" in the Islamic Revolutionary Movement, before they founded a new party of their own, by autumn 1994. Their credentials in the resistance were marginal compared to those of Masud. The same applies to Osama Bin Ladin, who arrived in Pakistan by 1984 and may have participated in one battle but boasted as a war veteran to his young idolaters. According to CIA agent Milton Bearden, Bin Ladin fought a battle only in spring 1987, although his biographer Yossef Bodansky, blessed with rather vivid imagination, credits him also with a couple of skirmishes in 1986 and 1989.

Actually, when the Palestinian organizer of Arab aid, Abdullah Azzam, wanted to send volunteers, money, and arms to assist Masud, Bin Ladin had his mentor assassinated in autumn 1989, took over the organization (Al-Queda), sent the volunteers back home (Kabul remained to be liberated, as well as the rest of Central Asia), and let Hikmatyar have the rest. Bin Ladin left his base in the Pakistani frontier town of Peshawar in an unexplained panic (telling that Saudi Arabia had hired the ISI to kill him), in 1991, while communists were still in power in Kabul, and just when things started to move in Soviet Central Asia. He had quite apparently no interest in destabilizing the Russian sphere of influence, and in contrary, directed the activities of Arab adventurers against pro-American governments.

During the Afghan war, Arabs hanging around in the region had been of little use (the Afghans detested them because of their religious fervour, lack of respect for traditions, and boasting habit), and although they pretended to be interested in Afghanistan, they were in fact hiding in Peshawar from their own police. When visiting Afghanistan, they were merely tolerated because of their connections to financial aid. Most of the "Arab Afghans" were Egyptians in exile, but some Arab countries dumped there common criminals. In 1991, they were recruited to fight in Algeria, and in 1993-1994, they were used by Hikmatyar to assist Aliyev and Russian-sponsored terrorists in Azerbaijan.

Bin Ladin returned to Afghanistan only when in need of refuge for himself, invited by Hikmatyar in 1996, and soon found out, that meanwhile, all his fellow terrorists had defected - alongside with the communist generals - to the self-appointed "Mullah" Omar. Bin Ladin followed suit.

Russia's sponsorship of the Taliban and Al-Queda

Post-Soviet Russia faked friendship with the legal Afghan government of Burhanuddin Rabbani (1992-2001), while its "former" communist generals (seven out of eleven) served Hikmatyar, with the main exception of Dostum. According to Peshawar University professor Azmat Hayat Khan, the communist army was divided with the explicit intention of continuing destabilization, and retaining their party affiliations and structures for future use. The Taliban was, however, sometimes suspicious about its former communists, many of whom may have been purged in September 1998, when three generals, twenty-two officers, and thirty other people were arrested for involvement in a communist conspiracy.

When Rabbani's defence minister Masud, the archenemy of the KGB, was about to restore peace in Afghanistan by 1995, against all odds, Russia promoted a new rebel movement, the Taliban. Money, arms and technological know-how were channelled not only through the above-mentioned agents, but also directly by flights from Russia, and probably overland through Turk-menistan. This started before Bin Ladin's arrival, and Bin Ladin - through his Egyptian connections, close to Hikmatyar - remained servile to Russian interests.

First of all, Russia was worried about the future of ex-Soviet Tajikistan, which enjoyed a short period of democracy at the very same time when Rabbani and Masud, both ethnic Tajiks, were restoring order in Kabul. The Russian army restored old communists to power in Tajikistan, fought a bloody civil war, and put pressure on the Afghan government not to tolerate Tajik guerrillas on its soil. Rossiiskiye Vesti wrote in September 1994, that the Tajik civil war could be finished only by pacifying Afghanistan.

Secondly, Saparmurat Niyazov, the communist leader of Turkmenistan, initiated, in November 1994, a project to build oil and gas pipelines through Afghanistan to Pakistan. This was further promoted by the mighty Gazprom Company, whose former manager Viktor Chernomyrdin is, as its shareholder, one of the world's richest men, and happened to be Russian prime minister from 1993 to 1998. This end of the pipeline project has received little attention from Western media, while the other end has produced speculations ever since the Californian-based UNOCAL and the Saudi Arabian Delta Oil companies were attracted to the project by October 1995.

Originally, also the Argentinean oil company Bridas was involved, but because it would have preferred a routing through Iran, it was dropped out of the project. Gazprom succeeded in having UNOCAL to sign a deal on August 13th, 1996. This became a political nuisance to the USA, and finally, UNOCAL cancelled it. However, neither the government of Turkmenistan, nor the Russian gas giant Gazprom, suffered from bad publicity. They met no political objections to continue negotiations with the Taliban. Niyazov personally put on hold the promising alternative, American-sponsored Trans-Caspian Pipeline Project for the export of Turkmen gas to Turkey.

Turkmenistan's Afghan connections, both economical and political, remained relatively unnoticed by the media, because the country was almost as closed from the outside world as it used to be during the Soviet times. After the Taliban's defeat and the escape of Al-Quaeda militants toward the north-east corner of Iran, or toward Turkmenistan, Niyazov had to cut his links by a thorough purge in the army and secret services. Muhammad Nazarov, chief of the KNB (Turkmen KGB), was publicly reprimanded, demoted from four-star general to lieutenant general, and dismissed on March 13th, 2002.

He was replaced by the interior minister. The defence minister and head of military counterintelligence, Gurbanduri Begenzhev, also lost his posts in disgrace. The same happened to Khosse Reyymov, another major general, who had been responsible for border controls. The changing of the guard came as a surprise as just weeks before, the security services were being presented as a pillar of Niyazov's authoritarian regime. Some sources suggested that the US ambassador had complained in private to Niyazov of crime within the Turkmen secret services. Niyazov's "fight against infection" within the KNB began immediately after the meeting.

While Niyazov and Chernomyrdin had personal financial interests to support the Taliban, US Vice President Al Gore signed the infamous 1995 US-Russian weapons agreement, which exempted Russia from sanctions, although Russia would sell arms to Iran. This secret agreement violated the rules of 1992, by the US Congress. Gore's excuse was that Russia agreed upon not selling nuclear technology, and to stop all arms exports to Iran by the end of 1999. This, of course, never happened, and when the failed agreement was leaked to The New York Times in October 2000, Russia declared its intention not to keep it anyway.

The case illustrates how deeply Chernomyrdin was involved in businesses with Islamic extremists, and how

Russia succeeded in having Bill Clinton's administration participate in shady deals against American public interests. There were also rumours of promised concessions in the pipeline projects, or in financial support to Gore's presidential campaign. Gore's loss at the November 2000 elections was a devastating surprise for Russian political establishment.

Thirdly, a KGB officer, Viktor But (Victor Bout), flew arms to the Taliban until 2001. The beginning of this business enterprise would have remained unknown, if a Russian airplane would not have been spotted at Kandahar airport. According to But's explanations, the arms shipment, originally intended to the government in Kabul, was forced to land at Kandahar by a MIG 21, on August 6th, 1995.

This happened exactly at a time when the Taliban was about to be routed. Instead of a rapid disaster at this critical point, the reinforced Taliban turned to attack, and took over the town of Herat by September 5th. The Russian pilots were kept as hostages in Kandahar until next August 16th, when they miraculously escaped and were decorated by the Russian president. Soon after, in September 1996, an well-armed Taliban advanced all the way to Kabul.

"By August the [Taliban] group was broke and deseperate. Yet suddenly they were rolling in cash and confidence. On Sept. 27 the Taliban marched into Kabul. Former mujahedin commanders close to the Taliban say the bonanza arrived courtesy of Osama bin Ladin... Afghan and Western sources say bin Laden's gift to Omar amounted to $3 million." According to Russian sources, the money, exactly three million US$, was a "ransom" paid directly by Russia. Perhaps it did not make much of a difference, who delivered the money - and much more than worth of that in arms - to the Taliban?

Viktor But was born in 1967, probably in Smolensk. He has used also the names Viktor Bulakin and Vadim Aminov. He carries five passports, two Russians, one

Ukrainian, and probably one Tajik and one Uzbek. He served as navigator in the Soviet air force, and graduated from the Military Institute for Foreign Languages in Moscow, known as a GRU spy school. By 1991, But had a career in the KGB, assisted by his father-in-law, who was no less a character than the Brezhnev family member Tsvigun.

After the disintegration of the Soviet Union, But served in UN peace troops in Angola. He still has a house in Johannesburg, now used as a brothel. In 1995, But appeared in Belgium as the owner of a cargo flight company. He flew arms to Afghanistan, since 1997 to East Congo, Rwanda, Burundi, and Uganda, and since 1998 to Liberia and Sierra Leone. Destinations may have included also Bosnia, Serbia, Iraq, Eritrea or Georgia (the end users are often unknown), Peru, and Sri Lanka (Tamil Tigers).

But's partners were Soviet-trained air force generals of the Taliban. To be closer to Afghanistan, he moved in 1997 to the United Arab Emirates. When UN sanctions forced the United Arab Emirates to check the cargo going to Afghanistan, in January 2001, Bill Clinton's administration did its last favour to friendly Russia by allowing an exception for carriers registered in Russia. For Clinton's administration, Russians were always above any suspicions as sponsors of Islamic terrorism. Once again, the British MI6 was needed to turn CIA's attention to the right direction.

Russian disinformation labelled the Taliban a client of Pakistan, although some observers had noticed already by 1997, that the ISI had surprisingly little leverage on the Taliban. Even if the Taliban were a creation by Benazir Bhutto's (1993-1996) interior minister, Nasrullah Babar, they had soon freed themselves from any gratitude and dependence.

In June 2001, a fax message from Peshawar, revealed by Pakistani intelligence, described But's role as Taliban's lifeline. Arms should be routed either overland via Turkmenistan, or by air to Uzbekistan or Turkmenistan -

the airplanes, flown by reliable Armenian pilots, would then fake emergency landings in Afghanistan.

But has 250-300 employees, probably mostly Russians, Ukrainians, and Armenians. According to a Russian newspaper, the Komsomolskaya Pravda, But's main source of arms is Transdnestria, the Moldovan slice of land occupied by Russian army and administered by Soviet-nostalgic communists. This is also where terrorists of the Turkish PKK have found refugee. According to Jane's Intelligence Review, February 2002, "Pakistani smugglers with ties to Ukraine" escorted possibly up to 200 Al-Queda militants to Ukraine. The "Pakistani smuggler" was, however, But's associate, and the destination probably Transdnestria.

But himself owns a five-storey house in Moscow, where he appeared in a radio studio to declare his innocence. Shortly before, the Russian Interpol officer had claimed that they had searched for But for years, and could guarantee, that he was not in Russia. But's brother had a house in Islamabad.

On February 28th, 2002, the head of the Russian Interpol office proudly declared, that after four years of investigations, Russian law-enforcement agencies could assure, that But was nowhere in Russia. At the same time, But appeared in the Ekho Moskvy radio programme, saying that he had lived all the time in Moscow. He evaded questions by claiming, that he was a businessman, envied and therefore persecuted by Americans, that he had no ties to Russian intelligence, that he was involved only in air transportation since 1992, and that he never went "into the arms trade as such" - after all, "What does 'arms trade' mean?" He asked philosophically. He repeated the common claim that "Americans helped in cultivating the Taliban and controlled it through Pakistan."

The same night, a Russian Interior Ministry spokesman explained that police were not seeking to arrest But, because they had no evidence of any wrongdoing. Instead, the Russian media started to explain that But was only working for a Ukrainian Jew, Vadim Rabinovich, who must be an Israeli agent. This claim had been originally presented by the reorganized Russian foreign intelligence service SVR.

The But affair may have required from Russia more than just diversion in the media. In mid-October 2001, tension between Russian and Abkhazian border was very high, and experts predicted an "anti-terror invasion" of Georgia by Russian forces. This did not happen, however, as suddenly everything cooled down. At the same time, Russia's foreign ministry had protested The Washington Times' report about Al-Queda's arms trade relations to "Russian mafia", asking for exchange of information between security services. When the But affair was discussed in public, in February 2002, Georgia invited US military assistance. This caused a fury in Russia, but unexpectedly, the Kremlin appeared paralyzed to react.

Some years ago, Clinton's Russia expert Strobe Talbott had entertained great expectations because the FBI was allowed to open an office and to train Russian colleagues to fight terrorism in Moscow. This was before the spy scandal of the FBI. They failed, however, to investigate the September 1999 terror wave, which was pinned collectively on Chechens, but was obviously committed by Russian secret services. At the end of October, 2000, FSB colonel Aleksandr Litvinenko sought asylum in Britain and claimed to have evidence of FSB's guilt for the bombings. Other Russians have expressed suspicions on GRU's involvement. Interpol, the FBI, and their Russian colleagues appear to be unable not only to investigate terrorism but also to apprehend well-known Russian "merchants of death" in Moscow, despite of international warrants for arrest.

Talbott's "post-Cold War" thesis was that simple good will, trusting Russian officials, and supporting financially Russia's supposedly reforming institutions, would pay back in the form of increasing mutual trust and genuine friendship. According to a polling conducted by the US State Department, quite the opposite has happened, over 70% of Russians had a favourable opinion of the USA in 1993, but only 37% in February 2000.

There might indeed be a Chechen connection, but hardly the like Interpol's Russian officials would be investigating, the former communist boss of Soviet Chechnya, and Russia's puppet president (1995-1996) Doku Zavgayev, was appointed as Russia's ambassador to Tanzania shortly before Bin Ladin's associates blew up buildings there. US federal prosecutors found a letter between terrorists, who repeatedly referred to the group's members in Kenya by the code name "the fish people". The arms flown by But's company to Afghanistan were listed as "fish from Tanzania". Where do fish dwell? Perhaps in an aquarium, which happens to be the nickname of the GRU headquarter in Moscow...

Also, the PKK leader Abdullah Öcalan's decision to fly to Nairobi, in February 1999, may be added to a list of curious East African coincidences.

We should also remember the career of Yevgeni Primakov, KGB operative in Egypt in the 1960s, chief of the SVR from 1991 to 1996, foreign minister from 1996 to 1998, and prime minister from 1998 to 1999. His appointment into Chernomyrdin's government in December 1996 followed two months after the sacking of Aleksandr Lebed, the popular general who made peace in Chechnya and advocated strong measures against the Taliban. "The rivalry between SVR and foreign ministry ... ended in decisive victory for the SVR with Primakov's appointment as foreign minister ... in December 1996."

Primakov appears to have carried with him a sharp policy change, instead of negotiating a final peace deal with the Chechens, as had been agreed by Lebed, the FSB encouraged provocative Islamists, who committed murders and kidnappings from 1997 to 1999, scaring most foreign aid workers and reporters out of the land, and providing the Russian government with an excuse for a renewed intervention. Obviously, this was a method successfully exercised in Afghanistan to oust the Rabbani government from Kabul.

During his travels in the Middle East in the 1980s, Primakov had been known to talk about Free Mason and Jewish conspiracies. According to a Russian newspaper article by Oleg Lurye, Bin Ladin's cousin had meetings with the daughter of Boris Yeltsin.

Soviet Islamists in Russia

Islamists in modern Russia are KGB-trained provocateurs, who fight traditions and nationalism, and dream about a re-established Soviet Union. Their perception of Islam resembles more a Communist caricature than the historical roots of ethnically mainly Caucasian and Tatar Muslims. To understand the development to this better, KGB's activities in the Middle East can be divided in five-year periods:

- 1968-1972 the KGB puts great hopes on international terrorism in general, and particularly on Palestinians, and other Arab Socialists. Focus on Egypt.
- 1973-1977 the KGB is disappointed and Arabs are frustrated, but Saudi-sponsored Islamism provides an alternative political ideology for promoting anti-American and pro-Russian sentiments. Focus on Iraq.
- 1978-1982 the KGB puts great hopes on the "Islamic revolution" of Iran, and its expansion to Arab countries, while exporting communism into Afghanistan. Focus on Iran. End of Andropov's era (1967-1982) in the KGB.
- 1983-1987 the KGB is disappointed, but accommodated by the dominance of Islamism over orthodox Communism in Iran. Focus on Syria and Afghanistan. End of GRU chief Pyotr Ivashutin's era (1963-1987).

- 1988-1992 the KGB withdraws its "active measures" inside the Soviet borders, and concentrates in provoking "ethnic conflicts" to divide and rule separatists in the Caucasus and elsewhere in the dis-integrating empire. The KGB is split (1991), and the GRU has chiefs with no intelligence background (1987-1991) but establishes huge post-Soviet military bases in Karabakh, Abkhazia, and Transdnestria.
- 1993-1997 the KGB (FSB and SVR) re-establishes communist power in former Soviet Republics (except the Baltic countries) but fails to do it in Chechnya.

Afghanistan remains divided as a new group of provocateurs, the Taliban, emerges to challenge the freedom fighters. The GRU under Fyodor Ladygin (1992-1997), has more resources at its disposal than the SVR under Primakov (1991-1996). Through these phases, Russian secret services gained a tight hold on international terrorism, and especially on Islamism. It was nothing new. During the 1920s, Soviet intelligence had succeeded in thoroughly infiltrating fiercely anti-Soviet monarchist emigrant organizations.

Furthermore, "dozens of mythical organizations came into being. One of these, the 'Trust', has become well known in both Western and Soviet writings. For many years the Soviet leaders claimed to have cunningly infiltrated a monarchist resistance organization, but in the 1970s they admitted that they themselves had created it. ... Similar ones attacked... the church hierarchy of every denomination; and 'nationalists' inside and outside the country, with a 'line' of provocation covering each political tendency within each major ethnic subdivision - Ukrainians, Cossacks, Armenians, Georgians, Central Asians. Fragmentary information on at least two dozen 'lines' has become known in the West through the years."

Unfortunately, "Soviet provocation... remains little understood in the West. People safe in a democratic system may find it difficult to conceive that rulers would systematically use such hostile techniques against their own subjects." Back in the 1920s, anti-Soviet emigrants were compromised in front of western governments to reduce their credibility, and they were used in domestic propaganda to stage sabotage actions, to scare the populace, and to provoke dissidents into revealing themselves. This excellent experience was certainly in the minds of post-Andropov and post-Ivashutin intelligence officers, who "may in fact have launched a new golden era of provocation. ... A blatant example was the work of the far-right anti-Semitic organization called Pamyat (Memory)."

For the development of Soviet Islamism, the years 1988-1992 were crucial. The KGB fought for its very existence, and the GRU too was called to fight internal enemies within Soviet borders, instead of its traditional foreign military intelligence work. Although the GRU had fewer agents abroad than the KGB (in relation 7 to 10), it was claimed to possess more financial resources by the mid-1980s. Where was the money spent when the "Cold War" was declared ended, traditional military intelligence lost motivation, and left-wing terrorist organizations of the 1970s vanished from sight? Obviously, GRU resources were concentrated to activities within Soviet borders, to arm and train provocateurs. It is known, that Special Forces were called from Afghanistan to crush Crimean Tatar demonstrations in Moscow, in July 1987. They appeared soon in the bloody incidents of Tbilisi (1989) and Baku (1990), and in Baltic capitals (1991).

GRU's Afghan experience was, how to manipulate Islamists and to make Communists (of the Khalq faction) to grow beards and join their declared enemies. This "Khalq strategy" provided a successful alternative to the more orthodox "Parcham strategy" that relied on ideologically less unholy alliances. When Soviet property was privatized, the GRU naturally made money out of sale of air craft and arms.

As Finnish researcher Anssi Kullberg has recently pointed out in his well documented master's thesis on Russian geopolitics, the Islamic Renaissance Party was founded in Astrakhan, in June 1990, under KGB surveillance, to argue for a Soviet and global Islam against separatist movements among Muslim nations.

The Islamic Party of Azerbaijan was founded in 1991 by a philologist, "a typical representative of the post-Soviet lumpen-intelligentsia", who was both anti-Turkic and anti-Semitic. Its members organized the burning of an Israeli flag and training of "Islamic brigades". The party fought an international Masonic conspiracy to spread the American model of civilization, until its leadership was arrested in 1996, and accused of spying for Iran.

Soviet sponsorship for Islamism has been exposed by a Chechen nationalist leader, Ahmad Zakayev, in a revealing booklet on "Wahhabism - Kremlin's drugs against national liberation organizations".

Finnish Polish researcher Zofia Grodzinska-Klemetti, who visited Chechnya during and between the war years, has also stressed how both Russian and Saudi intelligence were regarded by Chechens as parallel forces undermining the peace and liberty of Chechen society. She noticed in her lecture in Helsinki on October 23rd, 2001, that anti-Semitic propaganda was always in Russian language, and that God was always addressed in Arabic, as Allah, instead of using more popular appellations in local languages. It has been very typical for western Islamists to insist on the use of God's Arabic name. Obviously, anti-Semitism did not emerge from Caucasian or Russian Turkic (Tatar) cultures, but was imported in the name of Arab-centered Islam.

When the Soviet colonies had nevertheless declared independence in 1991, militant Muslims like the Chechen Basayev brothers, and some of Hikmatyar's "Afghan

Arabs", were invited by the GRU to join an "Islamic cause" on behalf of Abkhazia against Georgia. Although the war of 1992-1993 was depicted as a war of independence for the traditionally Muslim Abkhazians, the Basayevs and other Muslim volunteers soon found out, that this was far from the truth. The so-called Abkhazians were old-time Communists who refused to accept democratic changes. Instead of gaining more autonomy, Abkhazia - just like Karabakh and Transdnestria - became practically operated by Russian secret services, and engaged in international arms trade and training of terrorists.

According to American Turkish researcher Ali M. Koknar, Shamil Basayev went through military training in Afghanistan from April until July 1994; Indian researcher Vinod Anand dates his visit from March to May 1994 - anyway before the Taliban emerged. His host must then still have been Hikmatyar, or one of his Soviet-trained subordinates. There has never been evidence of any contacts between the Chechen leadership and the Taliban, except for a private mission of the former Chechen vice president in early 2000, when Russia had already invaded Chechnya for the second time.

The Chechen Republic of Ichkeria had declared independence in 1991, and for the first three years, Russia tried a variety of tricks to overpower it. What had succeeded by 1993 in Georgia, Tajikistan, and Azerbaijan, failed to bring results in Chechnya. In the end, Russia started two full-scale invasions against this tiny Caucasian nation. Very few Islamists have shown any sympathy for their fellow Muslims. Both Iran and Iraq have applauded Russia's invasions. Although Russia has blamed Muslim terrorists ("Afghan Arabs") for the tough Chechen resistance, more Ukrainian or ethnic Russian (!) volunteers have been sighted among Chechen freedom-fighters than Arabs or Afghans.

There are tactical similarities between Chechnya and Afghanistan. Equally sinister forces operated in both countries. Provocateurs were used by Russian secret services to destabilize governments, and the world media was largely kept misinformed about what was going on. At some point, while Afghans were accused for fighting in Chechnya, Chechens were accused for fighting in Afghanistan. Such astonishingly illogical accusations were uncritically transmitted by Western media.

Few journalists bothered to ask, why these "mercenaries" remained invisible, immortal (no bodies found on battle grounds), and impossible to be ever caught alive (unless Russia had its prisoners-of-war executed before they could be interrogated), or what sense would it make to have such a bold "students' exchange" between two countries without a common border or even a common neighbour. The logistic risks alone would certainly discourage such practices.

Beside this, the origins of such inconsistent claims could be traced quite easily. The myth of Chechens in Afghanistan was invented by the Times of India in December 1999, concerning at first only refugees, women and children. By April 2000, there appeared in The Indian Express and The Hindustan Times articles, distributed in the internet by well-known disinformation agents, stories about Arab, Pakistani and Afghan militants, who allegedly had been to Chechnya in August 1999, but returned to fight in Kyrgyzstan before retiring to Afghanistan. Indian newspapers have been always useful for launching Russian disinformation.

In April 2000, the alleged Afghans in Chechnya and Chechen refugees in Afghanistan were suddenly turned into Chechen fighters in Afghanistan, by the Russian media. When a Russian TV crew claimed on May 22nd, 2000, that Masud had admitted the existence of "not yet many" Chechens in Afghanistan, Itar-TASS news agency reported "dozens of Chechens" sighted in Afghanistan, which Reuters and BBC inflated into "thousands of Chechens".

So, a myth was born. Although Kazakstani Khabar TV searched 3260 prisoners in Afghanistan to find a Chechen, the only candidate turned out to be an Azerbaijani. A Russian newspaper reporter managed to meet a Circassian, who must have worked hard to explain his American interrogators the differences of Caucasian nationalities. There were more Westerners among Al-Queda prisoners.

Mysteriously, none of these Chechens could ever be interviewed - unlike two captured Chinese Uyghurs, who were presented in probably every respectable Western newspaper. This, of course, pleased China, but provided Russia little evidence to substantiate its own myths on terrorism.

It has been alleged that most Al-Quaeda militants in Afghanistan were of Saudi Arabian or Egyptian origin, but passports could be stolen or forged. Records captured in Kabul, include mostly Yemeni names, followed by Algerians, and individual Syrians, Lebanese, Palestinian, Kuwaiti, and Tunisians. Al-Quaeda's third man, "Abu Zubaydah", was first declared a Saudi Arabian of Palestinian origin, but then recognized as an Iraqi activist of the Arab Socialist Baath party. Although they are Arabs all the same, identities could provide clues about political backgrounds.

Chechens have been accused for various mischiefs in Russia. Some years ago, there were stories about toxic material hidden in Moscow parks by Chechen terrorists. Now we know that the Soviet Army had dumped chemical armament into a Moscow park 30 years earlier. (TOL 12.9.2001) All traces seem to lead back to the "Third Rome" and its "praetorians", the Russian military intelligence, GRU. According to the Russian president himself, in his speech at the "Aquarium" on November 5th, 2001, as many as 421 GRU officers had perished in Chechnya during two years of war, and the GRU continues to have a role in Russian foreign affairs.

The "number of the beast" of the Book of Apocalypse, Nostradamus' prophecies, astrology and numerological magic has entertained people for centuries. Even if history was not predetermined and predictable, it might be useful to present some scenarios, based on historical comparisons, presuppositions of repeating cycles, and warning examples. European history has been traditionally approached from a Western point of view, where the central point would be situated somewhere around Switzerland.

From the slopes of Sankt Gotthard, the great rivers flow to different directions, towards the North Sea, the Mediterranean Sea, and the Black Sea. The antagonism between Germany and France has been the dominant theme shaping European great power politics and European integration. However, the geographical central point of Europe has been located in Lithuania, the greatest river of Europe starts from the uplands of Valdai, and in the Caucasus, there are higher peaks than in the Alps. Perhaps then Europe's fate, too, has been more dramatically shaped by the centuries of antagonism between Turkey and Russia?

According to the Anglo-Saxon point of view, which has become familiar to us through all the movies, the ultimate goal of Napoleon Bonaparte and Adolf Hitler was the conquest of England. Campaigns into Russia were just fatal by-plots. The Nordic history, however, also remembers Charles XII [King of Sweden], who advanced as far as to Pultava, and escaped from there to the protection of Turkey. Were all these three conquerors just megalomaniac fools, obsessed by some kind of an odd Russia fever, which led them to a military suicide on the endless steppes? This romantic view understandably prevails in Russia and it has also been accepted by the dissidents who have criticized the adventurous policies of European great powers. However, serious historians have always known that Russia was by no means perfectly innocent to its great patriotic wars. Russia participated the partitions of Poland, the Molotov-Ribbentrop pact, and the Yalta division of Europe. The Russian army had wandered at the Alps before Bonaparte took power in France.

This means that the events of Russian history have shaped Europe far away in the West, too. Could we learn something useful for understanding Europe, by comparing Russia's reactions to its state of weakness after the Crimean War (1853-1856), after the First World War (1914-1918), and after the fall of the Warsaw Pact (1989-1991)?

The Crimean War was followed by seven hopeful years of reforms, during which the serfs (land slaves) were released, political control was eased, the Caucasus War was brought to an end, and the autonomy of Finland was strengthened. These years were followed by fourteen years of mixed hope and doubt, during which the Polish uprising was crushed, the Circassians were deported, political assassinations and terrorism increased, the state became indebted, Alaska was sold, but Turkestan was conquered. Then came five years of political violence, the war against Turkey (1877-1878), the assassination of the czar and the illegal cancellation of the constitution, and the pogroms against Jews (1881-1882).

The First World War was followed by seven years of chaos and disorder, which were highlighted in the rising hopes when the civil war was over and the economy had revived a bit. After Lenin's death and before Stalin established his tyranny, the administration had its own kind of a democratic flavor, and dissatisfied citizens were allowed to travel abroad. However, this period was changed to a period of fourteen years (1925-1939), during which the strangling grip of communism got worse. Finally, six years of war were experienced.

The liberation of Eastern Europe and disintegration of the Soviet Union (1991) were followed by seven hopeful years, although the first Chechen War (1994-1996) was heralding a change. Then came the devaluation (1998), Vladimir Putin's rise into power (1999), the second Chechen War (1999-), the gradual rehabilitation of Soviet symbols, the erosion of the freedom of speech, and the fading of democracy. We might presently witness a period of fourteen years, which most observers interpret in contradictory terms, but increasingly negatively. We can ask, whether this period will be followed by a political cramp including war and external threat. Then the year 2012 might be the time when Russia must explode against its neighbors.

The Baltic States got to enjoy their full independence 21 years (1918-1939), before they were again occupied. From their new independence (1991), same time will be past only in 2012. Before that there will be no reason to suppose that they would be permanently safe, and that the Russian leaders would have forgotten the "good old days" for good.

Putin's presidency will last until 2008. His re-election for the period 2008-2012 requires an exceptional law (as was the case in Finland with President Urho Kekkonen), or a change of constitution. This year, 200 years will be past from the year when Napoleon had himself crowned as an emperor. It is also easy to find similarities between Putin and Benito Mussolini, as well as many military dictators, who tend to seek life-time reign, and often also enjoy relatively large popular support in the beginning.

A basic problem of dictators is how to justify their power over a longer time, how to keep eternally youthful, and how to turn people's attention away from internal problems. Napoleon marched into Russia thirteen years after his rise into power, and Mussolini invaded Abessinia when he had been thirteen years in power. Where could Putin seek a glorious victory in 2012?

The Baltic States are now members of the EU and NATO, but will this decisively save them? First and foremost we have to ask, will the membership in the EU and NATO, still after eight years, raise enough respect in Russia to pre-empt Russian desires for expansion?

Right now it seems evident that the enlargement of the EU will get slower, and Turkey will not be able to enter by 2012. It may indeed happen that the Cyprus question paralyzes the EU foreign political decision-making as early as this year. The EU is torn by internal controversies - and not least on the field of foreign policy. The German government will change in the next election, but by 2012 it may change for a second time. When the Madrid bombings (March 11, 2004) have proved that terrorism is a successful method of changing pro-Western governments in Europe, the future right-wing government of Germany will have to live in a constant fear for terrorism.

The re-election of George W. Bush for a second term means the EU's relations with the US will remain cool. The situation was similar after the re-elections of the last three two-term Republicans Dwight Eisenhower (1956), Richard Nixon (1972), and Ronald Reagan (1984). Eisenhower, Nixon and Reagan disagreed with their European allies originally in their relationship with the Soviet Union, but soon also in their policies in the Middle East.

In Europe, "street parliaments" and "intellectuals" demanded unilateral disarmament, marched for peace, and made scorn of the intellect of the US president, but the governments in Western Europe still realized how dangerous the communist threat really was. How many of the European governments will be able to resist the defeatism agitated by left-wing media, or has the guts to commit itself to defending the Baltic States, even in theory? Will the healthy instincts of self-preservation and national defense of the Europeans survive to 2012?

The Baltic States and Poland have experienced enough many betrayals to not trust in the protection of the EU. The unity of NATO is also questionable, as Germany, France and Belgium refused to grant Turkey security guarantees a year ago. The Baltic States and Poland, even as NATO members, will have to count on their traditional ally, Turkey, in addition to the US.

The occupation of the Baltic countries would be prepared with a campaign, where the following arguments are expected to arise, fed into Western European media, and perhaps supported by conspiratorial operations and provocations:

- There are striking violations of human rights or discrimination against the Russian minorities in the Baltic States.
- The Baltic governments are protecting terrorists acting against Russia (Chechen refugees). [Mysterious bomb blasts could occur to support the claims.]
- Lithuania is causing troubles to the Russian transit to the special enclave of Kaliningrad [formerly known as Königsberg].
- The EU should grant Russians freedom of visa.
- Putin has to do something, because otherwise a radical nationalist would rise into power. [A provocateur could be activated for the purpose.]
- The Baltic States should pay themselves for their adventurous foreign politics.
- The Baltic countries have never really belonged to Europe.
- The possibility of a (nuclear) devastation of a third world war must not be even thought of.
- NATO has become anachronistic, and conflicts must be subjected to the OSCE or UN.
- Russia does not want to suppress Baltic independence, but just to keep Americans away.

Political trends in the Western countries have been changing in waves. The right-wing 1950s were followed by the "new-leftist" shift of the 1960s and 1970s, and the "new-rightist" 1980s. The support of the left in Western Europe peaked around the change of millennium, when Spain and Austria were the few countries in Western Europe dominated by the right wing - Austria ending in a EU boycott. It is relatively sensible to expect a rightist peak around 2010. The terrorists who have been inspired by the

Spanish experience in March 2004 could feel an irresistible temptation to try toppling down these rightist governments two years later.

Right-wing thought has changed its shape over times. A wave of anti-Semitism spread to the West from Russia in the 1870s, 1920s, and 1990s. It has been mixed with anglophobia (until 1946) and anti-Americanism (thereafter). After the extermination of any large populations of Jews, the Muslims have become a similar "alien" element and a suitable scapegoat. Local prejudices against Chechens (in Russia), Albanians (in Serbia and Macedonia), Turks (in Germany), North Africans (in France), and Pakistanis (in Britain) can be easily unified as a common all-European Islamophobia, where all Muslims are treated as terrorists, socially misfit and abusers of social welfare. Targeting xenophobia against Muslims serves well Russia's interests and helps in closing Turkey (as well as Albania and Bosnia) out of the EU.

In today's Europe, Islamophobia is just in the bud, just like anti-Semitism once upon the time. It is, however, fomented by the radical demands of Islamist communities, which irritate the dominant populations, and by international terrorism, which causes irrational fear. Sooner or later European citizens will grow weary of all the security measures and hope that Europe would have nothing to do with the Islamic world. While the US is actively participating in the defence of Israel, Turkey and Pakistan, in the reconstruction of Afghanistan and Iraq, in the returning of Lebanon's sovereignty, and other projects of the Middle East, the troubled Europeans will easily resign from all of them. This decision can easily be speeded up with terrorism.

Although the Islamists attempt to pose as the representatives of Muslims in general or Arabs in particular, we have to keep in mind that the Islamists are actually rebel groups fighting against their own governments (including the Saudi monarchy). Their relationship with inclusive ideologies like Pan-Arabism or Pan-Islamic thought is about as genuine as the relationship of European terrorist organizations of the 1970s (for example the ETA and the IRA) with the Pan-European thought [that is, non-existent]. Unfortunately it will take more than eight years before Europe starts to understand that al-Qaida doesn't work in favor of the Iraqis, just as the PKK doesn't work for the Kurds, the ETA for the Basques, or the IRA for the Catholic Church.

It might well happen that a shift from the policy of concessions to radical Islamists - which peaked in the Spanish election - towards general frustration and hatred against Islam will take place around 2012. First the Europeans will start to question the rationality of the overly tolerant immigration policy. The popularity of leaders like Jörg Haider and Silvio Berlusconi is not over.

The next thing to follow will be a wave of terrorism, which will first cause a reaction of panic, but gradually defiance will appear instead. The right-wing will adopt Islamophobic and xenophobic themes, which will be combined with anti-Americanism. In this way, a new extreme right will be born, and it will get many supporters from the former extreme left. Haider, Berlusconi and Putin are the pioneers of this forthcoming path.

The ones to lose are the conservatives and liberals of the "Old Europe", as well as their ideological brothers who might be in power in the "New Europe". However, when the described thinking prevails among the ruling left and new extreme around 2012, the Baltic governments and other "New European" conservatives and liberals will raise anger in the "Old Europe" for their sympathies for the US, Free Iraq or the Chechens.

They are treated as awkward troublemakers by the "Old Europe", which prefers to deal directly with Russia, deciding also about the fate of the Baltic countries and other borderlands with Russia, without endangering their good relations with Moscow, especially as the relations with the

US have deteriorated. European great power politics will become increasingly dominated by the spirit of Tilsit, the Holy Alliance, the Berlin Congress, the Molotov-Ribbentrop pact, and Yalta.

When it was declared that the Cold War is over and a wave of moderate leftism wiped all across Europe, adopting an optimistic stand at future. Because of this, the seven years of hope in Russia were left unused, Russia's democratic development was not supported, the Chechen wars were not prevented, Afghanistan and Iraq were allowed to sink into tyranny, millions of refugees joined the immigrants and moved left, political mysticism favoring conspiracy theories gained foothold in Europe, and the European unification was not fulfilled in the best possible way.

When, after visitation, realism again started winning support, the traditional right wing (conservatives and liberals) started to win elections (surprisingly also in the US as early as in 2000), but the left wing managed to turn the situation by exploiting terrorism and the situation in the Middle East. The right wing will probably recover and win crushing victories across Europe, but only after they have adopted fatal influences from the extreme left.

This radicalization will be, in turn, responded by the left by radicalization, but meanwhile Russia will have a chance for a partial restoration of the Soviet system. The only hope for Europe to avoid this fatal polarization will lie in the ability and willingness of US Republicans to stay in power and to stay active in world politics. If the Americans withdraw into isolationism (like after 1918, in 1945-1946, and in early 1990s), the Pan-Europeans will have to stand alone the challenges of 2012.

5

Post-Modern Terrorism

Individual perpetrators of terrorist acts may be psychopaths or suicidal personalities, but their mentors, protectors, and managers, are rational political players. Not only the techniques, but also the strategies of terrorism will follow general development, to suit better to the modern society. Terrorism is the art of manipulating political opinions and decisions by the use of violence and mass psychology, especially in a democracy - in dictatorships, carefully targeted assassinations would be more efficient. There are basically two strategies:

1. Collective blackmail;
2. Provocations.

In the former, the enemy is forced to pay such a high price for peace and security, that compromises or appeasement will get wide support. This is clearly the intention of the IRA against the United Kingdom, or the ETA against Spain. In some cases, the enemy may become a political pariah, shunned by potential allies. This is the case of various terrorist groups operating against Turkey (to prevent EU membership), Israel, and the USA.

The latter method was used for the "Bulgarian agitation" in 1876, and became the favourite strategy of Russian secret services throughout the 20th century. Provocations aim at compromising the "ordinary" suspects. Even the German

National Socialists were tempted to use Jews as scapegoats for staged acts of terrorism.

Both traditional terrorist strategies are, however, messy and risky. Terrorists have learned that the victims tend to react unexpectedly, by rallying around their political leaders and accepting tougher counter-terrorist policies. Many good men (from the terrorist perspective) have to risk their lives for committing terrorist acts, and even the most fanatic groups have a limited supply of voluntary suicide-bombers. In the case of provocations, on the other hand, terrorists may save man-power, but they have to sacrifice women and children in an attempt to earn sympathy and accuse their enemies for brutality. Would it not be possible to achieve the same results by less actual blood-shedding?

Terrorism needs media attention like plants need sunshine. If an airplane is destroyed, but everybody assumes it an accident by technical failure, terrorism gained nothing. If the reason of an air crash remains unsolved or doubted, a terrorist group may claim responsibility and celebrate it as their achievement. Why do the hard work of actually planting bombs in airplanes, if the most important factor is, to what and whom the media subscribes the incident?

Terrorists need journalists, but journalists too live of bad news and threats. Terrorists and journalists live in a symbiosis, mutually profitable relationship. Ideally, journalists provide terrorists with headlines and resulting public outcry, while terrorists provide journalists with the evidence required for verification. A maximal sensationalist "yellow press" needs a minimum of real bodies. If public hysteria can be created bloodlessly, just by media reports and threats, why fill the mortuaries?

In Iraq, coalition soldiers and civilians are killed almost daily. This has been chosen instead of open resistance, because killing 30 men in a battle once a month would, paradoxically, not produce the same net result. The ultimate aim is not to destroy the occupying military forces (Americans could easily afford to loose a thousand men in the whole war), but to keep the media occupied, and to make the "home front" tired of the whole issue. Killing military personnel would not be terrorism as such, but when the aim is to frighten the great public by continuous media attention, it could be classified as terrorism.

The remnants of the former Iraqi government and security forces are not the only people to have learned the might of the media, and how to influence it effectively. Terrorism is spreading all over the world as a substitute for old-fashioned fighting. High-profile kidnapping cases provide similar publicity, without body counts. During the Anthrax letter scare and SARS epidemics, ordinary people felt the temptation of jokes that could paralyze air traffic, mailing, private and public businesses. The media can be held hostage by so many different ways.

In long term, virtual terrorism may become a business-conscious enterprise. Advertisement and campaign bureaus, consults and lobbyists, belong to the 20th century, while the 21st century will see the privatization of full-service secret agencies with their trusted professional terrorists, provocateurs, media connections, stock exchange experts, life guards, arms merchants, human rights lawyers, and documentation centres. Disinformation is not even illegal.

Although this development may clean up terrorism somewhat, and save lives and limbs, there will follow the same problems that plague every expanding organization. Some terrorists become common criminals, but others may find the manipulation of financial markets more interesting. Airlines and insurance companies react to terrorist acts, and threats of such. There will be rivalries, and some terrorist organizations may turn into honest protection business.

Terrorism is a globally unevenly distributed phenomenon. The natural objects are free and democratic societies, where the media is not censored, justice is clement, and the decision-making process is open and predictable. The most successful organizers and sponsors, however, are internationally protected dictatorships with closed borders, secretive administration, hierarchical power structures, and cheap work force. This inequality determinates that terrorists will be harboured by dictatorships against democracies, until the latter make serious counter-threats of promoting democracy by force, which will prevent dictatorships of exploiting their natural advantage too far.

Countries like Turkmenistan and North Korea know, that their real or supposed capability to retaliate are their best guarantees against foreign demands of liberalization, but the recent fate of Afghanistan and Iraq warn them of testing the patience of democracies beyond all limits. Peaceful coexistence of dictatorships and democracies is possible only in a state of mutual balance of terror.

Russia has by far the longest tradition of state terrorism, global network of agents, propaganda machinery through international front organizations, and all kind of subversive tactics. The restoration of Soviet-style centralization, and the possession of destructive potential, accompanied with continuing economical and demographical problems, makes terrorism a temptation hard to resist. What would Russia have to loose by protecting terrorist groups and regimes?

In a postmodern world, Russia will cultivate and export the know-how and techniques it knows best. This will not necessarily mean that Russia would sell too much nuclear technology to Iran, because it prefers to keep a monopoly. Russia will not need to harbour Usama bin Ladin or Saddam Hussein in Moscow, because there are enough client states and nominally independent military bases to store them outside its borders.

Most likely, postmodern Russian terrorism will appeal to the media, and avoid unnecessary brutality. Why blow up innocent people, when all critical opposition by democratic societies can be paralyzed and eliminated by the mere threat of risking world peace? Who would seriously oppose bold demands of further credits, or the extradition of individual terrorists, if Russia would fully use all its potential? Journalists, researchers, and politicians could be relieved by the prospect of saving lives - perhaps even their own - through appeasement at the cost of taxpayers. Nevertheless, this would be the end of democracy.

Dark Web Terror

Global connectivity, rapid technological development, highly skilled professionals, experienced employee mobility and lack of knowledge, expose IT and network infrastructure to a myriad of risks of which the risk of a malicious cyber attack by terrorists is the most threatening because of its final goals. Debating the terrorist's capabilities to launch a sustained cyber-attack on networks and IT infrastructure argument, suffice to quote Kent Anderson in "Managing the Cyber Threat", "Traditional wisdom holds that insiders are the greatest threat to an organization. This is based on two assumptions: first, insiders have access and second, that they have knowledge of a company's systems, applications and processes".

This quote summarizes in essence the extent to which terrorists can reach into our supposedly protected systems. The restrictions and self-inflicted disabilities in checking certain information and background on employees, which could unveil inside terrorist activities is restricted either because of the fears of infringing privacy and civil rights or because of "profiling" deemed as inappropriate. This irresponsible way of providing crippled security serves as an opened invitation for Jihadi sympathizers, devoted supporters and dormant terrorists - especially among the newly converted - to take advantage of the security gaps in many ways. There are four critical factors, as seen above, which are sure to make a cyber attack devastating.

- Insider restricted information – usually available to employees
- Access to hardware and software (codes, PW, systems status, etc) – which are part of the professional tasks and interacting with other employees
- Knowledge of the systems – a "must" task in order to be able to perform the work-duties
- Opportunity – by the very fact that opportunity situations occur daily for insiders

Kent Anderson's quote should be a shining red light to all the experts and threat deniers ("until I see it I don't believe it exists"), and those that still believe that the threat level is low and that the terrorists lack the knowledge to launch a heavy duty attack.

Have they fallen prey to "consensus thinking" maybe. Given the above, should we be surprised that UBL and alike see the internet as an effective weapon to fight the West; should we again underestimate what they can do and to what extent?

A Deadly Scenario

It's Wednesday, December 24, 2008. The financial markets are closed, the banking systems is inactive and the entire commerce and business system is in a low-key, standby mode worldwide; people in the US are in a celebrating atmosphere following a good year without terror attack in the homeland. It is an ideal picture of pre-Christmas. But then, without warning, at 2:15 am, "the worm" roared.

An extremely sophisticated and complex virus, the "Storm Worm 2", launched by UBL's IT group three month before, was cleverly engineered to keep multiplying into and from itself, expending exponentially, constantly infecting and taking over the full control of more and more computers, servers and networks worldwide.

By December 31, Storm Worm 2 - or "The Jihadi Storm", the name given by Al-Queda's IT Chief Jawad Ramadan - has already penetrated and quietly installed itself in a dormant mode inside hundreds of vital financial, commercial, military and private infrastructure networks, ready to be activated.

In the early hours of January 2, 2008, at 1:20 am eastern time zone, twelve remote unmanned regional switching and control centers, and ten strategically located communication antennas towers and comm boosting and relay stations, were blown up by powerful C4 explosive charges planted in advance and activated by drive-by remote activation.

At 1:25 am, The Jihadi Worm, started drilling, neutralizing the network protection software programs and opened the gates for external unauthorized access. The systems were left "bare-naked" and helpless and the shift system administrators didn't even know, because no alarm was triggered and no sign of intrusion was detected.

At 1:28 am, Joseph Stapleton (alas Gibran Hammuda), the IT shift manager, opened the door to the main surveillance and monitoring control room at Google's HQ using his high-security special badge and his confirmation tag key, and deactivated the antivirus and protective systems, by running a short and simple command program from a CD that was sent to him by regular mail a day before, which was written based on the information supplied by him. In order to avoid his covert activity, Joseph wrote a short report message to his chief letting him know that "there is a glitch in the main frames but I believe the system will be up again shortly".

At 1:45, a bombardment of millions of e-bombs were launched from hundreds of locations all over the globe, using software that kept creating automatic messages, inundated public, government and open systems until the systems began collapsing, dragging with them a host of directly and related networks, which were suppose to be independent, therefore protected from exactly such an attack.

At 1:55 am, Hamzi Tauafik Hilal, the cook of the two million cubic meters LNG super-tanker "Independence Day", climbed up to the deck, and confirmed that the tanker is docked and is surrounded by several other LNG and LPG tankers within the perimeter of the Mississippi port. Being Muslim, he volunteered to remain on duty with a crew of other three shipmen.

He walked calmly into the control room and shut off the refrigerating system that kept the natural gas below the freezing point, went back to the kitchen, cut off the gas tube from its wall socket, prayed for a minute praising Allah for the opportunity to become a shaiid, and without hesitation pulled the trigger of his Ronson lighter; a monstrous explosion shattered the surroundings. An enormous ball of fire engulfed the entire port, triggering tens of secondary explosions farther from the center, in a terrible ripple effect.

On December 25, at 06:00 am, hell began, the West was on the verge of collapsing. There were no commanders, nor security forces to activate within a radius of 7 miles from the port. It was all but flatten scorched earth.

If this imaginary scenario sends an icy shiver down your spine, it should, because it much more realistic than what you think. It's not accurate in its details but makes sense, and if you're scared, you definitively should be. Given that so many security breaches occur daily, and so many local cyber attacks take place every minute on the internet, it can happen, and we've seen this degree of sophistication from Al-Queda in the near past.

No doubt that the new flat decentralized structure facilitates better coordination and synchronization through the internet. It takes time to put in place such a daring plan, but as mentioned in Part Two, terrorists have time and patience. And there is a continuous infiltration of Muslims with terrorist connections into government jobs, research institutions, and the military and security forces, including the FBI lately, (Nada Nadim Prouty, who also worked for the CIA).

Thousands convert to Islam every year and the government doesn't and shouldn't control or monitor the process, but do we know how many convert to Islam and don't tell their employer; is this detectable by security managers, I doubt it; and if the authorities would be able to acquire the details via legal venues, what could they do?

Is the above scenario realistic? Yes, because the accumulated threat of vicious, life-threatening cyber terrorism is far higher than the sum of its parts. Can this really happen? It sure can. It's not that the information and the warning signs don't exist, they are all over the place; in the media, on the web, in chat rooms and forums, in lessons learned from breaching events, deep penetration into highly-secured networks, through hacking into academic networks, banks, stock exchange and public domains, etc.

The problem stems from the same misunderstanding and arrogance which led us to military, security and moral defeat in the near past. It emanates from a sense of technological superiority many in the industry walk around with, which is factually true. What they miss though is the simple fact that the more they amass protective layers on the already sensitive systems and networks, the easier it becomes to find holes to penetrate it.

System administrators, computer engineers, programmers and security managers who battle every day with such problems, are actually very concerned. Again, like we've seen before 9/11, the executive management, driven by other than professional interests, prefer not to believe that it is much easier than what they've been manipulated to believe, to bring down their sophisticated grand networks. They are constantly tutored that terrorists using non-savvy internet "beginners", which they believe them to be, don't have the required knowledge to really expose the system to serious danger.

Instead they pay lip tribute to the media partially agreeing that dark-web terrorism may develop into a real danger, sometime in the future. Such statements are typical acts of self-protection in case the threat materializes faster than expected. But this is by no means an answer to the real threat which keeps growing by the day. Some eye-opening examples:

Immediately after 9/11, several studies have shown certain signs of dark web cyber attacks generated by terrorists. It was obvious as early as 2001-02 that the level of sophistication, the targets chosen, and the scope of the attacks, the sources and the numbers kept growing rapidly. Collection of data regarding those attacks indicated that the attacks focused on what terrorists perceived as very important targets, such as vital communications and critical infrastructure systems. In time, since 2001, cyber attacks developed and evolved exposing various problems and vulnerabilities of networks which were suppose to be untouchable.

It is extremely important to emphasize that studies and analysis of cyber attacks launched by terrorists have shown an interesting pattern:

- A cyber attack came shortly before the terror attack, or
- The cyber attack was launched almost simultaneously with the physical attack (maybe a field test designed to coordinate and synchronize cyber and physical attacks)
- The cyber attack began immediately after the physical attack – meaning that it was prepared in advance, intended to propagate the victory whether true or not

Very important data can be found in "Cyber attacks during the war on terrorism: a predictive analysis" released on September 22, 2001 by The Institute for Security and Technology Studies at Dartmouth College. The importance of this study is in that it was published just two weeks after 9/11, and while the research was all done much earlier, the conclusions are still viable today.

Run Away Logic

"Terrorist groups are increasingly using new information technology and the Internet to formulate plans, recruit members, communicate between cells and members, raise funds, and spread propaganda. Terrorist groups including Hezbollah, the Abu Nidal Organization, and UBL's Al-Queda Organization are using computerized files, email, and encryption to support their operations." stated Louis Freeh, FBI Director in his Congressional Statement, "Threat of Terrorism to the United States," as early as 2001.

Six years have passed since. Al-Queda's rebirth in many aspects, its fast-track evolution after 9/11 and how resilient they've become despite the flat non-centralized structure, should tell us a similar story as to the development of the cyber attack factor in their ideology. There are several UBL confirmed quotes indicating the importance of the internet and of cyber attacks as part of the total Jihad against the West; why shouldn't we take those threats seriously.

Gigantic intelligence mistakes were made by forcing explanations to questions that did not have a proper answer, simply because they didn't know. And most of those were assessment mistakes. The tendency exists to apply an expected or projected answer every time a real time answer is not available, which in turn leads to wrong analysis and wrong assessment. The run away logic is a subconscious way to find a "logic" reasoning thus allowing one to evade the need to deal with the bits and pieces that can't be placed in the puzzle that intelligence is; every time it is applied, run away logic "kills" the path to the problem, making it invisible or transparent. Running away from the problem or bypassing it results in the same "there is no problem", and that is very dangerous.

This quote from the Daily Telegraph article "How real is the threat of cyber terrorism?" is another telling example: "This is a difficult message for some, because these days anyone who causes widespread damage is being given the label "terrorist." But imagine for a minute the leadership of al Qaeda sitting in a cave somewhere, plotting the next move in their jihad against the United States. One of the leaders jumps up and exclaims: "I have an idea! We'll disable their e-mail...." The misconceptions and basic lack of understanding of the matter displayed speaks volumes. More concerning is the fact that the newspaper conveys the views of the experts and politicians who overwhelmingly believe the threat of a powerful terror cyber attack is nonsense and scary tactics.

The US Naval War College used a research group to simulate a massive cyber attack on the nation's information infrastructure. Government hackers and security analysts initiated in the summer of 2002 in Newport, Rod Island the "Digital Pearl Harbor" war game intended to confirm or dismiss the threat of a cyber attack with serious implications on the national level. According to reports, the results were far from devastating, the hackers failed to crash the Internet, although they did cause serious sporadic damage.

CNet.com reported in August 2002, that "officials concluded that terrorists hoping to stage such an attack "would require a syndicate with significant resources, including $200 million, country-level intelligence and five years of preparation time." This conclusion meant to be the last nail in the coffin of potential cyber attack, and the ultimate convincing argument that terrorists are not, and will not, be able to stage such an attack in the foreseeable future.

Yet by analyzing the details of their own conclusion, the exact opposite conclusion are more plausible, and this is why:

- The syndicate – this is what we see today – a conglomerate of terror organizations, Jihadi groups and Islamic radical movements, all cooperating with and through the internet, in an amorphous, almost fluid structure.
- Significant resources – Iran, Iraq, Syria and the terrorists' pact with syndicated crime provide a myriad of financial, support, backup and manpower sources, not to mention the "charity funds", internet and mosque donations, and high profits from other venues.
- Country level Intel – The deep involvement of Al-Queda and many other Jihadi groups in the Iraqi and Afghanistan wars, has transformed them into experienced fighters and very good information gatherers. From seized documents we know that terrorists have real-time intelligence which is quickly dissipated, and are very apt to acting upon it.

  Five years of preparation time – we enter now the seventh year since 9/11 and in spring 2008 it will be the fifth anniversary year of Operation Iraqi Freedom. Shouldn't we worry?

Therefore, by their own words, the conditions designed by the "Digital Pearl Harbour" war game managers as critical for terrorists to be able to launch a nation-wide cyber attack, are all fulfilled as detailed thereof. What other convincing reason experts can provide that would let to believe that terrorists are not ready yet? Wasn't UBL who claimed in 2002 that "hundreds of Muslim scientists are with me and will use their knowledge in computers and electronics against the infidels?"

Dan Verton in his book "Black Ice: The Invisible Threat of Cyber-Terrorism" quotes Sheikh Omar Bakri Muhammad, UBL's messenger: "I would advise those who doubt al Qaeda's interest in cyber-weapons to take Osama bin Laden very seriously". Verton further mentions that "The third letter from Osama bin Laden ... was clearly addressing using the technology in order to destroy the economy of the capitalist states".

Furthermore, why should we accept blindly the assessment and judgment of the same experts that failed repeatedly either in "connecting the dots" or draw the right conclusions. This in addition to what we've learned a-priory that information on our enemies is too often frivolous, based on unsubstantiated "facts", and often fed by terrorist sources as disinformation.

The Resulting Implications

A less known fact is that critical infrastructure, delivery systems and control center depend entirely on SCADA networks. Furthermore, SCADA is intermeshed with tens of thousands of sub systems who in turn control their own sub systems, and so on and so forth. Every crash, glitch or delay in any of those systems, secondary, tertiary and farther remote sub-networks, creates a ripple effect which can be tracked back thousand of miles away from where the actual event occurred.

A SCADA system monitors and controls all major industrial and civil networks among which:

- Air traffic and railways.
- Power generation and transmission.
- Oil and gas – from extraction through the refining process to delivery.
- Manufacturing and production.
- Water management, including sewage.
- Maritime control.

- Any and all daily public and civil activities, like elevators, refrigerating systems, backups, etc.

But more so, it is important to understand that SCADA is not one system, but a name given to any control network that is based on the specific supervising and collecting information methods from any system that uses a network of computers, servers and communication it is connected to. Therefore, virtually any private, public, industrial, business military and financial structured system is connected to, or makes use of certain SCADA version, adapted to its specific needs. As such, when a problem occurs, there is an immediate impact on a host of other systems which we aren't aware that they are connected somehow to each other.

Any combination of problems within any of the networks controlled by SCADA could trigger:

- Cutoff or water floods.
- Sewage getting mixed in drinking water.
- Open dams, release water and inundate lower grounds (i.e. Katrina storm)
- Massive power blackouts.
- Cutting off the central control room of nuclear power plants or shutoff of the cooling system, thus overheating the nuclear reactor (i.e. the Chernobyl incident).
- Explosions in refineries and processing plants.
- Overloading oil and gas pipelines causing it to burst and explode.
- Incapacitating defense systems by shutting them down or altering commands.
- Train collisions.
- Oil spillage in the ocean.
- Blocking financial systems and interfering in the stock exchange trade.

- Transfer huge amounts of money from financial institution, draining its sources and potentially creating a financial domino-effect collapse.
- Disrupt simple daily tasks such as office buildings, malls and government facilities air conditioning shutoff or over-heating.

SCADA (Supervisory Control And Data Acquisition, is designed to deal with mission-critical networks by definition. Yet SCADA's basic operation principles have raised security concerns from the very beginning, way before the threat of dark web cyber-terrorism was raised. Hundred of events all over the world since the mid 1990s, of which an estimate of 40% were defined as cyber attacks even then, define its innate vulnerabilities and security gaps:

- The common baseless belief that SCADA networks are fully protected networks are not connected to the internet, therefore not accessible from the outside.
- The lack of awareness regarding security design flaws, problems of authentication and protection and difficulties in upgrading existing operational networks without creating new gaps (patching).
- A false sense of security, emphasized by the developers and software designers and manufacturers, that the systems are well protected because unique specialized protocols and proprietary interfaces are used, thus making a successful break-in almost impossible.
- The typical mistake that leads to the false belief that SCADA networks – especially those defined as critical infrastructure - are safe from outside attacks by the very fact that they are physically secured, thus very difficult to penetrate and alter or change the system.

Obviously, any successful attack, local or partial, on a mission-critical SCADA system could cripple or destroy financial networks, prevent recuperate loss of data order destruction of critical information, distort commands and trigger physical destruction of sites; it could collapse a banking system, the stock exchange, or take over the air control causing airplanes to crash.

It is important to mention, that even today, in the era of total Jihad, there are still decision makers that resist the call of many not to patch up the existing SCADA, but develop more secure systems and build new architecture and configuration that fit today's threats. Those anti-change figures, both in the private sector and the government, believe yet that the benefits provided by the existing SCADA systems are greater than the risk of a massive attack. A comprehensive study by the British Columbia Institute of Technology showed that major companies in the US and four other nations have recorded about 135 SCADA security incidents in a little more than four years. Aren't the results of this study alone substantiated enough to prove that there is a growing threat of terrorists cyber attacks; must we wait for another devastating blowout to happen? The awakening time is now.

Well known SCADA security incidents:

- In 1992, Chevron's emergency system was disabled by an employee, causing the alert system to be shut off in 22 states in the US. The problem was discovered only when an emergency which had to be transmitted occurred.
- In 1997, a "kid hacker" broke into NYNEX, cutting off Worcester, MA airport for more than six hours, creating traffic problems which spread out farther that the specific location affecting airs traffic and creating delays and other local problems.
- NATO used information warfare against the Serbs in the war to liberate Kosovo. Russian hackers, who sympathized with the Serbs, launched a heavy attacked on NATO's computers. When US air forces accidentally bombed the Chinese embassy, Chinese hackers attacked computer systems in the US.

- In 2000 the Russian authorities confirmed that hackers were able to gain control over GazProm, the world largest natural gas pipeline network in 2000, Vitek Boden, a former employee took control of the SCADA system controlling the sewage and water treatment system at Queensland's Maroochy Shire in Australia. Using just a wireless connection and a stolen computer, he released millions of gallons of raw sewage and sludge into creeks, parks and a nearby hotel and the coastal waters of Queensland, Australia.
- In 2003, the east coast of America experienced a total blackout, which is indicative of what a cyber attack on such a network could create. It was found that many related and connected systems were infected with the Blaster Worm virus, which wouldn't have been detected shouldn't the blackout have happened. Computer glitches in Ohio caused inaccurate readings along First Energy's electric power lines, and cascading effects among northeastern utilities dealing with the summer heat prompted the shutdown of more than 500 generating units in the US and Canada.
- In January 2003, the Slammer Worm virus hit the Ohio based Davis-Besse nuclear power plant safety monitoring system, causing it to be off-line for more than five hours.
- Instruction manuals and computers seized by American troops in Al-Queda training camps in Afghanistan and Iraq, had lots of information regarding dams and other related critical structures.

Mitigating Factors

"Many in the cyber-security world - consultants seeking clients, academics chasing grants, companies selling software - were deemed to have a vested interest in exaggeration. As were politicians" wrote Simon Finch in his article "Cyber-terrorism is real - ask Estonia" in the British newspaper "Daily Telegraph".

This duality goes both ways, those that argue that it's much ado about nothing, and those that preach for a much serious approach in dealing with this new threat of cyber terrorism by Islamic terrorists. The problem is the fast global spread of networks which leads to the fact that almost all systems are interconnected. Software-wise the only means that maintain a partial independency of each network is the firewalls and its add-ons and derivates. With this easy to circumvent (instead of penetrate) protection software, viruses can easily infect networks that are regarded as being totally protected.

Another amazing fact is that most Islamist websites are hosted on servers located in the West, especially in the US as shown in MEMRI's recent research. Needless to say that Islamists, Jihadists and their supporters have learned to exploit Western freedom of speech, and use it in many creative ways to connect with each other, spread their message and prepare.

There is little doubt that the American IPs don't know what the content of the hosting websites is, mainly because the language of most of these websites is Arabic or other non-western language. The use of hacking to sabotage Internet sites becomes more prevalent. In those activities, which Jihadists call e-Jihad, they attack websites they believe to be anti-Islam or active enemies, aiming to create at this stage, as much as possible morale damages. Other hacking type focuses on attacking infrastructure, strategic, economic and military networks aiming to inflict substantial damage on western infrastructures. Many of these partial successful and failed attacks are seen as a real time proof to the terrorists' incompetence, but the notion that those are training activities and drills becomes more prevalent these days.

To understand the mini-revolution that the Jihadist groups undergo, suffice to study the depth of the online activity and the content richness of their websites, whether in indoctrination, collection of charity (da'wa) or military training and information. Today, the internet is seen by terrorists as an integral part of their total Jihad, an additional ramification to the military, economic, and political fronts carrying the same values as field activities. And more compelling is the fact that e-Jihad is characterized as the type of Jihad for those who cannot participate as field fighters. The name they've given is "The media jihad (al-jihad al-i'lami)".

Epilog/Afterword

Instead of an ordinary summary, I decided to list the main reasons why we should not panic but seriously worry. Because worry emphasizes the need for counter measures and encourages public pressure on the political and business leadership. Hereafter is the compiled "why should we worry":

- Authentication doesn't exist at all or is easy to brake.
- It is increasingly difficult to manage "rights" of entry/usage for each person and identity.
- Every time updating or patching is involved, there is a gap opened that allows penetration.
- Even if a network is designed, run and supervised as an independent closed-end network, there are many temporary uncontrolled interconnections through which an unauthorized entry is easy.
- The so-called "Stand-alone Systems" connect to the Internet through direct links, open, unprotected Wi-Fi, laptops, cellphones, etc as part of their routine activities. Interconnection with the main targeted core system is relatively easy to achieve by creating a VPN-like path via the SQL server which allows collection of data sent from the server to the system. Once inside, reaching the production controls is easy since it is usually not protected.

- A known fact is that there are always discrepancies between the diagram of a system and its actual deployment, especially if it is a relative "old". This flaw is an easy prey to hackers since system administrators consider self-contained – self-managed system as untouchable, and they have the diagrams to prove it, while in reality the system is indirectly connected to outside entities unauthenticated or unknown sources.
- A serious security flaw can be found on the production level, where many systems have to synchronize with NTP over the internet and the tech support of the supplier connects to the system remotely.
- Contrary to popular belief, targeted e-storms/e-bombing can cripple, disrupt and destroy, and shut down critical lines and processes. Proof of the threat level can be found in the creation of the new Cyberspace Command by the US AF, which will also develop a cyberspace warfare doctrine, following many past incidents topped by two major cyber attacks this year:
    - The barrage of cyber attacks emanating from Russia which crippled the banking, police, and government offices of Estonia in April.
    - The Chinese military hacked into a computer network used by top aides to U.S. Defense Secretary Robert Gates, in June.
    - In many cases, the production floor is the most vulnerable to invasion because it is the easiest to connect to from outside via many uncontrolled channels, such as suppliers, technical support, etc.

The hottest development in cellular connectivity is "the real world web" which merge GPS information with network connectivity via ad-hoc links, Wi-Fi and cellphones and Google's Android project. For example, your smart phone will tell you where to find what you're looking for, thus it will be much easier to find where a certain network's servers are physically located.

- There is news from the hackers' world as well. The old proven hacking method where hackers "zombify" computers by infecting them with viruses and worms creating what is called huge "botnets", a network of computers under their control. And in spite of the creation of new threats every day, software companies developed and constantly update protection and anti-virus software which have the capacity to deal with the problem, and they keep improving. The efficiency of the anti-virus software is entirely based on researching new viruses, but lately hackers are responding by attacking computers and systems used by professionals. It is done by and automatic "calling to duty" command of armies of zombie computers, when a new virus is probed, flooding that computer with useless data and chocking the system. The same technique could be used for terrorism purposes.
- Open entries into secured systems is also available due to common mistakes or lack of simple procedures such as not changing the initial password provided by the manufacturer, using predictable PW, sending critical data on the system without encryption, weak authentication by using generic names, etc.
- Attacks by direct dialing into systems.
- Problems in identifying penetration attempts and differentiating between a malicious entry and benign incident.
- Ineffective firewalls, sloppy patching and non-secured coding practices.

War between Right and Wrong

United States is the only country in the world, which not only hold absolute trust in God, but also announces such position proudly, while many of the nations in the world are rather shy in expressing their beliefs in God. One of the mightiest currencies in the world, US Dollar bears a very clear slogan saying "In God we trust". And, who knows, such trust in God is always helping United States in achieving prosperity and strength almost every hour. But, we really witness almost an opposite in the minds of less developed and undeveloped countries in the world, especially in Asian Continent, who believes that the most 'powerful' instrument for them in attaining progress and prosperity is either to denounce existence of God or in other words, embrace atheism. Such tendency is giving opportunity for socialism, communism, atheism and religious extremism to grow. Although there are no relations between secularism and atheism, but, in today's world, mostly socialists and atheists are trying to monopolize secular term as something of their own. In fact, secularism has nothing to do with someone's personal religious beliefs. A person, being devote in his religion may act in secular form in all worldly actions.

Take for the example, the case of Indonesia. Being world's largest Moslem nation, they rather feel shy in expressing their religious beliefs openly or at least officially. You will possibly never find any religious symbol in any of the government establishments in that country. Or, how about our own India? You will see Bapu Gandhi's portrait proudly displayed in various offices, but never any Hindu relic or symbol. Why? Because, India prefers to be called a secularist nation.

What is secularity? Secularity (adjective form secular) is the state of being separate from religion. For instance, eating and bathing may be regarded as examples of secular activities, because there is nothing inherently religious about them. (Note, however, that both eating and bathing are regarded as sacraments by some religious organizations, and therefore would be religious activities in their worldview.) Saying a prayer, worshipping, and attending Sunday School or Friday Mosques are examples of religious (non-secular) activities. All state universities in the United States are secular organizations, while some private universities are church-related; among many, four church-related examples are Brigham Young University, University of Notre Dame, Baylor University, and The Catholic University of America.

The public university system in the United Kingdom is also secular, although many primary and secondary schools are religiously aligned. Although in many of the western countries religious schools and educational institutions enjoy rather special and priviledged position in the society, there is always controversy centering Islamic religious schools in any part in the world. Because, in recent years such institutions unfortunately infected with jihadist motivations and also with culture of religious hatred. But, in original, Islam never preaches culture of religious hatred. There are numerous aruguments and confusions on the real connotations on Jihad even amongst Islamic scholars. Majority believe jihad stands for self purification and not killing others.

In English, the term atheism was derived from the French athéisme in about 1587. The term atheist (in French), in the sense of "one who denies or disbelieves the existence of God", predates atheism in English, being first attested in about 1571. Atheist as a label of practical godlessness was used at least as early as 1577. Related words emerged later, deist in 1621, theist in 1662; theism in 1678; and deism in 1682. Deism and theism changed meanings slightly around 1700, due to the influence of atheism; deism was originally used as a synonym for today's theism, but came to denote a separate philosophical doctrine.

Karen Armstrong writes that "During the sixteenth and seventeenth centuries, the word 'atheist' was still reserved exclusively for polemic ... The term 'atheist' was an insult. Nobody would have dreamed of calling himself an atheist." Atheism was first used to describe a self-avowed belief in late 18th-century Europe, specifically denoting disbelief in the monotheistic Abrahamic God. In the 20th century, globalization contributed to the expansion of the term to refer to disbelief in all deities, though it remains common in Western society to describe atheism as simply "disbelief in God". Most recently, there has been a push in certain philosophical circles to redefine atheism as the "absence of belief in deities", rather than as a belief in its own right; this definition has become popular in atheist communities, though it's mainstream usage has been limited.

Atheism in the 20th century, particularly in the form of practical atheism, advanced in many societies. Atheistic thought found recognition in a wide variety of other, broader philosophies, such as existentialism, objectivism, secular humanism, nihilism, logical positivism, Marxism, feminism, and the general scientific and rationalist movement.

In today's world, mostly Marxists, Communist, Socialist, etc. take refuge under cover of secularism and promote the ideology of non-existence of God in their own way. This is a very dangerous trend. Because, according to social histories of past several decades, people, having belief in existence in God, under various religious identities are abstaining from many evil or bad actions fearing wrath of God. Such strong belief in God is saving the world from many of the social and otherwise disorders. On the other hand, when people get more involved in his or her religious beliefs, it always turns them away from the lure of atheism or secularism.

For example, in marriage, believers go through religious rituals, which is a strong indication for them in making promise to God for a happy marital life. Such trend is saving millions of couples in today's world from being either separated or getting involved in extra-marital physical affairs. On the other hand, a secular, who does not apply religion in worldly affairs, may not go through such religious obligations. So, there is every chance for them in either becoming disobedient to husbands or wives. Look into Soviet Union. During those strict Communist rules, extra marital mixture and all forms of perversions were in practice at an alarming level. According a statistics, more than sixty percent of children born in Soviet-Communism did not know the identity of their genetic father. But now, things are changing. Russian society is embracing various forms of religious beliefs. This is saving the society from devastating level of divorce, perversion etc.

As I mentioned at the beginning, United States is amongst world's one of the most believer nations having firm trust in God. But, this is not applicable to a number of European nations, particularly Britain. This country in particular, despite being largely dominated by Christians is in reality becoming polluted with secular turn atheist ideology. Most of the social disorders such as gay or lesbian activities, or even extra marital and pre-marital physical relations are on increasing trend in that society. While in United States, when a Mayor of New York City lost his position just for having an illicit 'appointment' with a hooker, British Prince Phillip can afford to continue holding his position even after openly confessing of keeping extra-marital relations with Camilla Parker Bowls, thus pushing Lady Diana towards death.

One Monica Lewinsky became an object of great political disorder for mighty figure like Bill Clinton, while such affairs are very normal in British society and politics. This may have been very personal affairs of the British if they would have never tried to infect such practices in various nations in the world. Look into India or even

Bangladesh. A large number of British non government organizations in both countries are actively or tactfully promoting gay or lesbian culture. They are even provoking women from disobeying family principles and becoming perverts. Numbers of divorces in our societies are gradually increasing because of existence of such NGO activities. Even I know the cases of 'living together' or pre-marriage pregnancy are becoming a great headache.

Let us also look into a very recent hassle Bangladesh is experiencing. According to reports, religious extremists as well as moderates in that country are presently on severe protest because the military backed interim government is set to incorporate a property distribution law, which religious scholars term as anti Koran. Why such dangerous initiative by an unelected government, which is possibly over burdened with numerous problems and challenges, including the recent food crisis, power shortage etc.

There are international pressures on Dhaka in holding the general election by 2008. None of these are minor challenges. But, why authorities in Dhaka are extremely eager in introducing a law, which reportedly goes against majority's religious beliefs? Look into the names in the interim government in Bangladesh. Most of them are previously nourished by British money. Now, possibly they wish to implement some of the British agendas. It is not unknown to anyone, the stories of notoriety of NGOs in Bangladesh. And, Brac or Grameen Bank tops the rank as modern day's 'Shylock'. They extract interest from poor people even up to the level of 30 percent. They encourage Moslem women from doing anything unfit to their society.

Of course, I am not against freedom and rights of women. Nor does Koran endorse any such actions against women's right or freedom. Verse 'Nisa' (Women) in Koran describes in details the rights and freedom of women. But, the problem is, no one pays attention to it. Some Moslems even love to consider Koran as an outdated 'book'. This is the dangerous trend. If the government in Dhaka will fail to understand people's religious sentiment and continue attacking devotees and mosques, it may ultimately become boomerang for them. They should remember the instances of Hazrat Baal mosque in India, Lal mosque in Pakistan or even Golden Temple in Punjab. Attack on such religious places never brought anything good for any nation.

It is proven in history of time. Uncompromising attitude of Bangladesh government towards the demands of Moslem clergies and Moslem radicals will possibly open the doors for a near religious riot in various parts of the country. And, this is the opportunity; hidden objects of Al Qaeda would be looking for. Bangladeshi law enforcing agencies are now targeting Dhaka's national mosque as their prime suspect. Secular Medias in Dhaka are in synchronized campaign against mosques and all Moslems. Some are even giving provocations against Islam. I can see a similar situation in Dhaka now, which reminds me of Sunni-Shiite riots in Pakistan. In Bangladesh, Sunni-Shiite riot may not be possible. So, there is endless effort in creating a civil war within the society using a very sensitive issue.

What is terrorism? Basically activities and tactics the writer or speaker disapproves. Sometimes it can be extended simply to cover a cause of which the writer disapproves. Writers on terrorism fall into two schools: those that extend the term to include all forms of political violence and those that use a narrower definition which relates to political violence intended to intimidate. [Arblaster, 1977: 416] Because of the polemical and ideological nature of much of the writing on terrorism there is no universal definition of terrorism and a great deal of the problems stem from the fact that most commentators wish to include some groups as terrorist and exclude others on the grounds of legitimacy, naming them freedom fighters and the like.

Thus American commentators wish to exclude the Mujaheddin in Afghanistan and the IRA while including the PLO the Vietcong and similar groups who have had an impact on US citizens. Middle East commentators have great difficulty with the notion of 'Islamic fundamentalism' as being a source of terrorism and consider the use of the term evidence of antagonism on the part of western commentators towards their religion. Egyptian commentators wish to distinguish between the PLO which they see as a legitimate group and the PFLP-GC or the group around Abu Nidal, which they see as illegitimate. Although the question of when it is legitimate to resort to violence and when it is not is a fascinating one and has a history dating back to Aristotle, it does serve to obscure the actuality that terrorism is merely a set of tactics neither evil nor good in themselves which are used by certain political organisations at certain times. No organisation that employs terrorist tactics will ever spend all its time engaging in such tactics to the total exclusion of all other forms of activity.

There are a number of issues in the study of terrorism that will be relevant to the themes of this chapter. The first is what sort of violence is terrorist violence? Does it have to involve paramilitary methods and the technology of warfare, or can terrorist violence involve baseball bats, clubbings, petrol soaked rags through doors and other less sophisticated forms of violence? This question is not only relevant to violent political activity by the extreme right-wing, but also to "punishment beatings" during the IRA ceasefire, which Protestant politicians and others see as evidence of continuing IRA activity. The second is, how organised does violence have to be to be terrorism? Are there really command hierarchies, are there autonomous systems and 5 man cells or active service units or is the whole thing much more loosely organised with individuals part of particular operations at particular times but not necessarily part of a coherent permanent organisational structure? This latter question is very similar to the theoretical question of how organised is organised crime?

There are similar questions regarding organised crime. The literature is divided into a perspective which sees it as involving "foreign" structures within a state, a perspective which defines it by its employment of violence as a "state within a state" and a contemporary perspective which argues that it is simply individuals who wish to make money in ways made illegal by the laws of their state. "Governments in Waiting" as a recent conference speaker put it. As already stated, the issues are similar to those concerning terrorism, how "criminal" is it? How "organised" or hierarchical is it? How violent does it have to be? What sort of crimes does it have to be involved in? Finally, why do we wish to draw a distinction between terrorism and organised crime? Does the nobility of the cause excuse the criminality of the actions?

In the real world, there may sometimes be occasions when a group of people engages totally in some form of paramilitary activity to the exclusion of all other forms of activity. Nevertheless, this is rare. Terrorism is better seen as a set of tactics used by individuals, loose associations of people and tightly organised, cellularly structured political parties. Some of these people are engaged in promoting a single issue, others in seeking to supplant a government. The former are thus better thought of as armed pressure groups, the latter as armed political parties. The categorisation below derives from the European experience and in its original incarnation was intended to distinguish between phenomena on the basis of the reasons why violence was being used. Thus categories 2, 3 and 4 form a set related to armed-pressure group activity.

Categories 1, 6 and 11 are more clearly armed parties. Category 5 is close to civil war and Categories 7, 8, 9, 10 and 12 are phenomena related to international relations. 11 have also been in practice in that it has usually involved state-sponsorship of groups against a recent revolutionary regime and cross-border activity is involved. Examples are groups such as the Contras in Nicaragua and the Iranian Mojaheddin are a good example to demonstrate that such groups are not always US-sponsored and anti-Marxist. Category 13 is simply an interesting consequence of the existence of a paramilitary campaign. Any real-world group of people or cause can move between categories over time, or even overlap categories at a particular time.

	Type of Group or Scenario	Examples
	Domestic terrorism	
1.	Anticolonial	None inside UK since 1922
2.	Ethnic religious and cultural minorities	Scotland: sra, snla, tartan army, army of the provisional government of Scotland
		Wales: fwa, mac, mog Cornwall: an gof
		Immigrant communities: bla [?], sikh groups
3.	Ideological minorities, left	Angry brigade
		Freedom fighters for all
4.	Ideological minorities, right	Ss wotan 18, combat 18,
5.	Double minorities	Northern ireland: pira / inla v. Uvf/ uda/ uff
6.	Urban guerilla	None outside northern ireland context
	International terrorism	
7.	Exiles	Spanish anarchists, pflp, pflp-gc
8.	Exiles auxiliaries	Angry brigade,
9.	Internationalists	None
10.	Catspaws	Libyan individuals
11.	Counterrevolutionaries	None
12.	Islamic fundamentalist	None known
13.	Unorganised imitators	Many in mid-70s. Few now.

The framework has been updated to recognise a generally accepted division between domestic and international or transnational terrorism. The analysis that follows will concentrate on U.K. domestic terrorism after 1968, except where there is a link between a domestic group or scenario and an international group or scenario. The main focus is thus on categories 1-5.

Anti-colonial groups are not a major problem in the UK in the post 1968 period. With the exception of the Irish groups up to 1922 anti-colonial terrorism within the UK has hardly existed. The imperial experience however of the British security forces is quite considerable. From 1950 onwards the Malayan emergency, the Mau-Mau in Kenya, the insurrection in Aden and the conflict in Dhofar on the borders between Aden and Oman led to the production of a number of significant counterinsurgent strategies associated with names like Kitson and Thomson. Some Americans may consider Northern Ireland after 1968 to be an anti-colonial war of liberation but this represents a major misunderstanding of the nature of the majority population in Northern Ireland. Anti-colonial struggles against other colonial powers occasionally impinge on British politics. Most frequently in recent times the cause of an independent East Timor.

What the UK has suffered from is a whole series of terrorist incidents associated with ethnic, religious or cultural minorities. In Scotland the Tartan Army was probably the most prominent and flourished in the mid 1970s. There have also been episodes involving the Scottish National Liberation Army, the Scottish Republican Army and the Army of the Provisional Government of Scotland. With the exception of a small cell based on Stirling University none of these have amounted to very much and the police have found it fairly easy to identify the members of the group and deal with them through the courts in the normal way. The major Scottish problem has in fact been links with the Ulster Protestant paramilitaries.

Wales however has offered a greater level of activity. The Free Welsh Army that were hoodwinked in the famous

Fishguard trawler episode of 1967 (Sunday Times Insight team 1970]; Meibion Owain Glyndwr, and Mudiad Amddifyyyn Cymru [MAC] maintained a high level of activity mostly engaged in fire bombing second homes in North Wales though later developing into the firebombing of Conservative party offices and estate agents. Again police action seems to have disrupted these organisations successfully although a celebrated trial ended in not guilty verdicts. There were allegedly connections with Northern Ireland here again, especially in the provision of explosive technology.

Another small group, An Gof, was active in Cornwall at various times but the movement split in the mid 70s and violence seems to have departed the Cornish nationalist movement as Meibion Kernow wins the odd council seat and satisfies Cornish aspirations by so doing to all intents and purposes. The above groups thus, though active, have not sustained their violence over a period of time or achieved any high level of operational capability with the exception of the Welsh fire bombers. Again, with this exception, there has been no serious requirement of funding for a relatively large organisation or for the import of weaponry or explosives.

Links with organised crime are possible in that one or two of the anarchists allegedly involved in paramilitary activity in South Wales have spent time in jail after being involved in various escapades in London. One curious incident from the early 1970s illustrates the problem of differentiating between terrorism and organised crime. A group of Afro-Caribbeans were caught in the act of robbing a restaurant in South London. They promptly held the staff hostage and claimed to be the "Black Liberation Army". A siege developed, known in the literature as "the Spaghetti House Siege".

Subsequently, at the trial it was claimed that the BLA did not exist and the accused were simply criminals who wished to rob the restaurant for personal gain. It was frequently said at the time among cannabis users that "If you want to buy dope north of the river, you have to deal with the IRA. South of the river it's the Black Liberation Army." The author heard this said before the Spaghetti House Siege ever happened. In the late 60s it needs to be remembered that there were those who argued that crime was a revolutionary act. Abbie Hoffman for instance wrote a tract entitled "Steal This Book". Theft was considered an act of liberation of a piece of property, so revolutionary movements from this period did not draw the boundary between crime and revolutionary activity in the same place as the legal system does. The theft of explosives, cars or money was a necessary part of the activity of such groups.

The most serious religion related "terrorism" has been that in the Sikh community where there has been intimidation of Sikh temples into providing funding for a resistance movement opposed to the Indian government and fighting for an independent Sikh state. Deaths have occurred in relation to this campaign, most notably during the occupation and siege of the Golden Temple in Amritsar, but there are no known links with organised crime groups in the UK. There are allegations of links between members of the organisation and cocaine smuggling rings in South America but it always difficult to know the degree to which this is government propaganda against their cause. [Times 1984 June 16th, Sunday Times 1985 Dec 1st]

The fact is that the organisation has managed to continue in existence and appears to have reasonable amounts of money and weaponry at its disposal. If the argument to be outlined below is correct then it will have done so by acquiring the methods of organised crime to fund itself. Cultural minorities such as new age travellers and festival goers seeking to keep alive the spirit of the 60s have tended to possess an ideology of peaceful protest and are thus not usually of relevance here although their involvement in various activities is fairly well documented. However well the occasional violent confrontation with the police may be documented it would be stretching the various and exotic definitions that exist of terrorism to include a wish to live in tepees in the fields and smoke marijuana.

Left wing ideolological minorities though often stereotyped as terrorist in fact played little part in terrorism in the UK. Avoiding the definitional problems of left and right wing, for the purpose of this classification system this category include those of Trotskyite, Maoist and anarchist persuasion who choose to resort to paramilitary violence. The anarchist groups The Angry Brigade and Freedom Fighters for All being the only major groups to engage in bombing and issuing communiqués in a significant way. The Angry Brigade appears to have funded their initial efforts by offering to carry out symbolic attacks on Spanish property for the Spanish Anarchists opposing General Franco. In return for carrying out these attacks they would receive explosives to carry out their own. Since they consisted of one or at most two cells there was no extensive organisation that required funding nor was there a sustained operation over a long period of time.

Freedom Fighters for All made the mistake of organising their campaign to occur simultaneously with the opening of the IRA's mainland campaign in October 1973. This was presumably unwitting but they were quickly cleaned up in the heightened level of police activity that followed the more serious bombings elsewhere in the country. [Black Flag 1973-4 passim] Again therefore funding does not appear to come into the equation. According to Black Flag, a group of anarchists was accused of conspiring to carry out a social security fraud as a means of funding persons unknown to take part in terrorist activities but this made no major splash outside the anarchist press. [Black Flag 1974] It does raise the same issues as those raised earlier by the Spaghetti House siege, where the "terrorists" see crime as an essential and justifiable part of their " revolutionary" activity, can academics set a tight boundary between organised crime and terrorism?

The Trotskyite Fourth International, which elsewhere in the world went over to paramilitary activity, in the UK flirted briefly with Northern Ireland, but after the death of one or two activists returned rather rapidly to its more normal role in student agitation. There was no killing by armed police of an unarmed demonstrator which provided the impetus for violent terrorist cells elsewhere in Europe, usually bearing the name of the date on which the demonstrator had been killed, June the 2nd, May the 15th etc. Right wing violence, contrary to the work of most authors on the subject has been much more wide spread in the UK than violence by the ultra-left. It tends to be ruled out as terrorism because it is rarely paramilitary, in the sense of involving high-technology attacks.

It consists mainly of attacks on individual members of ethnic minority communities, bookshops and prominent left wingers, the intention of which is to intimidate these communities as a whole. This certainly fits in with at least one definitional school of terrorism. Searchlight documented a horrifying number of attacks of this sort and numbers of individual groups of right wingers were brought to trial. [Searchlight Special 1985] Interesting this was not depicted by the press or academics as a whole as terrorism although Paul Wilkinson did write a short book entitled The New Fascists Funding on the right has tended to come from prominent wealthy retired or semi retired sympathisers but again according to Searchlight the British Movement under Michael McLaughlin became very much involved in business activities. Indeed according to Searchlight McGloughlin set himself up as a wholesaler of military and survivalism and retired from leadership of the British Movement.

All this pales however in comparison with the Northern Irish groups which fall into the double minority category—a category not of this author's invention but an adaptation of Robert Mosses' coinage in his book Urban Guerilla. The problem of Ireland is that the Protestants form a minority in the island as a whole, which is predominately Catholic but in the Six Counties that form Northern Ireland, the Protestants form the majority and the Catholics the minority. Thus both sides can claim to be the majority depending on how you count them. On the side of the cause for a single, 32 county states in the island of Ireland the Provisional IRA [PIRA] and the Irish National Liberation Army [INLA] have been the main paramilitary protagonists, although INLA split at one stage and Saor Eire has also been significant at times. On the side of continuing union with the United Kingdom, the Ulster Defence Association [UDA] with its nomme de guerre the Ulster Freedom Fighters [UFF] and the Ulster Volunteer Force [UVF] have been responsible for the majority of violence. There have also been other groups such as the "shadowy" Ulster Resistance Movement and the Red Hand commandos.

IRA Fundraising

In the late 80s or early 90s Rowan. Bosworth-Davies and Barry Rider twisted my arm into producing a series of presentations on money laundering and terrorism. From this emerged a spoof prospectus for the IRA PLC which has been recently shamelessly plagiarized by journalists without attribution. A small international company providing executive and leisure services in the British Isles and North West Europe and overseas offices in the United States and Australia. Courier services available to various parts of the world.

Subsidiary companies provide construction and demolition services. IRA PLC also franchises clubs and a "get you home" service. Private security services also provided for housing estates. Insurance quotations against bomb damage can also be brokered. The company has recently secured a niche in the import-export market, particularly of livestock and CDs.

The problem with discussing the income and expenditure of the IRA is that one is immediately involved in problems of propaganda. It clearly suits the security forces to portray the IRA as no more than another organised crime group. This is of course to paint a distorted picture of the IRA, who are not primarily in business for the purposes of making money but who need to have ways of making money in order to stay in business. Indeed, although "IRA-PLC" is a catchy title, it would be more correct to talk of "Republican Movement PLC". Indeed Irish politicians prefer this latter term. The former title gives the impression that the IRA controls all branches of the republican Movement and this cannot safely be asserted.

Sinn Fein, the women's movement Cumann nam Ban, social clubs, Gaelic Sports associations, the Catholic ex-Servicemen's Association, prisoners support organisations and various businesses are all organisations within a broader movement. Who controls whom, who interacts with whom and how not only matters for research but occasionally matters are disputed before the courts. The money-making ventures alluded to in the prospectus may or may not be under the control of the Army Council, may or may not pay a percentage to the Army Council and may or may not take place in areas considered to be under Republican Movement "control".

Related problems may indeed appear frequently on the agenda of IRA army council meetings. How far should they engage in fundraising and how far in armed operations? Should the same personnel be involved in both? Should they be kept totally separate? How can they be used against the movement as propaganda? The essence of every act of terrorism is propaganda. Terrorism could be said simply to be armed propaganda. So fundraising in itself presumably should be used as a weapon to undermine British state. Fraud committed against the northern Ireland housing department would be legitimate, as would fraud against the ministry of agriculture food and fisheries, customs duties evasion or similar. Fraud against domestic Irish credit unions would presumably be unacceptable.

Equally dealing drugs in the UK might be acceptable where dealing drugs in Belfast would not be. Discussions by the author with senior police officers have indicated that the RUC denies any involvement in IRA drug dealing whereas police officers from further south are certain that IRA personnel are involved in trafficking if not in street dealing. Certainly the IRA has taken a leaf out of the pages of their Basque colleagues, ETA, in gaining popular support by kneecapping or placing orders of exile on well known drug dealers in Belfast, Derry city and elsewhere. Equally what the British security forces would call protection rackets the IRA would say are in the nature of a revolutionary tax, following the Basque model again.

Another problem discussing this subject is the nature of the sources. Various officers of the RUC and Garda Siochana have kindly briefed study groups led by the author in the past, but where documentary material has been shown, it has been on a confidential basis. The figures given above have had to be justified by reference to press sources, and these are often dubious. At one stage the stories were all about security forces' successes against the IRA's financial network, at another the IRA's links with the US are exaggerated to bring pressure to bear on visiting US politicians. At all times stories are exaggerated in order to sell newspapers and the Sunday Times clearly thinks IRA scare stories keep its readers interested. Nevertheless, it has received a number of major security forces leaks over the years and devotes more space and depth to Northern Ireland than its broadsheet rivals. The truth problem needs to be borne in mind constantly when considering the pseudo data of which the IRA-PLC prospectus consists.

Returning to the main theme of crime and terrorism: post office and bank raids throughout Ireland to be acceptable ways of blooding recruits and finding shows their commitment. Unattributable briefings given the author allege that 50% of post office and bank raids in the south have some form of IRA connection. The figure of contributions from overseas subsidiaries reflects published statements of the North American organisation Noraid which vary annually from $160,000 to $800,000. Added to this are contributions from the UK and Australia. Early in the 1970s contributions were also made by Libya.

This is generally presented as being money raised for the welfare of prisoners' families and that is balanced in the statement of expenditure by an estimate that money to prisoners' families costs the republican movement as a whole £2 million. This is of course where the problem starts in discussing the legal and illegal aspects of the business of the republican movement as a whole. Noraid would presumably claim that to support the families of prisoners is legitimate business and in no way relevant to the IRA as an armed illegal organisation. Nevertheless I have chosen to keep both these categories in my statement of income and expenditure.

Contributions from overseas obviously fluctuate. When the British security forces have carried out high profile operations such as the killings in Gibraltar the contributions tend to rise significantly. Collections are regularly made in various public houses in English and Scottish cities as well as the more formal fundraising organisations in the United States and Australia. One and a half million pounds is probably on the low side for these contributions. The point needs to be made however that very little of this money would have anything to do with weaponry or bomb making equipment in the 1980s and perhaps the 1970s because of the amount of munitions smuggled in from Libya during this period.

Libya apparently admitted to shipping 130 tonnes of weaponry between 1985 and 1987, of which about half has been used or found by security forces.[Sunday Times, 24 Dec 1995] Iran has also been accused of maintaining a £20 million slush fund in the mid to late 80s, of which some went to the IRA.[Sunday Times 21 Aug 1994]. Taking clandestine contributions from states together with declared and undeclared contributions through individual sympathisers, £1,500,000 seems a pretty good working average figure.

shebeen subsidiary is referred to as one of the curious consequences of the troubles. During the early 70s most pubs were bombed out by the republican side or the loyalist/ Protestant side. Most pubs were in fact owned by Catholics. As a result shebeens or illegal unlicensed drinking clubs grew up as places where the community could drink safely. In the 1970s it was very difficult to tell to what degree these were actually 'owned' by the paramilitaries on both sides. It is thus impossible to work out how these enterprises were used for fundraising or for money laundering. In 1989 new regulations were brought in by the authorities to try to estimate the income of gambling machines and so on and compare that with figures returned by the legal accounts of these businesses for taxation purposes. [Sunday Times 1st Aug 1993]

Again there is a problem discussing this in deciding where the republican movement ends and the IRA begins. Where these bars are run by committees from the community and everything is done in a legal fashion they may simply be involved in the payment of protection to the IRA rather than wholly owned businesses. The heading Import- Export Business covers the increasing allegations that the 'IRA" is involved in the import of counterfeit computer software, videos and music CDs. The security forces apparently attribute this to their "success" in clamping down on the drinking clubs, which they estimate cost the IRA £7 Million per annum [Sunday Times 1st Aug 1993] In which case the figure given is an under-estimate pre-1989 and an overestimate for post-1989.

This introduces the different problem as to the degree to which the IRA shades into Northern and Southern Irish organised crime groups and the degree to which propaganda is being engaged in to discredit the movement with the community. Nevertheless an early attempt to estimate income from these activities alleged £1 million per annum from fraud and extortion, £2 million from smuugled goods and video piracy, £750,000 from the black taxis, £500,000 from fruit machines , £250,000 from charities ,and £250,000 from overseas sympathisers. [Sunday Times 12 March 1995]

UCLAF, the fraud investigation unit of the European Commission, has alleged that the IRA is also involved in the movement of cattle across the northern-southern Irish border and back again in order to attract import subsidies and evade various forms of duty.[FAF] If this is being carried out by individual members of families normally associated with IRA membership, it may not necessarily follow that these individuals consider the activity to be IRA activity as opposed to private enterprise. Again our friends in the Sunday Times and the Times proper linked the "IRA" to a South African fraud of £41million,[Times 20 May 1995] a US heist of $7million, [Times 15 Nov 1993], a London bond robbery of £292 million, and a US bank fraud of £150 million [Sunday Times 22 May 1994].

If all this is true, then the IRA could probably buy Executive Outcomes to do its job for it! The above gives a more sober figure. The Sunday Times also has the IRA smuggling £2 million a year in stolen antiques to dealers in the British Midlands, selling illegal growth promoters for cattle to farmers, selling counterfeit designer jeans, computer games and videos and engaging in major building -site fraud. [Sunday Times 1st August 1993] Again, these activities may be taking place, but the IRA cannot have the time or the personnel to run them all. Much more likely is that, as with legal businesses, illegal businesses pay a "licence fee" to the IRA to operate.

This is one way of explaining the different signals coming from the security forces on drugs. Indeed, there are suggestions, that, in the case of drugs, some of this licensing was freelance. During the ceasefire, the IRA turned to attacking drug dealers to keep its activists battle-hardened, but it was possible to pay local commanders to prevent your name being put forward as a target to be approved by the Army Council [Sunday Times 31st Dec 1995]. Fire and bomb damage insurance refers to the allegation that various businesses pay money to the IRA to protect themselves from a bombing campaign.

The Sunday Times alleged that a major bakery chain for example paid £2 million a year to the IRA through an international security consultancy to prevent its bakeries being destroyed. In fact it appears that this was not an annual payment but related to the kidnapping of Don Tidey, an executive. A one-off payment of £2 million for one large business suggests that a total of £6 milllion for all businesses to insure against kidnapping and bombing is not actually that high and the income in this area may indeed be higher. Again the same paper, the Sunday Times, in one of its colour supplements, quoted a meeting of "black taxi" drivers as being called on to raise their weekly contribution to £8.

That would give a figure of £400 per driver per year, which needs to be multiplied by the number of drivers and one need to do similar calculations for other individual, small and large businesses, legal and illegal, around Northern Ireland. But as already mentioned above, elsewhere, the same paper has quoted security forces sources as calculating an income of £750,000 per annum from taxis. The heading Construction refers to fraud carried out against the Northern Ireland Housing Office during the reconstruction of bombed buildings. An estimate of £15 million lost has been given in newspapers. There have also been allegations of IRA involvement in social security fraud on the British mainland. Again the problem is that anything with an Irish connection is going to be called 'IRA'.

Turning to the expenditure statement, the category of "executives in the UK" is based on the assumption that the IRA have moved away from the totally independent 5 man cell [ASU] as their basic unit. They now use surveillance and intelligence teams whose job it is to set up particular operations. These are represented by the category "20 warehouse and support staff". Operatives tend to operate in pairs when actually carrying out a bombing or shooting. These are the "4 executives". The assumption made in the table is that if personnel employed full time as such an operative would be provided with an income of £20,000 per year and that the whole team would have access to a budget for hiring cars as well as stealing them and for obtaining legitimate accommodation.

These figures may be high and on the Northern Ireland side have been halved on the assumption the individuals concerned are drawing unemployment benefit or obtaining incomes from legitimate sources. The total assumed by the security forces of full time genuinely IRA units is about 100. ["If the politicians would only let us take 100 of them out, this nonsense would all be over"]. This table doubles that assumption to err deliberately on the expensive side. 50 are allocated to the South of Ireland 24 to the UK and 100 to Northern Ireland, 40 in the executive role and 60 in the warehouse and support role.

This may be a complete misunderstanding of the way the IRA operates and the idea that there genuinely are 100 full time personnel is probably be a security forces fantasy. Such an assumption leads to the conclusion that all that has to be done in Northern Ireland is to lock up 100 people and everything will stop. This is clearly not the case and the notion that there is such a thing as a full time IRA operative is not borne out by such memoirs as have been produced from within the organisation. In fact a survey produced in New Society in the late 1970s argued that something like three quarters of all the personnel in prison for IRA membership in the north of Ireland had actually been in work at the time of their imprisonment.

The notion that the IRA consists of unemployed personnel hanging around street corners waiting for a bombing to be suggested is a newspaper fantasy rather than a security forces one. The obvious point to be deduced from the Table is that the IRA is actually quite a cheap organi-sation to run. As the Libyan weapons and explosives cache is exhausted this will of course change. The second point is that it is a profitable operation. Somewhere those profits have been invested. The figures given are of course purely speculative, and other, more official sources would put the figure at £10 million profit per annum whereas this table estimates closer to £15 million. To reiterate a word of caution, these figures probably refer to the Republican Movement as a whole, and it may or may not be mistaken to leave the reader with the impression that the IRA runs the whole Republican Movement. It is certainly a matter of importance to the propagandist.

Terrorists in Prison

The IRA has a long history of involvement with various forms of what we now call money laundering and fraud. Back in the 1916-22 period money was raised for the independence of Ireland and according to Tim Pat Coogan's biography of Eamonn de Valera a large proportion of it was siphoned off by de Valera to found a newspaper under his own control. Not only did it remain under his own political control but also, as the majority share holder, it became his family's business and this lasted right through into the early 1960s. Tim Pat Coogan discusses the legality and morality of this. He also discusses the role of the famous American fundraiser Joe McGarrity who kept the IRA going during the 30s and 40s. There is further discussion of the role of members of the Irish government in the setting up, funding and arming of the IRA after 1968 in another of Tim Pat Coogan's books, simply called The IRA.

Certainly the leaders of the Provisional IRA had mostly been in prison during the 1956-62 campaign and mostly held in English jails because of a refusal to treat them as political prisoners. Without reading their memoirs, if they ever come out, it is impossible to know to what extent they formed links during that period. Joe Cahill, allegedly the IRA's financial expert, was in jail during this period. It is more certain however that the members of the IRA and other republican groups arrested during the mainland campaign after 1973 and held in British and Irish jails rather than the H-blocks would have had the opportunity to make links with organised crime circles . The criminal spirit of the 70s and 80s was certainly entrepreneurship.

Research may eventually demonstrate that the real intermediaries were the cannabis dealers of the early 1970s who saw themselves as part of an ideological commitment to change society rather than as simply involved in the process of making money. Howard Marks' autobiography suggests that such thoughts did motivate people like himself and entrepreneurs in the cities of Cork, Limerick, Dublin would almost certainly have been motivated similarly. His autobiography also describes a network of connections between himself, Jim McCann of the IRA and Dutch interests in the early 1970s.

He actually claims to have pointed out to McCann that, if you can smuggle arms you can smuggle drugs. The last four shipments from Libya were brought in by a professional smuggler, who was paid £100,000 fee for arranging shipment. The US fiasco alluded to above also involved an arrangement with an alleged professional arms dealer. [Bishop and Mallie] The arms trade is thus another source of contacts between terrorism and organised crime.

Increasingly in Dublin, Limerick and to a lesser extent other towns in Ireland the IRA finds itself coming into conflict with domestically based organised crime. The shooting of Martin Cahill "the General" in Dublin in 1994 by the IRA was a clear warning to organised crime that the true holders of the monopoly of violence were neither the state nor the state within the state of nonpolitical organised crime but the provisional IRA. There were allegations in the 70s that a street career structure went: join the Provisionals as a 16 year-old, graduate to the Official IRA in your mid-20s and move on to crime in your late 20s.

In addition, although it was found by the courts to be a case of CIA entrapment, during a US trial links were claimed between the American end of the Republican Movement and a figure "close to the Mafia" in a conspiracy to supply arms to the IRA. The USA is thus another possible place where connections to organised crime might have been created. The drugs business needs more research. Anecdotal evidence is that in the early 70s there was current an urban myth that north of the river in London you bought marihuana off the IRA, south of the river you dealt with the Black Liberation Army. The cannabis dealers of the late 60s and early 70s tended to see themselves as Robin Hoods with leftish political affiliations tweaking the nose of capitalism and part of the process of creating an alternative society.

They may have contributed to the funds of the IRA in the 70s particularly in the post internment period of 1972 when feelings ran highest in both Southern and Northern Ireland. Obviously it is difficult to research relationships in this or any other period until people start writing their memoirs. Nevertheless it is alleged that the Provisionals did briefly lose a lot of street credibility in the 70s when they were identified with heroin dealing in Belfast ghettoes and had very quickly to remove themselves from the trade. [unattrib] That they were involved in heroin suggests that they had been involved in other drugs previously and certainly it has been alleged that they remain involved in trafficking and wholesaling but not in retailing and street dealing both south and north of the border.

This has equally been alleged of protestant paramilitaries and there have been allegations that in drug terms all the paramilitaries actually work together and have the turf well divided up in northern Ireland.[unattrib] Protestant paramilitary organisation would presumably also reach into the west of Scotland where IRA organisation reaches down into the south of Ireland. If the intelligence organisations of the paramilitaries are as efficient as it is supposed to be, it is hard to believe that drugs can be sold in the areas under their control without their knowledge.

The introduction of Ecstasy as a youth drug of choice has created new opportunities for profit, not only by selling the drug but by providing the venues for "raves" to take place. Ecstasy has broader ideological acceptance in the community, being seen as the same category as marijuana rather than heroin. Like organised crime groups the IRA seems to have turned increasingly to fraud as a lower-risk, higher profit activity. Again, it is a matter for serious research to ascertain whether ideas were exchanged in prison, or whether accountants and lawyers taught the IRA's fundraisers the techniques.

In organised crime circles, it often appears that the children of criminals have been trained in these trades and have initiated changes in the modus operandi of the crime families. Perhaps the same family upward mobility operates within Irish Republicanism.

Organised Crime and Cellular Structure

It is important to remember that the Provisional IRA was in many ways a new organisation and represented a break with the organisational structures that existed previously. Most of the political agitators went off with the Official IRA when the split occurred. The hierarchy of the IRA tended to split on family lines - relatives becoming part of the same organisation as their other relatives. On some occasions a particularly charismatic individual kept a particular area's organisation intact and took it into whichever organisation he chose, be it the official or the provisional IRA.

Indeed for some time after the split in some areas individuals who were nominally members of one or the other organisation worked together on particular paramilitary operations without any problems. Internment however removed most of the old cadres and a new younger leadership took over and created a completely new structure.

In the period after the Sunningdale talks of 1973 and the collapse of power sharing in 1974 the Provisional IRA reorgainsed itself into a series of small active service units (ASUs) modelled on the classic 5 man guerilla cell. It is not clear to what degree this structure ever actually took hold and to what degree this simply facilitated the move to a much looser network of associations. There appear still to be individual organisations for different parts of the border area. For example, South Armagh appears to be organisationally coherent, as does South Tyrone and perhaps Newry. The organisational structures of the border areas appear to be suspicious of their nominal superiors in both Belfast and the South, and may keep their own fund-raising and smuggling operations quite separate from those of the Army Council.

It is not clear whether these units are typical or aberrations. As noted above there is some evidence of movement away from the ASUs and of the emergence of a network of different individuals specialising in different roles. To that extent the structure of the IRA appears to be converging with the changing structure of organised crime. A network of specialists is coordinated by some central planner for a one-off purpose or for a more long term enterprise. Just as organised crime has its 'enforcers', its specialists in violence, so too do the IRA. Equally organised crime has its smuggling or transportation specialists. Here the IRA either has its own or buys in a specialist from organised crime, as it did to move the consignment of arms and explosives from Libya.

Organised crime increasingly consists of different types of operative related in different ways to a central organisation. In the area of drugs, for example, there are different levels of dealer down to the non professional street pusher, above whom may be the apartment based dealer who sells larger quantities to specialist consumers and above whom are retailers, wholesalers and even importers. The street dealer may be considered part of the organisation in that there are rules that he will be punished for breaking. On occasion he may find that he is given a particular task to perform by the organisation.

Where organised crime groups have created "no go" or "high crime" areas, a number of different criminal activities take place. Traditional academic views were that this produced a pyramidical structure of parallel functional hierarchies held together by the violence disposed of by the criminal leadership. Ianni began to demolish this view in "Black Mafia". Gambetta and others now argue that much looser specialist structures and relationships exist, characterised by the nature of the business opportunity.

Similarly analytical structures can be applied to republicanism. In its early street fighting days the bottom of the pyramid was constituted by the youngsters who could be relied upon to follow the call to throw stones or to riot - a tactic copied by drug dealers in inner city areas to keep the police at bay, interestingly enough. Above then were the paper sellers and the Sinn Fein members in general who during the Hunger Strikes became active in canvassing and other forms of political work. Above them will be the councillors and whether one can say above, or beside, will be the paramilitaries in various forms. As suggested, the logistic specialists or the quartermasters with an expanded role, the intelligence and reconnaissance specialists and the bomb makers and designers and the actual bomb planters and assassins.

This picture still presents too hierarchical an impression. It Republican areas today individuals perform specialist roles rather than forming a hierarchical command structure. Since the ceasefire to this picture need to be added the baseball bat users who enforce community discipline. Like organised crime the IRA increasingly find itself responsible for law and order and obedience to rules in a particular estate. To some extent the nature of the housing estate in itself structures both the IRA and the organised cirme group.

With the collapse of policing between 1968 and 1974 and the problems of gaining legitimacy for a paramilitary Royal Ulster Constabulary after 1974 the provisional IRA found itself charged with more than simply providing the housing estate with security from attack by protestant gunmen. It also found that it had increasingly to take on police roles such as dealing with petty property crime, anti social behaviour and so on. The forms of punishment it chose began with tarring and feathering and then developed into a series of different forms of kneecapping. Indeed the IRA is now moving into housing estates north of Dublin in the south of Ireland on the basis of providing the same sorts of vigilante security and policing services.

It has always been a truism that where you have organised crime you have very little petty crime, because petty crime is frowned upon by the drug dealers and racketeers. This is an area in which there is definite convergence between organised crime and terrorism. The dynamics of excluding police personnel from a given territory produces a need to provide alternative policing structures akin to vigilantism.

Similarly the IRA has had to turn to the fashions of organised crime to raise money. At one time armed robbers were the aristocracy of organised crime and for a period the IRA obtained its funding by robberies. As mentioned above this still goes on, but like organised crime, the IRA flirted with drugs and now has followed organised crime into the much lower risk area of fraud, especially cross border fraud and the importing of counterfeit products. It has also been suggested that, in order to obtain guns, vehicles and forged documentation, IRA operatives on the British mainland have begun to pretend to be "normal" criminals and have "infiltrated the criminal infrastructure". [Independent 4 Mar 1996]

The Protestant Paramilitaries

The protestant paramilitaries had no need to exist between 1922 and the mid-1960s as the forces of law and order were very much behind the Protestant Ascendancy. With the advent of the Civil Rights Movement and the conciliatory response from the then Prime Minister of Ulster, O'Neill, the Ulster protestant Volunteers were created by the Rev, Dr. Ian Paisley, now [1997] the leader of the Democratic Unionist Party.

In 1966 the Ulster Volunteer Force [UVF] was recreated as, an urban working class based organisation that was not a supporter of Orangeism and other aspects of traditionalist loyalist politics. It drilled, collected weapons and robbed shops and an armoury. Its leadership then languished in jail until 1974. From the inter communal riots that drove the RUC form the streets of Belfast, the Ulster Defence Association emerged as a vigilante organisation.

Both groups engaged in sectarian murder of Catholics during the 1970s, but were in decline after the resurgence of the reformed RUC post-1976. The UDA rapidly became synonymous with its nom de guerre, the Ulster Freedom Fighters, in whose name the sectarian murders were carried out. These organisations at this stage had very little need for funding because there were many legally held weapons in Protestant hands and they were able to join the new Ulster Defence Regiment and gain access to training, weapons and intelligence. After the Hillsborough Agreement of 1985, however, many Protestants began to feel betrayed by the RUC and there were cases of the burnings of homes belonging to the police.

Networks of drinking clubs had begun to emerge as early as 1970 and provided a funding basis for the organisation. The rough and ready accounting systems of the clubs were used to launder the proceeds of bank robberies, and the Protestant paramilitaries began to branch into other areas, particularly a protection racket on building sites, which brought in hundreds of thousands of pounds. There are allegations of involvement in a whole series of rackets, including prostitution, drugs and pornography as well as the above-mentioned bank-robbery and extortion. There is evidence of a tendency of "some of it to stick to the fingers of those that raises it".

There was also a flirtation with the old apartheid South African government who linked with the Protestant paramilitaries in an attempt to obtain British made Rapier missiles and beat the arms embargo. This particular plot was foiled and the leaders arrested. More recently, allegations have been made in the press that Protestant paramilitaries have either begun to copy the IRA or even to cooperate with them in the sale of counterfeit products to the community.

Obviously, a great deal of further research is required, and the information on which much of this chapter is based is both controversial and unreliable. Nevertheless, the area requires further study. Long-lived terrorist groups clearly rely on wider popular movements to sustain and support them. Relationships between the components of these groups, who may be families, associates or merely resident in the same area are complex and non-hierarchical. The existence of a central paramilitary organisation means that coercive sanctions are available to impose discipline upon the wider movement, if necessary, although at the same time, there always exists the possibility of rival gangs emerging based on different territorial areas.

The shared political cause can impose an illusion of organisation, but can also create the possibility of ideological splits over the nature of the goal or the pace of the campaign. This creates a variable distinguishing these groups from organised crime, who may split over which leader to follow, or which business to prioritise, but will never find ideology getting in the way of business. The greater the devotion of manpower reources to fund-raising activities, however, the greater the likelihood the political group will become an organised crime group in fact, though not in name.

Such evidence as exists suggests that the form of organisation adopted by both organised crime and terrorism is dictated partly by the nature of police response. The interest in cellular structure and network arrangements is partly to make prosecution on the basis of "shared purpose" difficult to prove. The nature of business will affect the organisational structures of organised crime as a whole, but only the fund-raising structures of terrorist-related movements. The structure of the coercive apparatus will be governed by the relationship between the number required to deliver a violent event and the requirements of internal security. The specialised nature of a paramilitary arm of a political movement may make it attractive for organised crime to employ such a group for the purpose of contract enforcement on an occasional basis, but there is no evidence of this as yet, although ther have occasionally been allegations that individuals have been used to provide armed escort for consignments.

A group may set out with a political aim. If it cannot raise money, it will not survive. This chapter has discussed many small groups that passed briefly across the British political stage. On the other hand, if a group is successful in raising money but cannot find a peaceful political role for itself, it will increasingly take on the character of the organised crime groups whose methods it copies. History demonstrates that the Triads began with the aim of restoring the Ming dynasty after the Manchu invasion of China in 1644. 353 years later they have transformed themselves into a loose network of cross-border crime groups. [Chu passim] Similarly the Mafia began as a group opposing the imposition of a French dynasty on the kingdom of Sicily. Today they too have branched out into other businesses. Could it be that the profit motive will always conquer the political?

6

Religious Foundations of Suicide Bombings

Suicide terrorism has been the scourge of the last quarter century. A suicide bomb attack on the U.S. marine barracks in Beirut compelled Ronald Reagan in 1983 to withdraw peacekeepers from Beirut. Palestinian leaders deploy suicide bombers to force Israeli concessions, and Iraqi insurgents use suicide bombings to derail the new political order. Al-Qaeda terrorists attacked the U.S.S. *Cole* in Aden in 2000 and, on September 11, 2001, the World Trade Center and Pentagon. While some scholars argue there is no religious component to suicide bombing—often citing Sri Lanka's Tamil Tigers, who are not Muslims—they are wrong. All Muslim suicide bombers justify their actions with their religion and, more specifically, with the concept of jihad.

Muslim self-justification of suicide bombing lies in interpretation of jihad. While Western scholars of late argue that jihad refers primarily to internal struggle, Islamic writings feature jihad as physical warfare. Historian Bernard Lewis finds that "the overwhelming majority of classical theologians, jurists and traditionalists ... understood the obligation of jihad in a military sense."

Islamic jurisprudence has distinguished four different ways in which a believer may fulfill jihad obligations: 1) with faith in his heart; 2) by preaching and proselytizing with his tongue; 3) by good deeds with his hands; and 4) by confronting unbelievers or enemies with the sword. In practice, the first three are part of the *da'wa* (missionary activity), actions that support jihad by the sword.

Muslim theologians were explicit in the combination of nonviolent and violent jihad to spread Islam. Jihad is central to the Muslim perception of the world, dividing it into *dar al-Islam* (abode of Islam) and *dar al-harb* (abode of war) which is destined to come under Islamic rule. Jihad both purifies the *dar al-Islam* and is the tool to shrink and eradicate the *dar al-harb*. As a doctrine, the aim of jihad is clear, to establish God's rule on earth by compelling non-Muslims to embrace Islam or to force them to accept second class status if not eradicate them altogether.

Such an understanding constituted one of the main ideological bases of the dynasties that ruled the Islamic world from the late seventh century until Mongol hordes put an effective end to their control in the thirteenth century. A comparison between the concept of martyrdom in Islam on one hand and in Judaism and Christianity on the other illustrates the emphasis on violent jihad within Islamic jurisprudence. In Islamic practice, the martyr is one killed in jihad. He is entitled to special status in paradise and on Judgment Day. In Judaism and Christianity, a martyr is someone who endures torture and death rather than renounces his or her belief.

Jihad against Unbelievers

All four schools of Sunni Islam as well as mainstream Shi'ism consider idolatry (*shirk*), apostasy (*irtidad*), and hypocrisy (*nifiq, munafaqah*, or *riya'*) to be capital offenses. In each case, jihad is a means to counter such threats and assert the predominance of Islam.

There is little tolerance for idolaters within Islam, the first article of faith is the profession, *la ilah illa-llah* (there is no deity but God). Muslim jurisprudence considers *shirk* to be the worst form of disbelief. The Qur'an commands Muslims to kill those who commit *shirk* and is replete with examples calling for jihad against idolaters. For example, Sura 9:5 reads, "When the sacred months have passed, slay the idolaters whenever you find them, and take them captive or besiege them."

Sura 8:39 reads, "So fight them so that sedition might end and obedience is wholly Allah's"; and Sura 9:123 states, "Fight the unbelievers who are near to you, and let them find ruthlessness in you." Muslims living under the rule of idolaters are obliged to fight their rulers. The Qur'an likewise commands believers to conduct jihad against hypocrites, seize them, and do away with them.

All infidels, unbelievers, and hypocrites—those who commit blasphemy or treason—are relegated to hell. Prominent Muslim scholars consider the general jihad declaration against the unbelievers to be crucial to Islamic success. Those who sacrifice their material comfort and bodies for jihad win salvation. By their sacrifice, they obtain all the pleasures of paradise, be they spiritual—the close presence of God—or material.

As an additional incentive, Muhammad promised those mujahideen who fight in a jihad war a reward of virgins in paradise. Importantly, those conducting suicide bombings do not consider themselves dead but rather living with God. As Sura 2:154 explains, "Do not think that those who are killed in the way of Allah are dead, for indeed they are alive, even though you are not aware." Therefore the prohibition on suicide need not apply to bus bombers or other kamikaze jihadists.

Martin Lings, a British scholar of Sufism, argues that this linkage between martyrdom and paradise was probably the most potent factor that Muhammad brought to the annals of warfare, for it transformed the odds of war by offering a promise of immortality.

Jihad in the Hadith

The Hadith collections, the second important source of Shari'a after the Qur'an, devote considerable attention to jihad, most often in terms of military action against non-believers. Indeed, most Islamic theologians in the classical period (750-1258 C.E.) understood this obligation to jihad as military. There is a whole genre of hadith known as *fada'il al-jihad* (the merits of the holy war), based on the nine-volume Hadith collection of Muhammad ibn Isma'il al-Bukhari (810-70) and considered to be the most respected and authoritative collection.

He dedicates almost one-third of his fourth volume on jihad as physical holy war against infidels. For example, he relates a Hadith of Muhammad commenting that there are one hundred stages in paradise for those who fight for the way of God. Only those who participate in jihad deserve paradise without any checks and reservations. To exemplify this notion, Bukhari relates a story of a woman asking Muhammad if her son, who was killed in the battle of Badr, is in paradise, and he replied that her son is in a higher paradise.

Consistent with the Qur'an, these Hadith generally demonstrate the necessity for Muslims to spare no means to spread Islam by force and strike terror into the hearts of the enemies of God. The main motif of jihad in the Hadith reinforces the concept that death on the battleground in the cause of God leads to paradise and receipt of a "sacred wedding" to black-eyed virgins.

From among 262 traditions that are mentioned by Abdallah Ibn al-Mubarak (736-97), a renowned Khorasani scholar who concentrated on jihad warfare as the most important method to Islamic success, thirteen reinforce the concept of virgins in paradise as a reward for martyrdom.

The Hadith also emphasize the necessity for all believers, whenever called upon, to commit to a jihad war. In one example, Bukhari cites Ibn 'Umar, one of the transmitters of accounts about the Prophet traditionally accepted by Muslims, who relates, "Muhammad said: 'I have been ordered to fight against all the people until they testify that there is no god but Allah and that Muhammad is Allah's messenger, and offer the prayers perfectly, and give the obligatory charity.

So if they perform all that, then they save their lives and property from me and their reckoning will be done by Allah.'" And, in another, a transmitter narrated, "O Allah, you know that there is nothing more beloved to me than to fight in your cause against those who disbelieved your messenger."

Just as in the Qur'an, the Hadith give ample justification for those who would fight heterodox interpretations of Islam within their own society. Muslim jurists in four schools of law have agreed that the apostate should be given three days to repent and, if he did not, he was to be killed by believer's jihad.

Bukhari cites Abu Musa, another accepted transmitter, who related how "a man embraced Islam and then reverted back to Judaism. Ibn al-Mu'azz, one of the Hadith story tellers, said: 'I will not sit down unless you kill him, as the verdict of Allah and his messenger.'" In another Hadith, Ali bin Abu Talib, Muhammad's nephew and son-in-law, narrated, "I heard the Prophet saying ... whenever you find the apostates, kill them, for there will be a reward on the Day of Resurrection."

The Hadith are graphic about punishment for such apostates. According to Anas bin Malik, an Arab thinker and theologian from Medina and founder of the Maliki School of Islamic jurisprudence, "The Prophet ordered the apostates to have their hands and feet cut off. Then he ordered nails, which were heated and passed over their eyes, and they were left in the Harra [a rocky land in Medina], till they died."

Not as theologically important and seldom cited by modern jihadists are the Assassins, a twelfth and thirteenth century Shi'ite movement which staged assassinations against prominent political leaders who did not share their ideas. While their actions do not directly affect the intellectual evolution of contemporary suicide bombers, their actions demonstrate precedent and the ability of theologians to interpret Islamic doctrine to justify suicide terrorism. As with today's terror masters, the group's founder Hasan al-Sabbah promised its members paradise if they died in the course of their missions.

Contemporary Jihad

Early interpretations of jihad contributed a theological framework which proponents of suicide bombing adopted. First was the idea that jihad was violent. It was a tool not only to purify the domains of Islam and purge the heterodox but also to defeat non-Muslims. Today, academics and scholars may argue that jihad is peaceful and represents internal struggle, but they either obfuscate or misunderstand that for most Islamic theologians and as described in detail by Islamic historians, the first three nonviolent components of jihad form a larger, more violent aggregate.

Those who argue that jihad is peaceful base their assertions almost entirely on Qur'anic verses from the Meccan period, in which Muhammad and his band of followers were small and relatively weak and so prone to compromise. Islamists, though, justify their violence with verses revealed to Muhammad after his December 623 expedition to Nakhlah. Prominent classical scholars acknowledged the principle of *nasikh wa-mansukh* (abrogation) which placed greater emphasis on later Medinan verses of violence and jihad.

For contemporary Western scholars and journalists to down play Medinan verses suggest a critical misunderstanding of Qur'anic studies. Many Islamists are unapologetic about violent jihad. They use Qur'anic interpretation to justify terrorism, suicide bombings, and beheadings. They seek to emulate the aggressive jihad waged by Muhammad and his successors from 626 to 740 in their own struggle.

These are the Islamic apocalyptic terrorist groups of today who agree with the idea that jihad is so important that every believer must accept it as a compulsory duty, even when unbelievers have not started it. While some academics and commentators argue that jihad is restricted to religious wars, from an Islamic perspective, all wars against non-Muslims (or Muslims redefined by jihadists as non-Muslims) are religious. This is the reason why some Muslim scholars regard jihad as the sixth pillar of Islam, as it is in Shi'ite doctrine.

The most influential Islamist thinkers of the twentieth century—Abu al-A'la al-Mawdudi (1903-79), Hasan al-Banna (1906-49), and Sayyid Qutb (1906-66)—have addressed the centrality of jihad at length. Activists such as Muhammad Abd al-Salam Faraj, an Egyptian electrical engineer and a follower of Qutb, call it "the neglected duty," and interpret it to justify a fight against any ruler or government that does not adhere to the Shari'a.

Most recent jihadists have relied on Qutb to justify their own theories of violent jihad. 'Abdullah Yusuf 'Azzam (1941-89), a Palestinian who fled to Jordan after the Six-Day war, adopted many elements of both Ibn Taymiya, an early fourteenth century Islamic scholar who laid the philosophical groundwork for the Islamic fundamentalism adopted by Saudi Arabia centuries later, and Qutb to promote the belief in an inevitable clash of civilizations. He emphasized the necessity of violent revolution through jihad against both secular governments in majority Muslim states and against the West. He is credited with being the first Sunni Islamic figure to instill the Islamic community with a divine myth of invincibility of jihad and terrorism.

'Azzam was a major intellectual influence upon Osama bin Laden and Al-Qaeda. In his book *Knights under the Banner of the Prophet,* bin Laden's number two, Ayman al-Zawahiri, identified his organization's goals as *da'wa* and violent jihad against both an "internal enemy," i.e., existing Arab infidel regimes, and an "external enemy" in areas not controlled by Muslims. To Zawahiri, Muslims who accept Western values such as democracy and those who renounce jihad as a means to establish the Islamic state are infidels deserving of death.

The Islamic nation, he maintained, would be established only through jihad for the sake of God, compulsory duty vested upon all the Islamic community. He believed that a "Crusader-Jewish" alliance would mobilize all its resources to counter Islamic power. Bin Laden embraced similar logic. Beginning in August 1996, he used verses from the Qur'an and the Hadith to argue that jihad was compulsory to expel non-Muslims and Westerners from Saudi Arabia.

On February 23, 1998, though, he expanded his jihad when, with Zawahiri at his side, he announced the creation of the International Islamic Front for Jihad against the Jews and Crusaders. The writings of Qutb also influenced Abu Mus'ab al-Zarqawi, the late leader of Al-Qaeda in Iraq. Zarqawi peppered his speeches and declarations with verses from the Qur'an and Hadith to demonstrate God's promise of the inevitability of the creation of a pure Sunni Islamic state so long as Muslims fight jihad against the enemies of Islam by jihad. Zarqawi called jihad "the crest of the summit of Islam."

Bin Laden granted Zarqawi permission to kill Iraqi security forces and Shi'ites in order to achieve a "state of truth" and uproot the "state of the lie." Zarqawi did so with both car bombs and suicide bombers. On May 18, 2005, Zarqawi legitimized the killing of Muslims under the principle of overriding necessity and the victory of jihad. "Islamic law states that the Islamic faith is more important than life, honor, and property," and the Shi'ites are worse than the Crusaders, he argued.

He declared both collateral killing of Muslims and murder of noncombatant non-Muslims legitimate and, on September 14, 2005, declared jihad war on the Shi'ites. In the words of Rudolph Peters, an expert on contemporary Islam, the ultimate aim of jihad is the subjection of the non-believers and the eradication of non-belief. Islamic law is the ultimate solution, and it has full answers to all possible situations and problems, present and future.

This is why the fanatic Muslims of today—religious, ideologists, and practitioners—denounce all the existing political systems and demand their liquidation. The current Arab-Islamic system represents a "new age of ignorance" and the Western political systems are "the new Crusaderism," all doomed to extermination by jihad warfare.

Jihad becomes a binding duty on all Muslims as individuals. Abdulaziz A. Sachedina, an Indian Muslim expert on the Shi'ites who lives in the West, explained, "There is no doubt that the Muslim jurists conceived jihad in the sense of engaging in a war to increase the *Dar al-Islam* as an integral part of Islamic faith ... with the essential aim of uprooting unbelief and preparing the way for a creation of Islamic order on earth."

The violence of contemporary jihad was also apparent in the reaction of Islamists to cartoons published in the Danish newspaper *Jyllands-Posten*. Muslim rioters and Arab and Islamic governments seized upon the contention that it is against Islam to depict the Prophet Muhammad and to argue that the apostates and non-believers should be punished. Violence accompanied demonstrations in Europe and in Muslim countries. By far the greatest number of fatalities was in Nigeria, which is neither European nor Muslim.

In London, protestors marched under banners reading, "Slay those who insult Islam," "Butcher those who mock

Islam," "Behead those who insult Islam," "Exterminate those who slander Islam," "Massacre those who insult Islam," "Europe is the cancer, Islam is the answer," "Europe take lessons from 9-11," "Europe you will pay. Your 9-11 is on its way," "Be prepared for the real holocaust," and "Islam will dominate the world." To many jihadists, such threats are literal, not hyperbole. Suicide bombing becomes a legitimate technique to carry them out.

The Islamic Roots of Suicide Bombings

What is the connection between religious sources of over a millennium ago to the suicide bombings of today? There is a direct link between the jihadists of yesterday and contemporary jihadists. Many jihadists cite the works of Taqi al-din Ahmad Ibn Taymiya (1263-1328), an Islamic scholar born in Harran, in modern-day Turkey, who wrote extensively on the need for jihad and exalted it even above the Islamic obligations of fasting and pilgrimage (*hajj*). He attacked many practices prevalent among Muslims of his time and favored a literal interpretation of the Qur'an.

Modern jihadists have used his *fatwa*s commanding Muslims to fight the Mongols as precedents legitimizing suicide bombing. Mawdudi, Banna, and Qutb have also developed Ibn Taymiya's philosophy, writing extensively on jihad as the means to fight the re-emergence of the age of ignorance, with its tribal savagery and anarchy. They also suggested that the Islamic order can be maintained and protected, if not expanded, through violence.

In recent decades, the Palestinian Islamist group Hamas has embraced suicide bombings to lethal effect. Its 1987 charter shows its intellectual and theological justifications. It cites the Qur'an to promote the idea of Muslim exclusivity and Hadith from Bukhari and the *Sahih Muslim* calling for the murder of Jews to hasten the Day of Judgment. More recent exegesis also influenced Hamas. The charter cites Banna's call for Islam to obliterate Israel and is explicit about the violent nature of jihad: Article 13 argues that there is no solution to the Palestinian question but through jihad, and Article 15 declares the necessity to instill jihad in the heart of the Muslim nation.

The 9-11 suicide attacks sparked significant debate in the Islamic world about the merits of suicide attacks. Sheikh Muhammad Sa'id al-Tantawi, head of Cairo's Al-Azhar, the most prestigious university for Sunni jurisprudence, declared that the Shari'a rejects all attempts on taking human life, and Sheikh Muhammad bin 'Abdallah al-Sabil, a member of the Saudi Council of Islamic Clerics and imam at the Grand Mosque in Mecca, decried the suicide attacks on the basis that Islamic law forbids killing civilians, suicide, and protects Jews and Christians. But both Tantawi and Sabil sidestep the question of "martyrdom operations." Because preserving the life of *dhimmis* (Jews and Christians) is conditional to their acceptance of Muslim rule, suicide attacks upon Israelis or Jews and Christians outside majority Muslim countries may be permissible. Indeed, other Al-Azhar scholars, for example, 'Abd al-'Azim al-Mit'ani, say it is permissible to kill Israeli civilians in the cause of jihad.

Today's Al-Qaeda splinter and successor groups and their fellow travelers use the writings of Ibn Taymiya and those influenced by him. The linkage is concrete. They often cite the same Qur'anic passages and Hadith that justified the violent jihad of the seventh century. Religious clerics issue *fatwas* citing them. Perhaps the most prominent of these is Sheikh Yusuf al-Qaradawi, who has built upon such interpretations to justify suicide bombing, other acts of terrorism, and the murder of civilians, all in the cause of jihad. He has called suicide bombing a supreme form of jihad for the sake of God and, therefore, religiously legitimate.

Those who object to his ideas he labels as agents of ignorance. While he argues that the Qur'an does not allow attacks against the innocent, his definition of innocence is so narrow as to obviate such assurances. September 11 hijacker Muhammad Atta's last will and testament shows how deep such interpretations of jihad have penetrated Muslim life as his verbiage and instructions for burial showed how he believed himself a good Muslim, even as he participated in an event which murdered almost 3,000 civilians.

Suicide bombing in the Muslim world cannot be separated from religion. Its perpetrators believe jihad to be synonymous with war and mandate Muslims to strike not only at non-Muslims but also at co-religionists deemed insufficiently loyal to their radical cause. The ideological basis of such an interpretation has deep roots in Islamic theology, but it came to prominence with the twentieth-century rise of Muslim Brotherhood theorists such as Banna and Qutb and was further developed by their successors. While much of the exegesis developed out of Sunni jurisprudence, the Islamic Republic in Iran encouraged the phenomenon. Many of Tehran's proxy groups embraced the tactic.

It is fashionable among Western analysts and academics to explain away suicide bombing with discussion of "root causes" that omit religion. Many cite a history of exploitation by Western powers, Israel's existence, government oppression, poverty, lack of education, and alienation as reasons why desperate individuals decide to blow themselves up to murder others. But attention to suicide bombers' own justifications suggest that, for them, Islam and its call for jihad is the primary motivation.

Beheading in the Name of Islam

Images of masked terrorists standing behind Western hostages in Iraq and Saudi Arabia have become all too common on Arabic satellite stations such as Al-Jazeera and Al-Manar. Islamist websites such as *Muntadiyat al-Mahdi* go further streaming video of their murder. The February 2002 decapitation of *Wall Street Journal* reporter Daniel

Pearl, true to its intention, horrified the Western audience. Chechen rebels, egged on by Islamist benefactors, had adopted the practice four years earlier, but the absence of widely broadcast videos limited the psychological impact of hostage decapitation.

The Pearl murder and video catalyzed the resurgence of this historical Islamic practice. In Iraq, terrorists filmed the beheadings of Americans Nicholas Berg, Jack Hensley, and Eugene Armstrong. Other victims include Turks, an Egyptian, a Korean, Bulgarians, a British businessman, and a Nepalese. Scores of Iraqis, both Kurds and Arabs, have also fallen victim to Islamist terrorists' knives. The new fad in terrorist brutality has extended to Saudi Arabia where Islamist terrorists murdered American businessman Paul Johnson, whose head was later discovered in a freezer in an Al-Qaeda hideout. A variation upon this theme would be the practice of Islamists slitting the throats of those opponents they label infidels. This is what happened to Dutch filmmaker Theo Van Gogh, first gunned down and then mutilated on an Amsterdam street, and to an Egyptian Coptic family in New Jersey after the father had angered Islamists with Internet chat room criticisms of Islam.

The purpose of terrorism is to strike fear into the hearts of opponents in order to win political concession. As the shock value wears off and the Western world becomes immunized to any particular tactic, terrorists develop new ones in order to maximize shock and the press reaction upon which they thrive. In the 1970s and 1980s, terrorists hijacked airliners to win headlines. In the 1980s and 1990s, the car bomb became more popular; Palestinian terrorists perfected suicide bombings in the 1990s. But what once garnered days of commentary now generates only hours. Decapitation has become the latest fashion. In many ways, it sends terrorism back to the future. Unlike hijackings and car bombs, ritual beheading has a long precedent in Islamic theology and history.

Apologetics and Reality

Some American commentators say that Islamist decapitations are intended as psychological warfare and devoid of any true Islamic content. Imam Muhammad Adam al-Sheikh, head of the Dar al-Hijrah mosque in Falls Church, Virginia, for example, claimed incorrectly that "beheadings are not mentioned in the Koran at all." Asma Afsaruddin, an associate professor of Arabic and Islamic studies at the University of Notre Dame, also misrepresented Islamic theology and history when she told a reporter, "There is absolutely no religious imperative for this."

The Council on American-Islamic Relations (CAIR) as well as the American Anti-Arab Discrimination Committee (ADC) has both signed on to a statement that such killings "did not represent the tenets of Islam." Sam Hamod, former director of the Islamic Center in Washington, D.C., claimed that the Qur'anic passage on beheading unbelievers did not actually mean that people should be killed. Such fulminations have had an effect, the Western news media has, perhaps as a result of political correctness or its own bias, twisted the reality of Islamic history and propagated such revisionism. With such apologetics, Western academics either display basic ignorance of their fields or purposely mislead.

The intelligentsia's denial of any religious roots to the recent spate of decapitation has parallels in the logical back flips and kid-glove treatments in which many professors engaged in order to deny a religious basis for violent jihad. Afsaruddin and Hamod aside, Islamists justify murder and decapitation with both theological citations and historical precedent.

Decapitation in Islamic Theology

Groups such as Abu Mus'ab al-Zarqawi's Al-Tawhid wa al-Jihad (Unity and Jihad) and Abu 'Abd Allah al-Hasan bin Mahmud's Ansar al-Sunna (Defenders of [Prophetic] Tradition) justify the decapitation of prisoners with Qur'anic scripture. *Sura* (chapter) 47 contains the *ayah* (verse), "When you encounter the unbelievers on the battlefield, strike off their heads until you have crushed them completely; then bind the prisoners tightly." The Qur'anic Arabic terms are generally straightforward, *kafaru* means "those who blaspheme/are irreligious," although *Darb ar-riqab* is less clear. *Darb* can mean "striking or hitting" while *ar-riqab* translates to "necks, slaves, persons." With little variation, scholars have translated the verse as, "When you meet the unbelievers, smite their necks."

For centuries, leading Islamic scholars have interpreted this verse literally. The famous Iranian historian and Qur'an commentator Muhammad b. Jarir at-Tabari wrote that "striking at the necks" is simply God's sanction of ferocious opposition to non-Muslims. Mahmud b. Umar az-Zamakh-shari, in a major commentary studied for centuries by Sunni religious scholars, suggested that any prescription to "strike at the necks" commands to avoid striking elsewhere so as to confirm death and not simply wound.

Many recent interpretations remain consistent with those of a millennium ago. In Saudi-distributed translation of the Qur'an, 'Abdullah Yusuf 'Ali wrote that the injunction to "smite at their necks," should be taken both literally and figuratively. "You cannot wage war with kid gloves," Yusuf 'Ali argued. Muhammad Muhammad Khatib, in a modern Sunni commentary bearing the imprimatur of Al-Azhar university in Cairo, says that while traditionalist Muslims tend to see this passage as only applying to the Prophet's time, Shi'ites "think it is a universal precept." Ironically, then in this view, Zarqawi has adopted the exegesis of his religious nemeses. Perhaps the most influential modern recapitulation of this passage was provided by the influential Pakistani scholar and leading Islamist thinker S. Abul A' la Mawdudi, who argued that the Sura provided the first Qur'anic prescriptions on the laws of war.

Under no circumstances should the Muslim lose sight of this aim and start taking the enemy soldiers as captives. Captives should be taken after the enemy has been completely crushed. Accordingly, for soldiers of Islam, victory should be the only consideration. Status of prisoners of war was open to interpretation. Mawdudi maintained that the verse did not clearly forbid execution of prisoners but that "the Holy Prophet understood this intention of Allah's command, and that if there was a special reason for which the ruler of an Islamic government regarded it as necessary to kill a particular prisoner (or prisoners), he could do so."

As do many Islamists, Mawdudi cited historical examples of the Prophet Muhammad ordering the execution of prisoners, such as some Meccans captured at the Battle of Badr in 624 C.E. and at least one Meccan seized at the Battle of Uhud in the following year. While such examples do not directly address decapitation, they do allow for murder of prisoners-of-war. Mawdudi's interpretation, though, does not sanction the execution of hostages. Only the government, and not individual Muslim soldiers, could determine the fate of captives.

Another, albeit less-frequently, cited Qur'anic passage also sanctions beheadings of non-Muslims. *Sura* 8:12 reads, "I will cast dread into the hearts of the unbelievers. Strike off their heads, then, and strike off all of their fingertips." In the original text, the relevant phrase is *adrabu fawq al-'anaq,* "strike over their necks." This verse is, then, a corollary to Sura 47:3. Yusuf 'Ali is one of the few modern commentators who addressed this passage, interpreting it as utilitarian, the neck is among the only areas not protected by armor, and mutilating an opponent's hands prevents him from again wielding his sword or spear. The point of this opening phrase—to "cast dread" or, as some translations have it, "instill terror"—has now been adopted by Islamist terrorists to justify decapitation of hostages.

Decapitation in Islamic History

While some Islamists might justify murder of prisoners on Qur'anic prescription, others reinforce their conclusions by drawing analogies to events during the almost 1,400 years of Islamic history. Here beheading of captives is a recurring theme. Both Islamic regimes and their opposition have utilized beheadings as both military and judicial policy. The practice of beheading non-Muslim captives extends back to the Prophet himself. Ibn Ishaq, the earliest biographer of Muhammad, is recorded as saying that the Prophet ordered the execution by decapitation of 700 men of the Jewish Banu Qurayza tribe in Medina for allegedly plotting against him.

Islamic leaders from Muhammad's time until today have followed his model. Examples of decapitation, of both the living and the dead, in Islamic history are myriad. Yusuf b. Tashfin (d. 1106) led the Al-Murabit (Almoravid) Empire to conquer from Western Sahara to central Spain. After the battle of Zallaqa in 1086, he had 24,000 corpses of the defeated Castilians beheaded "and piled them up to make a sort of minaret for the muezzins who, standing on the piles of headless cadavers, sang the praises of Allah." He then had the detached heads sent to all the major cities of North Africa and Spain as an example of Christian impotence. The Al-Murabits were conquered the following century by the Al-Muwahhids (Almohads), under whose rule Castilian Christian enemies were beheaded after any lost battles.

The Ottoman Empire was the decapitation state par excellence. Upon the Ottoman victory over Christian Serbs at the battle of Kosovo in 1389, the Muslim army beheaded the Serbian king and scores of Christian prisoners. At the battle of Varna in 1444, the Ottomans beheaded King Ladislaus of Hungary and "put his head at the tip of a long pike ... and brandished it toward the Poles and Hungarians." Upon the fall of Constantinople, the

Ottomans sent the head of the dead Byzantine emperor on tour to major cities in the sultan's domains. The Ottomans even beheaded at least one Eastern Orthodox patriarch. In 1456, the sultan allowed the grand mufti of the empire to personally decapitate King Stephen of Bosnia and his sons—even though they had surrendered and, seven decades later, the sultan ordered 2,000 Hungarian prisoners beheaded.

In the early nineteenth century, the British felt victim to the Ottoman scimitar. An 1807 British expedition to Egypt resulted in "a few hundred spiked British heads left rotting in the sun outside Rosetta." Decapitation has also been quite common among Muslims whenever orthodoxy confronts Mahdist movements. According to Islamic tradition, the Mahdi, or "rightly-guided one" will come before the end of time to usher in a worldwide, perfect Islamic state. Every few generations, a charismatic leader emerges claiming to be the Mahdi. Since the Mahdi is the harbinger of just government, then any leader he challenges is by nature corrupt. The fervor of such claims often leads both the orthodoxy and the Mahdists to label the other unbelievers, allowing them to invoke Qur'anic verse 47:3 and behead captives.

A prime example of this occurred 500 years ago in the Gujarati sultanate of western India. Sayyid Muhammad Jawnpuri asserted that he was the Mahdi. His followers, who came to be known as Mahdavis, accused the Gujarati sultans and religious officials of *takfir* (unbelief). The sultans fought back, often displaying the severed heads of Mahdavi caliphs in order to intimidate would-be followers. The Gujarati brutality served its purpose and, by the end of the sixteenth century, the Mahdavis faded into oblivion.

Perhaps the most famous Mahdist movement—and one of very few to gain power—was that led by Muhammad Ahmad of Sudan in the late nineteenth century. In 1880, Muhammad Ahmad declared himself Mahdi and led jihad against the Ottoman Empire, its Egyptian subjects, and their

British allies. He and his followers beheaded opponents, Christian and Muslim alike. This Mahdi's most famous victim was Charles Gordon, a British general in Sudan on behalf of Anglo-Egyptian forces. Rudolf Slatin, an Austrian taken prisoner by the Mahdist army, later described the Mahdists' triumphant reaction to Gordon's execution in January 1885. One historian related how:

> Three black [Mahdist] soldiers were in the lead, one of whom he recognized as a man named Shatta. ... Shatta was carrying something wrapped in a bloody cloth. Slatin stood silent as they stopped in front of him, their faces triumphant. With a smile, Shatta undid the cloth while the crowd shouted. Slatin looked, it was Gordon's severed head ... "Is this not the head of your uncle, the unbeliever?"

While not as graphic as an Al-Qaeda video, the impact on Victorian society was the same. Revenge would take years. Muhammad Ahmad died, probably of typhoid or malaria, in 1885, but his state fell to the British army only in 1898. A half century later, in the years after Mustafa Kemal Atatürk founded the Turkish Republic and imposed secular government, a revolutionary religious leader named Mehmet led a short-lived but violent Mahdist revolt. Mehmet was a Sufi—an Islamic mystic—of the Naqshabandi order. Mehmet and his six disciples adopted the identities of the "Seven Sleepers" of the Qur'an, seven Christian youth who fell asleep in a cave during the time of Roman persecution of Christians in the third century C.E. and emerged, unscathed, over a century later when Rome had joined the faith.

By such identification, Mehmet and his Mahdist disciples sought to invoke the Qur'anic imagery of the small band of true believers standing against state idolatry. From Manisa, in west-central Turkey, Mehmet and his followers trekked to Menemen on the Aegean coast where, in the main mosque, Mehmet declared himself the Mahdi and called for the reestablishment of Islamic law canceled by

Atatürk. Mehmet's enthusiastic supporters overwhelmed the local Turkish army garrison. They killed the commander and put his severed head on a pole and paraded it around town. The uprising was short-lived, though. The Turkish army rallied its forces and crushed the revolt, executing all involved.

Beheading has particular prominence in Saudi Arabia. In 2003 alone, the Kingdom of Saudi Arabia beheaded more than fifty people. This number included both Muslim and non-Muslim workers. Over the past two decades, the Saudis have decapitated at least 1,100 for alleged crimes ranging from drug running to witchcraft and apostasy. The Saudi government not only uses beheadings to punish criminals but also to terrorize potential opponents. One famous example involved a Saudi national guardsman named Juhayman al-'Utaybi. In late 1979, the start of the fifteenth century in the Islamic calendar, 'Utaybi declared his brother-in-law Muhammad bin Abd Allah al-Qahtani to be the Mahdi.

They seized control of the holy mosque in Mecca and called on all Saudis to rise up against the government in Riyadh. The house of Saud responded forcibly with a shock-and-awe campaign. After a bloody battle, they regained control of the holy mosque. Within weeks, they had hunted down and either killed or captured the Mahdists. In early 1980, the Saudi government publicly beheaded 'Utaybi and his imprisoned followers. While outsiders may consider the Saudi practice barbaric, most Saudi executions are swift, completed in one sword blow. Zarqawi and his followers have chosen a slow, torturous sawing method to terrorize the Western audience.

All these various justifications contribute to the rash of beheadings in Iraq and elsewhere in the Middle East. Because Zarqawi and his followers consider the Iraqi and Saudi governments to be illegitimate, they find no injunction within Islamic law that would prohibit execution of prisoners. Indeed, Zarqawi has commented that he would "accept comments from ulema regarding whether his killing operations are permitted or forbidden according to Islam—provided that the ulema are not connected to a regime and are offering opinions out of personal conviction, and not to please their rulers" Islamist beheadings may be condemned by the imam of the great mosque of Mecca and by religious leaders in Egypt, Jordan, and Lebanon, but like self-styled mahdis throughout Islamic history, Zarqawi and Islamist terrorists simply dismiss these *fatwa*s (religious rulings) as empty rhetoric from lackey regimes.

Osama bin Laden's Al-Qaeda is also on record as supporting beheadings, including that of at least one Egyptian worker in Iraq whom they classified as a "nonbeliever" by virtue of his citizenship in an apostate regime, as well as his presumed approval of the U.S. actions in Iraq. Increasingly, Islamist groups conflate "unbelievers," "combatants," and prisoners of war, which, coupled with their claim to Islamic legitimacy, provides them with a license to decapitate.

Islamic civilization is not a historical anomaly in its sanction of decapitation. The Roman Empire beheaded citizens (such as the Christian Saint Paul) while they crucified non citizens (such as Jesus Christ). French revolutionaries employed the guillotine to decapitate opponents. Nevertheless, Islam is the only major world religion today that is cited by both state and non-state actors to legitimize beheadings. And two major aspects of decapitation in an Islamic context should be noted, first, the practice has both Qur'anic and historical sanction. It is not the product of a fabricated tradition. Second, in contradiction to the assertions of apologists, both Muslim and non-Muslim, these beheadings are not simply a brutal method of drawing attention to the Islamist political agenda and weakening opponents' will to fight.

Zarqawi and other Islamists who practice decapitation believe that God has ordained them to obliterate their enemies in this manner. Islam is, for this determined minority of Muslims, anything but a "religion of peace." It is, rather, a religion of the sword with the blade forever at the throat of the unbeliever.

Marching for Hamas

Hamas is a bully aided by a bigger bully, Iran. And, just as strident and threatening human bullies get away with their aggression so long as no one calls their bluff, so Hamas has been getting away with murder and torture because the UN and many states won't call its two-faced self-portrayal as the victim in the piece. In the struggle to take over Gaza from Fatah, it went on a rampage that killed hundreds of Palestinians. Even during this most recent assault, in early January, it executed Fatah members for violating their house arrest. A few weeks ago, Hamas determined to hurt yet more of its compatriots by introducing Islamic *hudud* punishments to the Strip, from amputations and stonings, to crucifixions and hangings.

Like all bullies, it likes to taunt its victims. It did just that for years after Israel left Gaza, firing rockets every day into towns like Sderot or Netivot. No one who has dismissed these rockets as harmless homemade toys has ever had the guts to spend a few weeks in Sderot, scurrying from shelter to shelter. And, oh yes, it also built up an arsenal (supplied by Iran) of Grad missiles that certainly aren't anybody's toys.

Like all bullies, Hamas likes to make boastful threats. Its 1988 Covenant is replete with them. It threatens to destroy the State of Israel by violence and violence alone. It says it will never accept the work of conferences or peacemakers, and only jihad will solve its problems. Meanwhile, the Palestinians see their lives drained away in a culture that embraces death and martyrdom, their children exposed to a steady diet of military training and preparation for violent death as suicide bombers.

Even if the Palestinians want peace, Hamas won't let them have it, because Hamas knows best, and jihad "is the only solution." Don't believe me, read the Covenant. It likes nothing better than killing Jews, and the bigger bully in Teheran thinks that's a damn fine thing too. No one says a word, because the UN is dominated by the Islamic states, and the Western governments know where the oil comes from, and nobody likes the Jews much anyway. The people calling for the end of Israel while they march on the streets of London and Dublin aren't all Muslims by any means.

There can be no greater indication of this boastfulness than what has happened in recent days. Having taken a heavy battering from Israel, Hamas now proclaims a "great victory," and its supporters dance in the ruined streets of Gaza, drunk on their own demagoguery. For all its bluster, Hamas, like all bullies, is a coward at heart. Watch those films of Hamas gunmen dragging screaming children along with them to act as human shields, watch how they fire from behind the little ones, knowing no Israeli soldier will fire back. And even as they put their own children's lives at risk, they shout to high heaven that the Israelis are Nazis and the Jews are child-killers.

This blatant pornography spreads through the Western media, and people never once ask "what does this look like from the other side," because they are addicted to the comforting news that the Yids are baby-killers as they'd always known, that they do poison wells, that no Christian child is safe come Passover. Hamas has become proficient at resurrecting the blood libel, just as its fighters use the Nazi salute, just as their predecessor in the 1930s and '40s, Haj Amin al-Husseini, conferred with Hitler about building death camps in Palestine and raised a division of SS troops in Bosnia to fight for the Reich.

We watch *The Diary of Anne Frank* on television, and some of us attend Holocaust Remembrance Day events, and others pay lip service to Jewish victimhood; we like our Jews emaciated and helpless under the SS boot. But the moment real Jews stand up and show themselves the stronger for all their deaths, it awakens an atavistic fear, and people recoil from them. Jews in uniform, how unseemly, Jews beating the bully, how unheard of and Jews with their own state what upstarts.

In my home country of Ireland, we glamorize the great nationalist heroes who rebelled against the bullying forces of imperial Britain in the uprising of Easter Sunday 1916. In France, they venerate the heroes of the Resistance against the occupying forces of Nazi Germany. In Spain, they have not ceased to heap praise on those who fought against the forces of fascist bullies and lost. To stand up against an enemy bent on your destruction is everywhere counted an act of bravery. But not when it comes to Israel. In 1948 and 1967 and 1973 and 2006, Israel fought off overwhelming forces that made no secret of their plans for an imminent massacre of the Jews. But nobody now seems to care, no one lauds the courage the Israelis displayed, and no one praises the extraordinary restraint they showed in victory.

In a bizarre reversal of all their commitment to human rights and the struggle of men and women for independence and self-determination, the European Left has chosen again and again to side with the bullies and to condemn a small nation struggling to survive in a hostile neighborhood. It is all self-contradictory, The Left supports gay rights, yet attacks the only country in the Middle East where gay rights are enshrined in law. Hamas makes death the punishment for being gay, but "we are all Hamas now." Iran hangs gays, but it is praised as an agent of anti-imperialism, and allowed to get on with its job of stoning women and executing dissidents and members of religious minorities. If UK Premier Gordon Brown swore to wipe France from the face of the earth, he would become a pariah among nations. Mahmoud Ahmadinejad threatens to do that to Israel and is invited to speak to the UN General Assembly.

Israel guarantees civil liberties to all its citizens, Jew or Arab alike, but it is dubbed "an apartheid state"; Hamas, ever the bully, kills its opponents and denies the rest the most basic rights, but we march on behalf of Hamas. The Left prefers the bully because the bully represents a finger in the face of the establishment? Almost no one on the Left has any understanding of militant Islam. Their politics is a politics of gesture, where wearing a keffiyeh is cool but understanding its symbolism is too much effort even for intellectuals. I have personally had enough of it all. The whining double standards, the blatant lies, the way their leaders have forced Palestinians to suffer for 60 years because peace and compromise aren't in their vocabulary and because they won't settle for anything but total victory.

Painful as it was, in the 1920s Ireland created a republic by compromising on the status of the North. Ireland subsequently became a prosperous country and, in due course, one of the hottest economies in the world. When the Israelis left Gaza in 2005, they left state-of-the-art greenhouses to form the basis for a thriving economy. Hamas destroyed them to the last pane of glass. Why? Because they had been Jewish greenhouses.

One Nation under Secularism

In Campaign 2004, secularism has become a dirty word. Democrats, particularly Howard Dean, are being warned that they do not have a chance of winning the presidential election unless they adopt a posture of religious "me-tooism" in an effort to convince voters that their politics are grounded in values just as sacred as those proclaimed by President Bush.

On one level, the impulse to capitalize on the religiosity of Americans can be seen as transparently, and at times comically, opportunistic. Late last year, Ed Kilgore, policy director of the Democratic Leadership Council, earnestly advised his party's candidates to invoke "God's green earth" in supporting stronger environmental laws. Mr. Dean, the candidate stuck with the label (or libel) of being the most secularist Democratic aspirant, seems to be heeding the advice to get religion. He recently informed an Iowa audience that he prays daily, and in New Hampshire last week, he demonstrated his ecumenism by using the Muslim -expression "inshallah," which means God willing.

On a deeper level, the notion that elected officials should employ a religious rationale for policy decisions is rooted in the misconception, promulgated by the Christian right, that the American government was founded on divine authority rather than human reason. When I lecture on college campuses, students frequently express surprise at being told that the framers of the Constitution deliberately omitted any mention of God in order to assign supreme governmental power to "We the People."

Dismissing this inconvenient fact, some on the religious right have suggested that divine omnipotence was considered a given in the 1780's that the framers had no need to acknowledge God in the Constitution because his dominion was as self-evident as the rising and setting of the sun. Yet isn't it absurd to suppose that men as precise in their use of language as Benjamin Franklin, Alexander Hamilton and James Madison would absentmindedly have failed to insert God into the nation's founding document? In fact, they represented a majority of citizens who wished not only to free religion from government interference but government from religious interference.

This deep sentiment was expressed in letters to newspapers during the debate over ratification of the Constitution. One Massachusetts correspondent, signing himself "Elihu," summed up the secular case by praising the authors of the Constitution as men who "come to us in the plain language of common sense, and propose to our understanding a system of government, as the invention of mere human wisdom; no deity comes down to dictate it, nor even a God in a dream to propose any part of it."

The 18th-century public's understanding of the Constitution as a secular document can perhaps best be gauged by the reaction of religious conservatives at the time. For example, the Rev. John M. Mason, a fire-breathing New York City minister, denounced the absence of God in the preamble as "an omission which no pretext whatever can palliate." He warned that "we will have every reason to tremble, lest the governor of the universe, who will not be treated with indignity by a people more than individuals, overturn from its foundations the fabric we have been rearing and crush us to atoms in the wreck." But unlike many conservatives today, Mason acknowledged even as he deplored the Constitution's uncompromising secularism.

Americans tend to minimize not only the secular convictions of the founders, but also the secularist contribution to later social reform movements. One of the most common misconceptions is that organized religion deserves nearly all of the credit for 19th-century abolitionism and the 20th-century civil rights movement. While religion certainly played a role in both, many people fail to distinguish between personal faith and religious institutions.

Abolitionists like William Lloyd Garrison, editor of The Liberator, and the Quaker Lucretia Mott, also a women's rights crusader, denounced the many mainstream Northern religious leaders who, in the 1830's and 40's, refused to condemn slavery. In return, Garrison and Mott were castigated as infidels and sometimes as atheists a common tactic used by those who do not recognize any form of faith but their own. Garrison, strongly influenced by his free-thinking predecessor Thomas Paine, observed that one need only be a decent human being not a believer in the Bible or any creed to discern the evil of slavery.

During the 20th-century civil rights struggle, the movement's strongest moral leaders emerged from Southern black churches. But the moral message of the Rev. Dr. Martin Luther King Jr. obviously ran counter to the religious rationales for segregation preached in many white churches in the south. In addition, Dr. King welcomed the help of nonreligious allies like Stanley Levison, his friend and lawyer, and the outspoken labor leader A. Philip Randolph. Michael Schwerner and Andrew Goodman, murdered in Mississippi in the summer of 1964, were nonobservant Jews who died not in the name of religion but because of their secular humanist commitment to racial justice.

Many politicians today, including President Bush, use the civil rights leadership of African-American ministers as an argument in favor of "faith-based" government financing. But those ministers were free to pursue their moral vision within American society precisely because they were independent of both government money and government control. Government officials, by contrast, have a very different constitutionally mandated obligation to devise public policies based not on religious interests but on a secular concept of public good.

When President Lyndon B. Johnson proposed the Voting Rights Act of 1965 and declared, in his memorable Texas twang, "We shall overcome," he was articulating a moral position that could and did command the respect of citizens of any or no religion. That is real leadership. Not a scintilla of bravery is required for a candidate, whether Democratic or Republican, to take refuge in religion. But it would take genuine courage to stand up and tell voters that elected officials cannot and should not depend on divine instructions to reconcile the competing interests and passions of human beings.

Abraham Lincoln, whose spiritual beliefs were so elusive that both atheists and the devoutly religious have tried to claim him as their own, spoke eloquently on this point during his long period of deliberation before issuing the Emancipation Proclamation. "I am approached with the most opposite opinions and advice, and that by religious men, who are equally certain that they represent the divine will," he told a group of ministers in September 1862. "I hope it will not be irreverent for me to say that if it is probable that God would reveal his will to others, on a point so connected with my duty, it might be supposed that he would reveal it directly to me. . . . These are not, however, the days of miracles. . . I must study the plain, physical facts of the case, ascertain what is possible, and learn what appears to be wise and right."

Today, many voters, of many religious beliefs, might well be receptive to a candidate who forthrightly declares that his vision of social justice will be determined by the "plain, physical facts of the case" on humanity's green and fragile earth. But that would take an inspirational leader who glories in the nation's secular heritage and is not afraid to say so.

The war in Iraq was winding down as I stood in the checkout line at the supermarket. The elderly lady behind me picked a morning newspaper out of a nearby rack and scanned the headlines touting a suicide bomber killing of several U.S. soldiers in Iraq. She forlornly cried, "Why does the world hate us so much?" I turned in time to see the elderly gentlemen behind her shrug his shoulders as a sign of bewilderment. Several others overheard the lady's anguish but said nothing.

The truth is that , the large majority of non-Americans don't hate us. It may come as a shock to our collective egos, but the rest of the human race does not sit around wringing their hands over anything American. They're too busy worrying about their own families and trying to make a living. In the rare times they are confronted by America, they will opt for their own culture. Why should that surprise us? Nationalism and pride in one's own culture are common. They may think us weird or crazy, but they don't hate us.

Obviously, there are people out there who hate us with such intensity that they are willing to die to kill as many of us as possible. We've labeled these people as terrorists. Unfortunately, the number of terrorists may be growing. Although there are a number of nationalistic liberation organizations, the terrorists threatening U.S. and Western security are driven by Islamic religious impulses. In fact, we would do well to understand the danger inherent in all religious expressions.

Nothing stirs human emotions like beliefs associated with supernatural beings. Parents have even killed their children for religious beliefs (several cases were recently reported). Many preliterate people sacrificially killed their children on an altar to their gods and the same religious views justified the slaughter of their neighbors. Lest my Christian colleagues feel a sense of superiority, we should remember that we have historically killed non-Christians and, incredibly, one another in the name of Jesus Christ. All religious systems justify the killing of others in the name of their deity.

The historical U.S. tilt toward Israel is a strong element in driving Islam's terrorism. But even if we change that imbalance, Islamic fundamentalists will continue acts of terrorism. And hatred will continue to beat in the hearts of Islamic fundamentalists even if al-Qaida is eliminated. This is because Islamic fundamentalism's hatred is driven by a deep fear of modernity. Western modernity, with its scientific world view, stresses secularism and the rights of individuals to choose their own values and life style. This is believed to undermine Islamic authority. It does.

Americans should be able to understand this view. We have a number of Christian fundamentalists fighting modernity. This is our nation's "dirty little secret" that we loathe to acknowledge and confront. Look at the evidence:

- The bombing of abortion clinics is an act of terrorism. Supposedly, "these are evil places operated by evil people and need to be eliminated for the sake of creating a godly society. This is the same rationale used by Islamic terrorists.
- Christian fundamentalists work to ban books and magazines as a means of "protecting people from evil ideas. Islamic fundamentalists do the same.
- Christian fundamentalists also fear science, since it refutes biblical literalism and undermines the church's moral authority. Christian fundamentalists correctly view scientific evolution as undermining the authority of the Bible.

The modernist genie is out of the bottle. It permeates and drives Western civilization. It liberates the individual and questions historic, taken-for-granted world views, replacing them with what most Westerners consider being more accurate and useful views. It's unfortunate that religious fundamentalists, of whatever brand, seem unwilling to adapt to it. No matter how many Saddam Husseins we displace, religious fundamentalism, wherever found and however disguised, is the real breeding ground for terrorism.

7

Origins of Suicidal Terrorism

Attention deficit disorder seems to flourish under conditions of late modernity. The past becomes itself more quickly. Memories, individual as well as collective, tend to be recycled and consulted only by the old. For everyone else, there are only current affairs, reaching back a few months at most. Orwell, of course, predicted this, in his dystopic prophecy that may have been only premature; but today it seems to be cemented by post-modernism (Delouse), and also by physicists, who are now proclaiming an almost Ash'arite skepticism about claims for the real duration of particles.

This is a condition that has an ancestry in the stirrings of the modernity which it represents. Hume anticipated it in his stunning insistence on the non-continuity of the human self, we are 'nothing but a collection of perceptions which succeed each other with inconceivable rapidity and are in perpetual flux and movement;' or so he thought. Modern fiction may still explore or reaffirm identities and thus define human dignity as the honourable disposition of at least some aspects of an accumulated heritage. But this is giving way to the atomistic, playful, postmodern storytelling of, say, Elliot Perlman, which defines dignity - where it does so at all - in terms of freedom from all stories, even while lamenting the superficial tenor of the result. It is against the backdrop of this culture that the scientists, now far beyond Ataturk's 'Science is the Truest Guide in Life', raise the stakes with their occasionalism, and, for the neurologists, the increasing denial of the autonomy of the human will - a new pre-destinarianism that makes us always the consequence of genes and the present, not the remembered past.

Our public conversations, then, seem to be the children of a marriage of convenience between two principles, neither of them religious or even particularly humanistic. The elitist mystical trope of the moment being all that is, significantly misappropriated by some New Age discourses, has become the condition of us all, albeit with the absence of God. Journalism thus becomes the privileged discourse to whose canons the public intellectual must conform, if he or she is to become a credible guide. More striking still is the observed fact that amidst our current crisis of wisdom it also seems to provide the language in which the public discussion of faith is carried on. Thus Catholicism becomes the humiliated cardinal of Boston, not St Augustine. Its morality is taken to be that which visibly clashes with the caprice of characters in *Home and Away*, not a severe but ultimately liberating cultivation of the virtues rooted in centuries of experience and example.

Judaism, in its turn, becomes the latest land-grab of a settler rabbi, not a millennial enterprise of faith and promise. Of course, our new occasionalism does invoke the past. But it does so with reference either to scriptures, stripped of their normative exegetical armature, or to those events which remain in the consciousness of a citizenry raised on enlightenment battles with obscurantism. So again, we recall Galileo, not Eckhart; we recall the interesting hatreds of the Inquisition, not the charity of St Vincent de Paul. Otherwise, our culture is religiously amnesiac. Winston Churchill, near the end of his life, began to read the Bible. 'This book is very well-written,' he said. 'Why was it not brought to my attention before?'

It is in this frankly primitive condition that we seek to discuss religious acts which, against all the predictions of our grandparents, claim to interrupt the progress of history towards a world in which there will be no continuity at all. To our perplexity, history, despite Fukuyama, does not seem to have ended. Humans do not always act for the economic or erotic now; Tamino still seeks his Sarastro. A residue of real human diversity persists. For the human soul is not yet, as Coleridge wrote,

This failed ultimacy, this sense that we, the Papageni, have to dust down the armour of an earlier generation of moral absolutes, when history was still running, when the victory of the corporations and of Hollywood was not yet assured, accounts for the maladroit condition of the world's current argument about terrorism. The most active in seizing the moment, as they elbow impatiently past the *fin de siécle* multiculturalists and postmodernists, are the oddly-named American neoconservatives, who invoke Leo Strauss and roll up their sleeves to defend Washington against Oriental warriors who would defy the dialectics of history and seek to postpone the apotheosis of Anglo-Saxon consumer society, which they see as the climax of a billion years of evolution. But despite such ideologised adversions to the *longue durée,* secularism seems to have little to offer that is not short-termist and reactive, and determined to reduce the globe to a set of variations on itself.

Traditionalists, who should be more helpful, seem paralysed. Much of the fury and hurt that currently abounds in the Christian and the Muslim worlds reveals a sense that the timetable which God has approved for history has been perverted. Christendom is not a virgin in this respect; in fact, it was first, with scholastic and Byzantine broadsides against Christian sin as invitation to Saracenic chastisement. Then it was the turn of Islam, when, from the seventeenth century on the illusion of the Muslims as materially and militarily God's chosen people was dealt a series of shocking blows. Now it is, once again, the turn of Christendom (if the term be still allowed), which is currently wondering why history has not yet experienced closure, why a former rival should still be showing signs of life, either as the result of a misdiagnosis, or as a zombie-like revenant bearing only a superficial resemblance to his medieval seriousness.

Certainly, the American president and his frequently evangelical team see themselves in these terms. Architects of a society which, Disney-like, appropriates the past only to emphasise the glory of the present, these zealots appeal to a prophecy-religion in which the Book of Revelation is the key to history. For them, too, the promised closure is imminent, and its frustration by the other an outrage. President Reagan, while less captivated by end-time visions than his successors, could offer these thoughts to Jewish lobbyists:

> You know, I turn back to your ancient prophets in the Old Testament and the signs foretelling Armageddon and I find myself wondering if we're the generation that is going to see that come about. I don't know if you've noted any of these prophecies lately, but, believe me, they certainly describe the times we're going through.

The protagonists of the current conflict, then, are unusual in their confidence that history has not ended, although millennialism seems to hover in the background on both sides, helped along by the frequently Palestinian scenery. The triumph of the West, or the resurgence of an Islam interpreted by bestselling Pentecostal authors as a chastisement and a demonic challenge, signals the end of a growing worry about the religious meaninglessness of late modernity. Tragically, however, neither protagonist seems validly linked to the remnants of established religion, or shows any sign of awareness of how to connect with history. Fundamentalist disjuncture is placing us in a kind of metahistorical parenthesis, an end-time excitement in which, as for St Paul, old rules are irrelevant, and Christ and Antichrist are the only significant gladiators on the stage. Fundamentalists, as well as mystics, can insist that the moment is all that is real.

Sunna Contra Gentiles

In such a world of pseudo-religious reaction against the postmodern erosion of identity, it follows that if you are not 'with us,' you are with the devil. Or, when this has to be reformulated for the benefit of the blue-collar godless, you are a 'cheese-eating surrender monkey'. Where religion exists to supply an identity, the world is Augustinian, if not quite Manichean. The West's ancient trope of itself as a free space, perhaps a white space, holding out against Persian or Semitic intruders, is being coupled powerfully, but hardly for the first time, with Pauline and patristic understandings of the New Israel as unique vessel of truth and salvation, threatened in the discharge of its redemptive project by the Oriental, Semitic, Ishmaelitic other.

In the West, at least, the religious resources for this dualism are abundant and easily abused. Take Daniel Goldhagen, for instance, who in his most recent book suggests that the xenophobia of the Christian Bible is qualitatively greater than that of any other scripture. New Bibles, he urges, must be printed with many corrections to what he describes as this founding text of a lethal Western self-centeredness. Semites of several kinds would be well-advised to beware a culture raised on such a foundation.

It is remarkable that both sides, in constructing themselves against a wicked, fundamentalist rival, mobilise the ancient trope of anti-Semitism. The Self needs its dark Other, preferably nearby or within. That Other has standard features, in the case of Christian anti-Semitism it is that it stands for Letter rather than Spirit, for blind obedience rather than freedom, for a discreet but intense transnational solidarity in place of Fatherland and Church. It is sexually aberrant (hence the Nazi polemic against Freud). It hides its women (who should, instead, join the SS, or practice *nacktkultur*). It imposes archaic and unscientific taboos, diet, purity, circumcision. Such are the categories in which an almost dualistic West historically defines its relationship to its nearest and most irritating Other.

Anti-Semitism is, in Richard Harries' words, a 'light sleeper'. But part of its strength is that it is not asleep at all; and never has been. As Christendom seeks its identity, the Dark Other today is now more usually Ishmael. Torched mosques, terrified asylum-seekers, bullied schoolchildren, and, we may not unreasonably add, a journalistic discourse of the type that is now being labelled 'Islamophobic', are less new than they seem. They represent a vicarious anti-Semitism. 'Islamic law is immutable' is a chorus in the new Horst Wessel song. 'Circumcision is barbaric.' 'Their divorce laws are medieval and anti-woman.' 'They keep to themselves and don't integrate.' Such is the battle-cry of the resurgent Western right, Pim Fortuin, Jean-Marie Le Pen, Jorg Haider, Filip de Winter. It has become startlingly popular, though always volatile at the polls. Thus is the old antisemitic metabolism of Europe and its American progeny being reinvigorated by the encounter with Ishmael. Again, history has started up again, and again our amnesiac culture ignores the vast cogwheels, deep beneath the surface, which move it.

On the other side, now, crossing the Mediterranean, or the Timor Sea, we generally find not a bloc of sincere fundamentalist regimes, but an archipelago of dictatorships, Oriental despots after the letter, which are in almost every case answerable not to their own electorates - for they recognise none - but to a distant desk in the State Department. These are the neo-mamluks, ex-soldiers and condottieri of a system that penalises ethics. Ranged against them we observe the puritans, iconoclasts with El Greco eyes, whose claim it are to detest the modernity of the regimes. Such puritans, led by the memory of Sayyid Qutb, have no illusions about the nature of secular rule. They see clearly that the regimes are *more* modern than those of the West, because more frank in their conviction that science plus commerce does not equal ethics. Where the Western journalistic eye sees retardation, the Islamist sees modernity. Hitler and Stalin were more modern than Churchill and Roosevelt, more scientific, more programmatic, and more distant from the past. The future is theirs, and it is neither Christ's millennial reign nor the triumph of small-town America. It is Alphaville.

The Islamist, then, is not the caricature of the envious, uncomprehending Third Worlder. Typically he has spent much of his life in the West, and is capable of offering an empirical analysis, or at least a diagnosis. Sayyid Qutb, in his writing on what he calls 'the deformed birth of the American man,' sees Americans as advanced infants; advanced because of their technology, but puerile in their ignorance of earlier stages of human development. There is something of Teilhard de Chardin in his account, which inverts Tocqueville to identify an American idiot-savant mania for possession. Technology made America possible, and ultimately, America need claim nothing else. Linked to Christian fundamentalism, it is an enemy of every other story; and unlike the East, it will not remain in its place. It must send out General Custer to subdue all remnants of earlier phases of human consciousness rooted in nature, spirituality or art.

Its client regimes are therefore its natural, not opportunistic, adjuncts in its programme to subdue the world. They are not a transitional phase; they are the end-game. Anti-Semitism forms part of this vision too, certainly. But since, as Goldhagen confirms, this is an essentially Christian phenomenon, to be healed by correcting the views of the Evangelists, in an Islamic context which lacks a letter-spirit dichotomy it seems a hazier resource for identity construction. Qutb was influenced by the Vichy theorist Alexis Carrel (1873-1944), through his odd, vitalist tract *L'Homme, cet inconnu*, which remains an ultimate, though unacknowledged, source text for much modern Islamism. No medieval Muslim thinker of any note wrote a book against Judaism, although homilies against Christianity were quite common. If medieval Islam had a dark Other, it was more likely to be Zoroastrianism than Judaism, which, in Samuel Goitein's phrase by which he summed up his magisterial work *A Mediterranean Society*, enjoyed a close and 'symbiotic' relationship with Islam. But today's Qutbian Islamist purges midrashic material from Koranic commentary, and studies the Tsarist forgery *The Protocols of the Learned Elders of Zion*, and, even, *Mein Kampf*. Nothing can be discovered, it seems, in the Islamic libraries, so that this importation into an ostensive nativity and xenophobic milieu becomes inescapable - the fundamentalist's familiar appeal to necessity.

As he surveys the wreckage of Istanbul synagogues and Masonic lodges, the journalist, as *ibn al-waqt*, is oblivious to the happier past of Semitic conviviality in the Ottoman Sephardic lands. And perhaps he is right, perhaps, under our conditions, the past *is* another religion. But the paradox has become so burning, and so murderous, that we cannot let it pass unremarked. The Islamic world, instructed to host Israel, was historically the least inhospitable site for the Diaspora. The currently almost ubiquitous myth of a desperate sibling rivalry between Isaac and Ishmael is nonsensical to historians.

Here, at the dark heart of Islam's extremist fringe, we find what may be the beginnings of a solution. No nativist reaction can long survive proof of its own exogenous nature. And no less than its Christian analogues, Islamic *ghuluww*, at least in its currently terroristic forms, betrays a European etiology. It borrows its spiritual, as well as its material, armament from Western modernity. This, we may guess, marks it out for anachronism in a context where intransigence is xenophobic.

This is an unpopular diagnosis; but one which is gaining ground. It cannot be without significance that outside observers, when not blinded by xenophobic needs to view terrorism as islamically authentic, have sometimes intuited this well. Here, for instance, is the verdict of John Gray, in his book *Al-Qaeda and What it Means to be Modern:*

No cliche is more stupefying than that which describes Al-Qaida as a throwback to medieval times. It is a by-product of globalisation. Its most distinctive feature - projecting a privatised form of organised violence worldwide - was impossible in the past. Equally, the belief that a new world can be hastened by spectacular acts of destruction is nowhere found in medieval times. Al-Qaida's closest precursors are the revolutionary anarchists of late nineteenth-century Europe.

And Slavoj Zizek, a still more significant observer, is convinced that what we are witnessing is not 'Jihad versus MacWorld' – the standard leftist formulation - but rather MacWorld versus MacJihad. This implies that if *ghuluww* has a future, it will be because modernity has a future, not because it has roots in Islamic tradition. That tradition, indeed, it rules out of order, as it dismisses the juridical, theological and mystical intricacies of medieval Islam as so much dead wood. The solution, then, which the world is seeking, and which it is the primary responsibility of the Islamic world, not the West to provide must be a counter-reformation, driven by our best and most cosmopolitan heritage of spirit and law.

A point of departure, here, and a useful retort to essentialist reductions of Islam to Islamism, is the fact that orthodoxy still flies the flag in almost all seminaries. The reformers are, at least institutionally, in the Rhonnda chapels, not the cathedrals. Perhaps the most striking fact about regulation Sunni Islam over the past fifty years has been its insistence that religion's general response to modernity must not take the form of an armed struggle. There have been local exceptions to this rule, as in the reactive wars against Serbian irredentism in Bosnia, and Soviet intrusion into Afghanistan. But a doctrine of generic *jihad* against the West has been conspicuous by its absence.

It is not immediately clear how we gloss this. In the nineteenth century Sunni Islam frequently elected to resist European colonial rule by force, giving rise to the figure of the Mad Mullah who formed part of the imperial imagination, in the fiction of John Buchan, or Tolstoy's *Hajji Murad*. In the twentieth century, however, the traditional pragmatism of Sunnism seemed to generate an ulema ethos that was certainly not quietist, but had nothing in common with Qutbian Islamism either. Hence the Deobandi movement in India, and its Tablighi offshoot, supported the Congress party, and generally opposed Partition. Arab religious leaders sometimes resorted to force, as with the Naqshbandi shaykh Izz al-Din al-Qassam in mandate Palestine; but the independence movements were overwhelmingly directed by secular modernists. The ancient universities, al-Qarawiyyin, al-Zaytuna, al-Azhar and the rest, regarded the modern period as a mandate for doctrinal retrenchment and the piecemeal *ijtihad*-based reassessment of aspects of Islamic law. In other words, mainstream Islam's response to the startling novelty of a modernity that was forced on its societies at the point of an imperial or postcolonial bayonet was self-scrutinising and cautious, not militant.

Traditional wisdom and the texts, of course, were the reason for this. Sunnism, as inscribed by the great Seljuk theorists, had put its trust in prudence, pragmatism, and a strategy of negotiation with the sultan. So in British India, the Hanafi consensus decided that the Raj formed part of *dar al-islam*. In Russia, Shihab al-Din Marjani took the same view with regard the empire of the Tsars. But for Qutb, all this was paradigmatic of the error of classical Sunni thought. Islam was to be prophetic, and hence a liberation theology, challenging structures as well as souls, not by preaching and praying alone, but by agitation and revolution. Given his education and *sitz im leben* in the golden age of anti-colonialism, probably nothing could have extricated Qutb from his critique of what he saw as Sunni indifferentism, rooted, he suspected, in Ash'ari deontology and a presumed Sufi fatalism. The prophetic is not *meant* to be accommodating; it fails, or it succeeds triumphantly. The normative political thinkers, Mawardi, Nizam al-Mulk, Ghazali, Katib Çelebi, and their modern advocates, had to be jettisoned. Technological empires had made the world anew, and, if it was to cope with an increasingly bizarre and offensive Other, Islamic thought had to be reformed in the direction of an increasingly unconditional insurrectionism.

Qutb's resurrection of Ibn Taymiya, via Rashid Rida, became paradigmatic. In the fourteenth century this angry Damascene had attacked ulema who acquiesced in the rule of the nominally Muslim Mongols. Loyalty could be to a righteous imam alone. Rida and others had taken pains to dissociate this from the Kharijite slogan 'No rule other than God's', for an unpleasant odour hung about the name of Kharijism. But *de facto*, the hard wing of Hanbalite Islam seemed vulnerable to a Kharijite reading. Prototypical al-Qaida supporters wrote to condemn the Syrian neo-Hanbali scholar Nasir al-Din al-Albani, when he released a series of taped sermons entitled *Min Manhaj al-Khawarij*, 'From the Method of the Kharijites', in the early 1990s. Often the word used by less radical puritans in Saudi Arabia for those engaged in terrorism is, precisely, 'Kharijite'.

What everyone agrees, however, is that al-Qaida is far, far removed from medieval Sunnism. For some, it is Kharijite; for others, an illicit Westernisation of Islam. As Carl Brown puts it, 'it cannot be stressed too often just how much Qutb's hardline interpretation departs from the main current of Islamic political thought throughout the centuries.' For Brown, Qutbism is kharijism *redux;* but we would add, with Gray, that it is a Westernised kharijism. Like all identity movements, it ends with only a very arguable kind of authenticity.

The convergence between a malfunctioning Hanbalism and modern revolutionary vanguardism may owe its strength not to a shared potential for instantiated xenophobia, although this will attract many party cadres; instead, I suspect, it relates to deeper structures of relationality with the world and its worldliness. The new Islamic zealotry is angry with the Islamic past, as Ibn Taymiya was. For Ibn Taymiya, the ulema had not adequately polarised light and dark. In the case of the mystics, they had disastrously confused them. There is something of the Augustine in Ibn Taymiya, a concrete understanding of a God who is radically apart from creation, or, in patristic terms, alienated from it, and a consequently high view of scripture that challenges Ash'arite and Maturidi confidences in the direct intelligibility of God in the world, and revives essentially dualistic readings of the Fall narrative. It may be that Ibn Taymiya's roots in Harran, scene of neo-Gnostic and astral speculations, parallel Augustine's Manichean background. But there is certainly a furious, single-minded zeal in both men that expresses itself in a deep pessimism about the human mind and conscience, intellectuals, poets, logicians, and mystics. In such a cosmology, which deploys the absolute polarity abhorred by Deleuze's *Pli* (his love of nomadic arts, with their 'blocs of sensations' is islamically suggestive) gentilizing becomes first, not second nature.

Seljuk accommodationism, by contrast, had been driven by an ultimately Ghazalian moralism that feared the spiritual entailments of this crypto-dualism. Nizam al-Mulk, paradigm of high Sunni realpolitik, does not enforce a norm, but enforces the toleration of many norms. He finds that like all scripture, the Koran is super-replete, overflowing with meaning, and no exegete may taste all its flavours; this destabilising miracle may express itself in schism, historically the less favoured Islamic option, or in *adab al-ikhtilaf*, the forced courtesy of the scholar-jurist well aware of the ultimately unfixable quality of much of holy writ. The Sunni achievement, which was a moral as well as a pragmatic achievement, was to incorporate a wide spectrum of theological and juristic dispute into the universe of allowable internal difference. For zealotry, as Ghazali puts it, is a *hijab*, a veil? It is a form of, in the Rabbis' language, loving the Torah more than God. A besetting *odium theologicum* can only be healed through self-scrutiny and a due humility before the often baffling intricacy of God's word and world.

It was on the basis of this hospitable caution that non-Qutbian Sunnism engaged with modernity. Reading the fatwas of great twentieth-century jurists such as Yusuf al-Dajawi, Abd al-Halim Mahmud, and Subhi Mahmassani, one is reminded of the Arabic proverb cited on motorway signs in Saudi Arabia: *fi'l-ta'anni as-salama* - there is safety in reducing speed. Far from committing a pacifist betrayal, the normative Sunni institutions were behaving in an entirely classical way. Sunni piety appears as conciliatory, cautious, and disciplined, seeking to identify the positive as well as the negative features of the new global culture. Thus it is not the orthodox, but the merchants of identity religion, the *Sunna Contra Gentiles*, who insist on totalitarian and exclusionary readings of the Law and the state.

If this is our curious situation, if al-Qaida is indeed a product and mirror not of the Sunni story, but of the worst of the Enlightenment's possibilities, if it is, as it were, the Frankenstein of Frankistan (as Zionism is a *golem*), how effective can be America's currently chosen antidote? This takes the form of killing, imprisoning and torturing the leadership, and many of the rank and files, using the methods which have been reported by British and other detainees released from Guantanamo Bay, and by Red Cross officials disturbed by news from Bagram air base in Kabul. Again, our occasionalism has allowed us to forget the history of revolutionary movements, which suggests that such measures are self-defeating, sowing the dragon's teeth of martyrdom, and announcing to the world the depth of the torturer's fear. A civilisation confident of victory would not resort to such desperate means. For after violence and internment, there is no last resort. Both moral advantage and deterrent threat have already been used up.

Traditional Sunnis intuit that al-Qaida is a Western invention, but one which cannot be defeated in a battleground where the logic is Western. This was one of the messages that emerged from the 2003 summit meeting of eight hundred Muslim scholars at Putrajaya. Al-Qaida is inauthentic, it rejects the classical canons neither of Islamic law and theology, and issues fatwas that are neither formally nor in their habit of mind deducible from medieval exegesis. But it is not enough for the entire leadership of the religion to denounce al-Qaida, as it did at Putrajaya, and then to hope and pray that the same strange logic of modernity that bred this insurgency can spirit it away again. The West inseminates, but does not so easily abort. Faced with this, the Sunni leadership needs to be more alert to its responsibilities. Even the radical Westernisation of Islamic piety remains the responsibility of Muslim ulema, not, ultimately, of the Western matrix that inspired it. And it has to be said that the Sunni leadership has not done enough. Denunciations alone will not dent the puritan's armour, and may strengthen it; this the Counter-Reformation learned by experience.

The war against neo-Kharijite ideology can only be won by Sunni normalcy. Washington's rhetoric of 'religion-building' disguises either a Texan missionary instinct or the triumphant relativism of the secular academy. Franklin

Graham and the Ashcroft Inquisition will fail, as Christianity always does against Semitic monotheism, while liberalism, at once its rival and its hypocritical bedfellow, cannot be relied on to supply ethics under conditions of stress. For the Occidental energy all too often responds to such conditions either by apathy (remember the wartime Parisian intelligentsia), or by suspending the ethical teleologically, the classic revolutionary gambit since the days of the Paris commune, if not the English civil war.

The zealots of both sides insist that the validating of 'soft targets' is a representative Islamic act. How might they respond to evidence that it is, in fact, a representative secular-Western one? The evidence, as it turns out, is compelling, being a matter of historical record. Despite its claims in times of obese complacency to abhor the killing of the innocent, the secular West reverts with indecent haste to Cicero's maxim, *Silent enim leges inter arma* - laws are silent during war. And it is in this Occidental culture, and not in mainline Islam, that we should seek the matrix of radical Islamism. Let us survey the record.

W.G. Sebald has been a recent and helpful contributor here. He writes lyrically of the vengeance visited by the RAF on Germany's cities in the early 1940s, focussing on the thirty thousand who died in Operation Gomorrah (!) against the city of Hamburg. The object of such campaigns was military only in a very indirect way, for Churchill's purpose in what he called 'terror bombing' (where it was not straightforward vengefulness) was to sap the morale of Germany's civilian population. As Sebald shows, Parliament restructured the whole British economy to support the area bombing campaign, for one reason alone, it was the only way in which Britain could successfully strike back.

In 1930, the British population had generally shared the view of one politician that to bomb civilians was 'revolting and un-English.' But with its back against the wall, the population changed its mind with impressive speed. In 1942,

Bomber Command's Directive No. 22 identified the 'morale of the enemy civil population' as the chief target. By the end of the war, a million tons of high explosive had rained down on German cities, and half a million civilians were dead. By that time a majority of Britons explicitly supported the bombing of civilian targets. As the MP for Norwich put it, 'I am all for the bombing of working-class areas of German cities. I am Cromwellian - I believe in "slaying in the name of the Lord",' while after Operation Gomorrah, a popular headline crowed that 'Hamburg has been Hamburgered.'

A third of the war economy was directed to serve this onslaught, with the development of new weapons of mass destruction, such as incendiary bombs, designed specifically to maximise devastation to private homes. Yet after Dresden, which the postwar official history hailed as the 'crowning achievement' of the bombing campaign, Churchill was forced to reconsider:

> It seems to me that the moment has come when the question of bombing of German cities simply for the sake of increasing the terror, though under other pretexts, should be reviewed. Otherwise, we shall come into control of an utterly ruined land.

This was no sort of repentance. To his last breath Churchill defended the terror campaign which he had instigated and which underpinned so much of his popularity. Mass destruction from the air of a target whose details were often obscured by clouds or the absence of moonlight was not, for this icon of English defiance, a moral problem. A largely secular person of the stamp of our wartime Prime Minister was clearly following a fairly standard Enlightenment philosophy which had replaced the wars of kings with the wars of peoples. Clausewitz, the chief architect of post-medieval military thought, was certain that 'war is an act of force which theoretically can have no limits,' a view that the most influential military theorists of the twentieth century extended to the use of airpower to terrorize civilians.

One might have hoped that this illustration of the moral calibre of secularity was found appalling by the Christian conscience of the day. But the stance taken by the leaders of British Christianity was already deeply influenced by modernism. The Archbishop of Canterbury William Temple, followed by his brother bishop of York, consistently refused to join the anti-terror minority within the Anglican Church. As a historian records, 'only a handful of the clergy objected outright to area bombing;' George Bell, the outspoken Bishop of Chichester, was a lonely exception in upholding earlier ideals of a just war which had regarded women and children as sacrosanct.

After the war, the victors reset the moral template to its rhetorical default position, and their earlier *fatwas* in favour of terror bombing were relegated to an outer, uncomfortable edge of the national memory. Once again, England and America (which had carried on its own targeting of civilians in Japan) reverted to the traditional notion of civilian immunity, with its pre-Enlightenment roots. So five years later, the British press felt able to excoriate Menachem Begin as a terrorist, simply because, as he puts it in his memoirs, 'our enemies called us terrorists [...] but we used physical force only because we were faced by physical force.' And today, who can claim that Al-Qaida's logic is different? The 777 has become the poor man's nuclear weapon, his own Manhattan Project. Again, he has turned traitor to the East by embracing the utilitarian military ethic of his supposed adversary. He, even more than the regimes, shows the cost of Westernisation.

In this light, how may we take the pulse of the West's denunciation of 'Muslim terror'? Let us recall Adorno's First Law of sexual ethics: always mistrust the accuser.

Samson Terrorists

The targeting of civilians is more Western than otherwise; contemplating the Ground Zero of a hundred

German cities, this can hardly be denied. Yet it will be claimed that suicidal terrorism is something new, and definitively un-Western. Here, we are told by xenophobes on both sides, the Islamic suicide squads, the Black Widows, the death-dealing pilots, are an indigenously Islamic product. And yet here again, when we detach ourselves from the emotive chauvinism of the Islamists and their Judeo-Christian misinterpreters, we soon find that the roots of such practices in the Islamic imagination are as recent as they are shallow. The genealogy of suicide bombing clearly stretches back from Palestine, through Shi'a guerillas in southern Lebanon, to the Hindu-nativist zealots of the Tamil Tigers, and to the holy warriors of Shinto Japan, who initiated the tradition of donning a bandanna and making a final testament on camera before climbing into the instrument of destruction. The kamikaze was literally the 'Wind of Heaven', a term evocative of the divine intervention which destroyed the Mongol fleet as it crossed the Yellow Sea.

Hindu and Buddhist tributaries of Middle-Eastern suicide bombing are conspicuous, and it is significant that the Islamists, driven as ever by nativist passion, recoil from them in fits of denial. (How happily, in the sermons, *hunud* rhymes with *yahud*!) Yet some scenic images may be instructive for those who take the philosophy of *isnad* seriously. After describing the Christian martyr Peregrinus, who set fire to himself in public, Sir James Frazier records:

> Buddhist monks in China sometimes seek to attain Nirvana by the same method, the flame of their religious zeal being fanned by a belief that the merit of their death redounds to the good of the whole community, while the praises which are showered upon them in their lives, and the prospect of the honours and worship which await them after death, serve as additional incentives to suicide.

But it was in South India that holy suicide seems to have been most endemic:

In Malabar and the neighbouring regions, many sacrifice themselves to the idols. When they are sick or involved in misfortune, they vow themselves to the idol in case they are delivered. Then, when they have recovered, they fatten themselves for one or two years; and when another festival comes around, they cover themselves with flowers, crown themselves with white garlands, and go singing and playing before the idol, when it is carried through the land. There, after they have shown off a good deal, they take a sword with two handles, like those used in currying leather, put it to the back of their necks, and cutting strongly with both hands sever their heads from their bodies before the idol.

The *atmaghataka*, the suicidal Hindu, was a familiar sight of the pre-modern Indian landscape, where 'religious suicides were highly recommended and in most cases glorified.' Suicide often functioned as the culmination of a pilgrimage: 'the enormous *Tirtha* literature (literature on pilgrimage) curiously enough describes in detail suicide by intending persons at different places of pilgrimage and the varying importance and virtues attached to them.' Ibn Battuta and al-Biruni, among other Muslim visitors, had been particularly shocked by Hindu customs of sacred suicide, particularly bride-burning and self-drowning. Altogether, in such a culture the development of suicidal methods as part of war is hardly surprising; they are deeply rooted in local non-monotheistic values.

Today's Tamil extremists extend this tradition in significant ways. Each Tamil Tiger wears a cyanide capsule around his neck, to be swallowed in case of capture. The explosive belt, used to assassinate hated politicians as well as Sinhalese marines and ordinary civilians, predates its Arab borrowing: the first Tamil suicide-martyrs in modern times appear in the 1970s. The Tiger's Hindu roots thus nourish the current Palestinian practice; as one observer notes, 'the Black Tigers, as the suicide cadres are known, have been emulated by the likes of Hamas.'

But there is also a strong Western precedent, in pagan antiquity, in early Judaism, and in Christianity. Suicide had been a respectable option for many ancients. Achilles chooses battle against the Trojans, knowing that the gods have promised that this will lead to his death. Ajax takes his own life, in the confidence that this will not affect his honour. Chrysippus, Zeno, and Socrates all opt for suicide rather than execution or dishonour. Marcus Aurelius praises it to the skies. It was only the neo-Platonists and late Platonists (who not coincidentally became the most congenial Hellenes for Islam) who systematically opposed it.

The Biblical text nowhere condemns suicide. (Judas is condemned for betrayal, not for taking his own life; although Augustine will claim otherwise.) On the contrary, it offers several examples of individuals who chose death. Saul (the koranic Talut) falls on his own sword rather than be humiliated in Philistine captivity (I Samuel 31). Jonah (Yunus) asks the frightened mariners to cast him into the sea (Jonah 1.12), and begs 'Take my life from me,' (4.3) for 'it is better for me to die than to live' (4.8-9). Job (Ayyub) prays: 'O that I might have my request, and that God would grant my desire; that it would please God to crush me' (Job 6:8-13), and even 'I loath my life' (7:15). Later, during the Maccabean revolts, the hero Razis falls on his sword to avoid falling into the hands of the wicked (2 Maccabees 14:42, 45-6). A notion of vicarious atonement has developed, so that the militant's suicide which enrages the enemy brings a blessing to the people (4 Maccabees 17:21-2).

The early rabbis typically accept self-immolation in situations of military desperation, to avoid humiliation and to impress the enemy. The deaths of Saul and Samson were regarded as exemplary. And in 'the Jewish Middle Ages, enthusiasm for martyrdom (at least in Ashkenaz - northern Europe) became so great that it proved a positive danger to

Jewish existence.' Religious voices raised in support of 20th century Zionism could link this tradition to their own militancy. Hence Avram Kook, the first Ashkenazy Chief Rabbi of mandate Palestine (in Walter Wurzburger's words) permitted individuals to volunteer for suicide missions when carried out in the interest of the collective Jewish community. In other words, an act that would be illicit if performed to help individuals would be legitimate if intended for the benefit of the community.

In the nascent Christian movement, Jesus came to be presented as a suicide, albeit one who knew that he would be resurrected. Some historians are convinced that Jesus, having armed his band with swords, formed part of the larger Zealot movement against Roman oppression, while others adhere to the orthodox view that his deliberate death was to be a cosmic sacrifice for human sin; but in either case, the dominant voice in the New Testament presents him as going to Jerusalem in the awareness that this would bring about his certain death. Hence the insistent courting of martyrdom by many early Christians praised by Tertullian (here in the words of a modern scholar):

> In 185 the proconsul of Asia, Arrius Antoninus, was approached by a group of Christians demanding to be executed. The proconsul obliged some of them and then sent the rest away, saying that if they wanted to kill themselves there was plenty of rope available or cliffs they could jump off.

And for Chrysostom, blasting the infidels, the Christians were better than the ancients, since Socrates had had little choice, while Christians volunteered for martyrdom. In fact, most orthodox Christian martyrs appear to have been volunteers, many of them appearing from nowhere to clamour for the death penalty, or emerging from the crowds to join the flames consuming one of their brethren. It was only with Augustine that this self-immolating behaviour came to an end, as involuntary martyrdom was established as the only acceptable Christian norm in the West.

Orthodoxy, however, remained closer to the primitive tradition. As Frazier records 'whole communities hailed with enthusiasm of the gospel of death and hastened to put its precepts into practice.' Although at first the volunteers were dropped into doorless rooms in which they starved to death 'for Christ', fire became the most popular method.

Priests, monks, and laymen scoured the villages and hamlets preaching salvation by the flames, some of them decked in the spoils of their victims; for the motives of the preachers were often of the basest sort. They did not spare even the children, but seduced them by promises of the gay clothes, the apples, the nuts, the honey they would enjoy in heaven. [...] Men, women and children rushed into the flames. Sometimes hundreds, and even thousands, thus perished together.

Combining the practice of suicidal martyrdom-seeking with the pursuit of warfare, resulted, for Europeans as well as for Tamils, in what would today be called suicidal warfare. This had the advantage of generating tremendous publicity for the cause in worlds such as the Indic and the Greco-Roman which, like today's, had a penchant for the bizarre. And for this, the most spectacular precedent was in the Bible. Brian Wicker, a modern Catholic interpreter, remarks that 'to us, Samson just appears like a cross between Beowulf and Batman,' while Bernhard Anderson in his book *The Living World of the Old Testament,* neutralises the Samson story by viewing him as the object of divine punishment.

Yet he is presented by the narrator of Judges 13 to 16 as an unambiguous hero, and traditionally the churches regarded his self-destruction and his massacre of three thousand Philistine men, women, and children, as a valid act of martyrdom. Augustine and Aquinas both pose the question: why is self-murder not here a sin, and answer, because God had commanded him, and the normal ethical rule was thus suspended.

This suicide-warrior rises to the top of Western literature in *Samson Agonistes*. Milton is here smarting from the horror and shame of the Restoration. Once again, England is under the idolatrous law of king and bishops, a kind of *jahiliyya*, and Cromwell's city of glass has been shattered. His poem, then, is autobiographical, Samson is a true hero, humiliated, blinded by an unjust king, kept captive in the world of the dark Other.

His duty, confronted by a hypocritical War on Terror, is to take effective revenge by any means necessary. His father, recognising this grim necessity, makes the usual statement of fathers of suicide bombers everywhere:

> Nothing is here for tears, nothing to wail,
>
> Or knock the breast, no weakness, no contempt,
>
> Dispraise, or blame, nothing but well and fair.
>
> And what may quiet us in a death so noble.

The theme continues, through Handel, to reach Saint-Saens. In the latter's opera *Samson and Delilah* the Samson legend, far from falling by the wayside of progress and *fraternité*, seems the perfect icon for France's contemporary humiliation before Prussian technology. The guns of Krupp have frustrated France's destiny in her *mission civilatrice*, and the chosen people must be avenged. The story seems perfectly modern, there is the theme of the tragic power of sex - Delilah becomes a second Carmen - and we witness the inevitability of total destruction in a grand, cast-iron *Götterdammerung*. Ernst Jünger, Stalingrad, and the suicidal B-52 captain in *Doctor Strangelove* are not far behind.

But perhaps the most recent, and also the most fascinating, mobilisation of the Samson 'ideal' in Western literature is the novel *Samson* by the Zionist ideologue Vladimir Jabotinsky. 'Homeland, whatever the price!' is the captured Israelite's slogan. Like the Islamist, the Zionist hero stresses the impossibility of conviviality:

> The second thing I have learned in the last few days is the wisdom of having boundary–stones [...] Neighbours can agree so long as each remains home, but trouble comes as soon as they begin to pay each other visits. The gods have made men different and commanded them to respect the ditch in the fields. It is a sin for men to mix what the Gods have separated.

Like a good Islamist, the Zionist Samson combines this xenophobia with a passion to acquire the Other's technology. When asked if he had a message for his own people, he cries:

> They must get iron. They must give everything they have for iron – their silver and wheat, oil and wine and flocks, even their wives and daughters. All for iron! There is nothing in the world more valuable than iron. Will you tell them that?

Like the Islamist, too, Jabotinsky's suicide-hero is envious of the unbeliever's skills at organisation:

> One day, he was present at a festival at the temple of Gaza. Outside in the square a multitude of young men and girls were gathered for the festive dances [...] A beardless priest led the dances. He stood on the topmost step of the temple, holding an ivory baton in his hand. When the music began the vast concourse stood immobile [...] The beardless priest turned pale and seemed to submerge his eyes in those of the dancers, which were fixed responsively on his. He grew paler and paler; all the repressed fervor of the crowd seemed to concentrate within his breast till it threatened to choke him. Samson felt the blood stream to his heart; he himself would have choked if the suspense had lasted a few moments longer. Suddenly, with a rapid, almost inconspicuous movement, the priest raised his baton, and all the white figures in the square sank down on the left

knee and threw the right arm towards heaven – a single movement, a single, abrupt, murmurous harmony. The tens of thousands of onlookers gave utterance to a moaning sigh. Samson staggered; there was blood on his lips, so tightly had he pressed them together [...] Samson left the place profoundly thoughtful. He could not have given words to his thought, but he had a feeling that here, in this spectacle of thousands obeying a single will, he had caught a glimpse of the great secret of politically minded peoples.

Lest this be thought an aberrant, marginal use of the suicide-hero, let us recall the words of another Zionist thinker, Stephen Rosenfeld, 'All our generation was brought up on that book.' Samson provides an important Biblical archetype for the national hero who is a semi-outcast among his own people, but who saves them nonetheless. In the dying months of Nazi Germany, *selbstopfereinsatz* missions were flown by Luftwaffe pilots against Soviet bridgeheads on the Oder.

In 1950, Cecil B. DeMille used Jabotinsky's novel as the basis for his film *Samson and Delilah*. And a still more recent example is the film *Armageddon*, in which a group of socially marginalised Americans sacrifice their lives by detonating their spacecraft inside a comet that is on a collision course with Earth. In doing so they are defying tradition and even lawful orders, but they earn thereby the eternal gratitude of their people. As Robert Jewett and John Lawrence have shown, this image of the American hero as the ordinary man impatient of traditional authority who. risks or destroys himself to save the world, is the great monomyth of today's West.

In some Eastern parts, the popularity of magically vanishing Bin Laden figures, who emerge from undistinguished lives to break conventional laws in order to save the world, offers another suggestion of how deeply Westernised Arab culture has become. Let no-one claim, then, that suicide bombing is alien to the West. It is a recurrent possibility of Europe's heritage. What needs emphasizing, against the snapshot thinking of the journalists, is the absence of a parallel strand in Islamic thinking. For Islam, suicide is always forbidden; some regard it as worse than murder. Many Biblical stories are retold by Islam, but the idea of suicidal militancy is entirely absent from the scriptures. Saul's suicide is not present in the Koran, nor do we find it in Tabari's great *Annals* (which wish simply to record that he died in battle).

The Koranic Jonah does not ask to be pitched overboard, and Job does not pray for death. Similarly, the suicidal *istishhad* of Samson is absent from the Koran and Hadith, no doubt in line with their insistence on the absolute wickedness of suicide. The same Islamic idealism that cannot accept David's seduction of Bathsheba, or Lot's incest, has here airbrushed out Samson's killing of the innocent and his self-destruction. Again, the point is clear, the scriptural and antique sensibilities which provided some cultural space for suicidal warfare in Western civilisation appear to have very thin foundations in Islam. Flying into a skyscraper to save the world is closer to the line which links Samson to Captain America, with a detour through the Book of Revelation, than to any Muslim conception of *futuwwa*.

Here are Buruma and Margalit, in their important study of Westernised anti-Westernism:

Bin Laden's use of the word 'insane' is more akin to the Nazis' constant use of *fanatisch*. Human sacrifice is not an established Muslim tradition. Holy war always was justified in defence of the Islamic state, and believers who died in battle were promised heavenly delights, but glorification of death for its own sake was not part of this, especially in the Sunni tradition. [...] And the idea that freelance terrorists would enter paradise as martyrs by murdering unarmed civilians is a modern invention, one that would have horrified Muslims in the past. Islam is not a death cult.

Let us now move on to consider other hints of the Western roots of radical Islamism. One symptom may be detected in a shared fondness for conspiracy theories. The messianic importance of the hidden deliverer is emphasised by the machinations of the forces of darkness which are ranged against him. The *mu'amara,* or Plot, is everywhere, as Robert Fisk, that dauntless lamenters of Mid-East fantasies, regularly observes.

A sadly typical example is given by Abdelwahab Meddeb:

When I was at Abu Dhabi in May 2001, a number of my interlocutors, of various Arab communities (Lebanese, Syrian, Sudanese, etc.), confirmed the warning, spread by the local newspapers, to the public of the countries of the Near East not to buy the very inexpensive belts with the label *Made in Thailand*. These belts, the people told me, were actually Israeli products in disguise and carried a kind of flea that propagated an incurable disease, one more Zionist trick to weaken Arab bodies, if not eliminate them. These interlocutors, otherwise reasonable and likable, gave credit to information as fantastic as that. Those are the fantasies in which the symptoms of the sickness of Islam can be seen, the receptive compost in which the crime of September 11 could be welcomed joyfully.

Again, this is historically unusual for Muslims. Healthy communities far from Western influence find it incredible. The current prevalence of a kind of Islamic McCarthyism, often hysterical in its attempts to reduce a complex and enraging modernity to a monomaniac opposition, is simply another indication of how far the Islamists have travelled from the tradition. Religion makes us more attentive to reality, while secularity bereft of real disciplines of self-knowledge and self-disdain, permits a dream-self. 'They think that every shout is against themselves,' says the Koran of the hypocrites (63:4), while praising the believers for their clear sighted faith that only God is simple, and it is only He that should be feared. The correct mindset is specified in scripture:

Those to whom the people said, 'The people have gathered against you, therefore fear them!' But it increased them in faith, and they said, 'Allah is enough for us, an excellent Guardian is he!'

So they returned with grace and favour from Allah, and no harm touched them. They followed the good-pleasure of Allah, and Allah is of great bounty.

It is only the devil who would make [men] fear his allies. Fear them not; fear Me, if you are believers. (3:173-5)

The context is the aftermath of Uhud, when waverers warned of the strength of the combined enemies around Medina. Paranoia thus becomes the marker of imperfect faith and undue respect for the *asbab*. But despair is *kufr*, Islam's Samson could never say:

Hopeless are all my evils, all remediless;

This one prayer yet remains, might I be heard,

No long petition, speedy death,

The close of all my miseries, and the balm.

Moreover, it requires an apparently unbearable humility for the Islamist conspiracy theorist to recognise that until very recently Muslims have seldom been perceived by the United States as a noteworthy enemy. For most of its history, America has opposed and feared and stereotyped Englishmen, Rebels, Red Indians, Spaniards, Huns, Reds or Gooks. The current preoccupation with Muslims is shallow in the US memory, if we discount the brief and long-forgotten enthusiasms of the Decatur episode.

Again, as with the conspiracy theories which urgently needed to see 9/11 as the work of Mossad, and the utilitarian justification of the vanguard's suspension of the ethical, the radical Islamists are an expression of the very Westernising alienation they profess to defy. In a sense, the West hates them because they are more modern than it, and thus remind it of the unbearable risks it has taken by following the road of Enlightenment. It is as Meddeb reminds us, 'Who are those who died while spreading death in New York, Washington and Pennsylvania? [...] They are the sons of *our* times, the pure products of the Americanisation of the world.'

Self-immolation in Gaza to bring down the unbelieving temple. This is tragedy in Wagnerian mode. It is suicide, *selbstmord,* not really prefatory to redemption, but to publicity and therapy. It was Nietzsche, not any Islamic sage, who wrote, 'The thought of suicide is a great source of comfort: with it a calm passage is to be made across many a bad night.' After being 'eyeless in Gaza, at the mill with slaves,' Samson experiences 'calm of mind, all passion spent' - the English idiom begins with Milton's ending, linking, as do some readings of the Samson legend, *eros* and *thanatos,* desire and death.

But it is Nietzsche who introduces the modern superhero. If 'the splendrous blond beast, avidly rampant for plunder and victory' cannot take the revenge which heals his heart, he will end his unworthy existence in a magnificent, Hitlerian funeral pyre. Samson thus becomes an anticipation of modernity.

Religion, if it has the right to exist at all, must consider this a spurious healing. Neither vainglory nor despair can have a place in the metabolism of a religion based on the idea of God's unique mastery of history, the polar opposite of dualistic paganism, or of the romantic Enlightenment dream which found its tragic moods congenial. The scriptures denounce *hamiyya,* the feverish identity-politics of the pagan Arabs; the post-orthodox Islamist admits it to his heart. 'Roots of Muslim Rage' is the title of Bernard Lewis' most notorious piece on Islamism. His pathology of the roots is far astray; but the rage is undeniable. How are we to understand such rage in the heart of a religion built on submission to the Divine will, *hulwihi wa-murrihi*, the bitter and the sweet of it? Which insisted that 'it is not the wrestler who is strong; it is the man who masters himself when angry'? Why did the Blessed Prophet pray for 'a certainty by which you render slight in our eyes the calamities of this world'?

The roots are, as it turns out, instrumental reason, natural causality, and the enthroning of Aristotle over Plato or Newton over St Denys. Without the certainty of an omnipotent God (and is not Islam here better at restraining passion than all other faiths?) the experience of adversity leaves us prey to wild emotion. It was this same *jahili* craving for revenge that led Churchill astray, as one historian suggests, 'In this superheated and bloody time emotion may have masqueraded as political thinking in a rationalizing Prime Minister's mind.'

Religion is never more tested than when our emotions are ablaze. At such a time, the timeless grandeur of the Law and its ethics stand at our mercy. 'Let the qadi not judge when he is angry,' as it is said. But here is the reality of Gaza:

'Hamas operations are not directed and have never been directed against children,' says Hamas political leader Ismail Abu Shanaab. 'It is directed at military targets.' When pushed, however, he goes further. 'To be frank with you, there are a lot of the moralities which got broken in this war,' he says. 'They are letting the Israelis kill Palestinians and they want the Palestinians to be moderate, to be moral. We cannot control the game because it has no rules, it has no limits.'

Revenge, rage, the teleological suspension of the ethical. It is Churchillian, but also aromatic with a not-yet-dispersed Marxism. Here, for instance, is Mawdudi, a tributary of the Hamas vision:

'Muslim' is the name of the international revolutionary party which Islam organizes to implement its revolutionary program and Jihad is that revolutionary struggle which the Islamic party carries out to achieve its objectives. As Abdullah Schleifer goes on to remark:

> Mawdoodi took as his enduring model a progression of dynamic relationships - the movement, the party, revolutionary struggle, the revolution - defined by one of the major desacralizing forces in contemporary times, in pursuit of a concept of state that draws its substance from non-Islamic sources and all with that same innocence of the modern Muslim importing his 'value-free' technology.

The antinomian quality of this furious insurrectionist method confirms Gray's suggestion that Islamism is simply another modern weapon against religion. For theists, the ethical can never be suspended; on the contrary, it is needed most when most under strain. Yet the militant transgressions of radicals form only part of a much wider picture of covert but deep surrender to Enlightenment thought.

Islamism, that *soi-disant* hammer of the Franks, is ironically modern in very many ways. It is modern in its eagerness for science and its hatred of 'superstition.' It is modern in its rejection of all higher spirituality (Qutb recommends, instead, *'al-fana' fi'l-'aqida'*). It is modern in its rejection of the principle of tradition, and, despite itself, cannot but impose the insecurities of Western-trained minds (and are they not all engineers and doctors?) on scripture. Intertextuality and the community of sages are barred. The theo politics of classical Islam, where both scholarship and the state are invigorated by mutual tension (the Men of the Pen and the Men of the Sword), is replaced by the finally Western model of the ideological totalitarian state, with a self-appointed clerisy (albeit composed of technocrats) requiring absolute control over policy and the Shari'a. The modular diversities of pre-modern Muslim societies, where villages, tribes, and *millat* minorities regulated themselves, give way to the Islamist appropriation of the machinery of centralised post-colonial etatism. Social subsets which flourished for centuries under, say, Ottomanism, already eroded by centralising colonial regimes, are finally liquidated by a vision that is purely Western, albeit camouflaged by loud religious language.

As Maryam Jameelah puts it, in a courageous article in which she publicly announces her disillusionment with the Islamist model:

> The tragic paradox of the life and thought of Maulana Sayyid Abul Ala Mawdoodi was his subconscious acceptance of the very same Western ideas he dedicated his entire life to struggling against.

In such a system, those who should be serving God end up obeying the men of the state who are His all too fallible interpreters. They worship in fear of the police, not in fear of God. Dissidence becomes a simultaneous treason and blasphemy. The failure of this totalitarian model of the 'Islamic State', this 'carceral Islamism' which makes a Muslim land a prison rather than a landscape of options and regional variety, is today everywhere apparent, and is a sign, perhaps, that God will not allow victory to such a perversion. For the Muslims will not long be allowed to bow before any other than God.

Is this attack on tradition modernity with a future? Zealotry itself is not normally refuted, it has to subside. Often that subsidence is enabled by schism, Cromwell could not be replicated because of the powerfully fissiparous quality of Dissent. Calvin's Geneva hardly outlived him. Hutterites, Levellers, Anabaptists, and the other fragments of the Protestant detonation could perpetuate themselves, but their energy source seemed to have a half-life. Islamic extremism, what has historically been called *ghuluww*, excess, and has occasionally, though not often, troubled the religion's equilibrium, usually knows a similar deflation through internal factionalism and the disappointment which seeps into all annunciatory movements when the world does not either improve or come to an end. In the case of Muslim Puritanism, we see, currently, infighting, as in Algeria, and on the streets of Riyadh. Apathy may not be long postponed.

This seems likely, to the extent that Islamism is the product of indigenous decay, a second Reformation. But will its porosity to Enlightenment thought prolong or accelerate this decay? (How ironic that Islam's Reformation should come after its Enlightenment!) Here predictions about Islamism may not be so different from predictions about a certain kind of exhibitionist postmodernism. Take Foucault, for instance. On his death, he had been praised by *Le Monde* as 'the most important event of thought in our century.' He was an iconic Western iconoclast, but more honest about the consequences of modernity than most liberal seekers after virtue. He had been strongly pro-Khomeini, and had also praised the Baader-Meinhof terrorists. Like many Islamists, he was a lapsed Marxist, concerned with making a statement, with angering the middle-class West, with disruption. A second Bakunin, he was concerned not with advancing a detailed and realistic agenda, but with a passionate desire to shock. And like his hero Nietzsche, he died of a venereal disease, his immensely careless sexual habits indicating the powerful allure of suicide for the sake of making a statement. We need to ask, is this too close for comfort to radical Islamism, with its penchant for *épater les blancs* by whatever means? For how long can the West portray the Islamists as its own polar opposite? Will it be harder to forget the zealots than to forget Foucault?

This is less hopeful, Foucault has not been forgotten. The ambient vacuum which permitted a philosophy of the absurd in France and in the Middle East shows no signs of abatement. Capitalist shortsightedness wedded to postmodern philosophy may offer the only real life-support system that the Muslim reformation can hope for. Thus the defeat of the Muslim aberration may depend on nothing less than the defeat of the current global system, and its replacement with an order grounded in the ethical brilliance of the monotheisms. This diagnosis places us far beyond both Qutb's chauvinism and the narcissism of the neocons. The same classical Islamic strength through cosmopolitanism that helped our ancient order to endure as a non-totalitarian expression of certainty must be remobilised to affirm the Other's heart, in order to reconnect the global system with religious reality. That is, a successful 'war on terror' cannot be detached from a humanly consensual war on environmental loss, on unfair trade, on identity feminism, and on genetic manipulation. If it is so detached, it will be lost.

Blake portrays the spirit of the industrial age as Urizen, blind ignorance, fettered in laws of causality unveiled by Newton, and sunk in feral emotionalism. Religion is indispensable to the nurturing of a true humanism because it fights this, and insists that humanity has a *telos*, and that the soul is therefore sacrosanct.

To succeed, then we must be able to realise that self-judgement, that greatest and most irreplaceable gift of the Abrahamic religions, is more than an evolutionary confidence trick. Consider Jürgen Habermas' latest book, which reflects on human nature as challenged by genetic science. Postmodernism seems to problematise self-judgement; and its associated ethical practice seems to reduce Aristotle's greatness of soul, which he, against later monotheist reaction, considered a virtue, to *superbia*, greatest of the seven deadly sins. But Habermas reminds us that confronted by genetic science, we are required, after a long hiatus, to judge ourselves. For science seeks our permission to rebuild our bodies to reduce the suffering of future generations; yet in the process it must ask us to define what we presently are. Liberal ethics, which resist both such definitions, and any exercise in using human beings for our own purposes, however idealistic, are thereby interrogated. Habermas is quite clear that the West's conception of virtue is a Christian ghost, rooted in a Kantianism that has been the basis of liberal notions of individual autonomy. Yet he seems convinced that this ghost still lives, and can be maintained perpetually, and may even serve as the stable basis of ever more ambitious projects for universal codes of human rights, in the arena of bioethics, as elsewhere. This will include, presumably, the war on Carrelian Islamism.

John Gray, iconoclastically again, is unsure that this is as coherent as it is helpful. Gray, whose understanding of Al-Qaida as an Enlightenment project we noted earlier, would rather we revisited Schopenhauer's deconstruction of Kant. Frightened ethicists have deceived themselves that there is no Christianity in this Christian ghost. Yet true Kantianism would reject the categorical imperative as a false projection upon the Noumenon. Our desperate desire to find a new moral anchorage after the sinking of Christian scholasticism blinds us to what is for Gray the unanswerable insight that without God, we are beyond good and evil. Schopenhauer saw, as Gray put it, 'that the enlightenment was only a secular version of Christianity's central mistake.'

There is no soul, only the individual will, and we have no reason to suppose that we are any freer in our decision-making than the animals from which religion taught us that we were so categorically distinct. Our consciousness is just one more part of the world. Heidegger turns out to be worse: he insists that he excludes Christian paradigms, but internalises them implicitly in his consideration of the human plight, suffering, guilt, and the paradox of being. And while Schopenhauer maintained a pure and private pessimism, Heidegger sought to intuit Being in his tribe. 'The Führer himself and alone,' he exclaimed, 'is the present and future German reality and its law.' Hitler's xenophobia allowed the philosopher to repair his wounds, and reconnect with Being. Qutbian fundamentalism is not far away.

It is impossible to exaggerate the debt Giddens' 'runaway world' owes to Christianity, for showing so much vitality even after Nietzsche proclaimed the death of its God. But for the Gospels, the Western empire would not have benefited from Kant's conjuring trick or Rawls' benign adversion to 'good people'. Yet the fact of its precariousness remains; and the risk of a tribal resolution is enormous. Science harnessed to *Geist* dragged up Hitler; and something similar has beset Islam. Solidarity, mythologically voiced, technologically imposed, is to be the cure for our desperate alienation. Remember the words of the Furies in Aeschylus:

> For many ills one attitude is the cure
>
> When it agrees on what to hate.

The danger, then, is that liberalism will prove too weak to prevent one form of Enlightenment chauvinism – carceral Islamism – from triggering a sudden revival of another such form – Hitlerian essentialism. The prosperity of the far-right across the liberal West shows how far this march has already come. Post-modernity is methodologically incapable of resisting this; and monotheism must step into the breach. A monotheism, however, which bears all the arms it has acquired and sharpened during its travels, its intellectual appropriation of Athens, its hospitality to the autochthonous non-Semitic, its insistence on diversity, all enabled and preserved by the centrality of spiritual purgation. The civil war within Enlightenment modernity that Gray identifies as the essence of the 'war on terror' is suicidal. Only a *ressourcement* in the anchored past can deliver us.

The Worst Enemies of Islam are from Within

On September 11th our lives changed forever. We witnessed an act of aggression that in many ways does not have a parallel in past or present times. There are several elements that make this act unique, from the use of civilian planes as weapons of mass destruction to the attack on the most widely recognized skyscrapers in the world. Nor have we ever witnessed the terrible indictment of Islam as having a part to play in such a heinous crime.

Muslims were seen rejoicing in some parts of the world in a display of what can only be called shamaatatul 'aadai', which is rejoicing at the calamities of ones' enemies. This is something explicitly prohibited in Islam and was never practiced by the Prophet of Mercy, upon him be prayers and peace. We have seen images since of American flags burning to further arouse the wrath of a nation filled with grief, confusion and anger. Again, Islam prohibits the burning of flags according to the explicit verse, "Do not curse [the idols] of those who call on other than Allah, thus causing them to curse Allah out of animosity [toward you] and without knowledge." This verse prohibits even the cursing of false gods because of the consequences. We have also seen image after image of Muslims with beards and turbans, who by all outward means look religious and pious - but are they really?

Unfortunately, the West does not know what every Muslim scholar knows; that the worst enemies of Islam are from within. The worst of these are the khawaarij who delude others by the deeply dyed religious exterior that they project. The Prophet, peace be upon him, said about them, "When you see them pray you will consider your own prayers insignificant. They recite the Quran but it does not exceed the limits of their throat." In other words, they don't understand the true meanings. The outward religious appearance and character of the khawaarij deluded thousands in the past, and continues to delude people today. The Muslims should be aware that despite the khawaarij adherence to certain aspects of Islam, they are extremists of the worst type.

Our Prophet said, peace be upon him, "Beware of extremism in your religion." Islam is the middle way between excess and neglect. Zealots are a plague upon religion. These extremists come in two types. The first is a reactionary extremist who falls far right of a center-point. Reactionary extremists do not want any pluralism; they view the world in melodramatic, black and white, good and evil terms. They are good and anyone who opposes them is evil. From among the Muslims these are people who 'excommunicate' any Muslim who fails to share their interpretations of the Quran. They use takfir [denouncing a Muslim as an unbeliever] and character assassination as a tool for marginalizing any criticism directed at them. They are used often by the Western media in order to scare simple people and cause them to believe that Muslims are insane. Unfortunately, our communities provide them with much fuel to fire their incendiary flames.

The second group is radical extremists, who while they are almost identical with the former group, differ in that they will use violence to further their cause. They are actually worse than the first. They believe like every nefarious secret society before them that 'the end justifies the means.' They see any act as acceptable if it will further their 'cause.' This is blatantly anti-Islamic for a number of reasons.

Firstly, Islam's means must reflect its noble ends. Any means that does not embody the core truths and ethics of Islam is not from Islam and thus denounced as aberration. Secondly, Islam is not a secret society of conspirators who no one knows what they are planning. Islam declares openly its aims and objectives and these are recognized by good people everywhere as pure and congruent with their own wisdom and traditions. In the case of many of these extremists even the non-Muslims recognize that no religion of any weight could sanction the taking of innocent lives. The Quran says that the Torah and the Gospel have guidance and light and that the Quran came to fulfill these prior dispensations. Good Christians and Jews who believe in God and live ethically upright lives have no frame of reference for such acts, so how could these acts be from Islam, which confirms what has come before it?

Thirdly, they are invariably people who have never taken a true spiritual path to God and nor have they studied the humanities. I can almost guarantee that you will not find a scholar of poetry among the whole vile lot of these people. They have no true knowledge of Arabian culture, which is centered in the idea of *futuwwa*; a word akin to the western word chivalry. The terrorists posing as journalists who killed Ahmad Shah Masud [Afghan Northern Alliance leader] were cowards of the worst type. Killing themselves was not bravery but stupidity, but killing one's enemy in such a way is the worst form of treachery and the Arabs have many poems denouncing such type of people.

Our real situation is this, we Muslims have lost theologically sound understanding of our teaching. Islam has been hijacked by a discourse of anger and the rhetoric of rage. We have allowed for too long our mimbars [pulpits] to become bully pulpits in which people with often recognizable psychopathology use anger - a very powerful emotion - to rile Muslims up, only to leave them feeling bitter and spiteful towards people who in the most part are completely unaware of the conditions in the Muslim world, or the oppressive assaults of some Western countries on Muslim peoples. We have lost our bearings because we have lost our theology. We have almost no theologians in the entire Muslim world. The study of kalaam, once the hallmark of our intellectual tradition, has been reduced to memorizing 144 lines of al-Jawhara and a good commentary to study it, at best.

The reality is we are an Umma [worldwide Muslim community] that no longer realizes that Allah is the power behind all power; that it is Allah who subjugates one people to another; that He gives dominion to which He pleases and He takes it away from whom He pleases. Our understanding of tawhid [oneness of God] has fallen into such disarray that we can no longer introspect when afflictions befall us and then wonder in amazement at why the Americans seem incapable of introspection. Indeed, I personally attended a memorial service in San Francisco with over 30,000 people and the Reverend Amos Brown said in no uncertain terms that America must ask herself what she has done either wittingly or unwittingly to incur the wrath and hate of people around the world. Muslims on the other hand, generally prefer to attack the West as the sole reason for their problems when the truth is we are bankrupt as a religious community and our spiritual bankruptcy has led to our inability to even deliver the message of Islam to Westerners in a time when they were giving us platforms to do so.

It is ironic that the Western media while producing many vile programs on Islam has also produced and aired material of the highest quality with a high level of accuracy only to be vilified by Muslims because it was not good enough. Where is our media? Where are our spokespeople? Where are our scholars? Where are our literary figures? The truth is we don't have any - and so instead of looking inward and asking painful questions such as why we don't have such things and such people, we take the simple way out by attacking people whom Allah tells us will do mean things, say bad things and plot against us. And always when we are warned we are told to be patient, to work for the good, to trust in Allah, to return to Allah, to implement our *deen* [religion].

Conspiracy or not, we are to blame for the terrible backlash against Muslims. The simple reason is that when a crazy Christian does something terrible, everyone in the West knows it is the actions of a mad man because they have some knowledge of the core beliefs and ethics of

Christianity. When a mad Muslim does something evil or foolish they assume it is from the religion of Islam, not because they hate us but because they have never been told by a Muslim what the teachings of Islam are all about.

8

Religion of Terror

A bomb goes off in a marketplace in Jerusalem. A suicide bomber launches himself into a bus full of women and children in Tel Aviv. Foreign tourists get massacred at a holiday resort in Luxor, Egypt. Villages upon villages get annihilated in Algeria. The list of events worldwide which have come to symbolise the 'Islamic terror' are endless. From the times in the 70's and 80's when Pan Am and TWA aeroplanes would be high jacked, to the mid 80's in war torn Lebanon where Americans and Europeans would be held as hostages for years; all such incidents have come to be identified with the religion of Islam.

Such incidents from past and present have undoubtedly affected Muslims worldwide and more so in the West. Any Muslim, who wants to practice his/her religion and expresses the pious desire to live under the banner of Islam, is labelled a fundamentalist or extremist. Any Muslim man who walks down a busy street in London or Paris (and Paris moreso) with a beard and a scarf on his head, is looked upon as being a terrorist who's probably got an AK47 stashed somewhere on his person. Muslim women who are veiled can't go anywhere in the Western world without being taunted as being oppressed or being mad (for covering up). However, are such beliefs and opinions about Islam really justified?

Exploding the Myth

One of the many shortcomings which have arisen in the West is judging Islam by the conduct of a minority of its people. By doing this, segments of Western society have deliberately played off the desperate actions of many Muslims, and have given it the name of Islam. Such behaviour is clearly not objective and seeks to distort the reality of Islam. For if such a thing was done Judge a religion by the conduct of its people) then we too could say that all Christianity is about is child molesting and homosexuality whilst Hinduism was all about looting and breaking up mosques.

Generalising in such a manner is not seen as being objective, yet we find that the Western world is foremost in propagating this outlook on Islam. So what is the reality of Islam? How does one dispel the myths which have been created and spread so viciously? The only way to examine Islam is to simply examine its belief system. Look at its sources, the Qur'an and Sunna, and see what they have to say. This is the way to find the truth about what Islam says about terror, terrorism and terrorists. One who is sincerely searching for the truth, will do it no other way. The very name Islam comes from the Arabic root word 'salama' which means peace.

Islam is a religion which is based upon achieving peace through the submission to the will of Allah. Thus, by this very simple linguistic definition, one can ascertain as to what the nature of this religion is. If such a religion is based on the notion of peace, then how is it that so many acts done by its adherents are contrary to peace? The answer is simple. Such actions, if not sanctioned by the religion, have no place with it. They are not Islamic and should not be thought of as Islamic.

The word jihad sends shivers down the spines of many Westerners. They readily equate this term with violence and oppression. However, it must be said that the meaning of jihad, as a 'holy war', is something which is totally foreign and not from Islam. If anything, such a description belongs more so to Christianity and its adherents. It was terms like this which were used to justify the slaughter and pillage of towns and cities during the crusades by the Christians. By simply looking into the sources of Islam, one is able to know that the true meaning of jihad is to strive/make effort in the way of Allah. Thus striving in the way of Allah can be both peaceful and physical.

The Prophet Muhammed (saws) said, "The best jihad is (by) the one who strives against his own self for Allah, The Mighty and Majestic". In the Qur'an, Allah also says, "So obey not the disbelievers, but make a great jihad (effort) against them (by preaching) with it (the Qur'an)".

By controlling and fighting against ones desires, the Muslims can then also physically exert themselves in the path of Allah. It is this physical or combative jihad which receives so much criticism. Because of the sheer ignorance of this type of jihad Islam is regarded as terror, and Muslims are regarded as terrorists. However, the very purpose of this physical jihad is to raise the word of Allah uppermost. By doing this, it liberates and emancipates all those who are crying out for freedom all over the world. If the likes of the pacifists of this world had their way, then the world would indeed be full of anarchy and mischief.

The combative jihad seeks to correct this as Allah says in the Qur'an,"And if Allah did not check one set of people by means of another, the Earth would be full of mischief. But Allah is full of bounty to the worlds" (Surah Al-Baqarah 2:251)

Such would be the corruption on this Earth if there had never been a combative jihad that Allah says, "For had it not been that Allah checks one set of people by means of another, monasteries, churches, synagogues and mosques, wherein the name of Allah is mentioned much, would surely have been pulled down. Indeed Allah will help those who help His (cause). Truly Allah is All strong, All mighty" (Surah Al-Hajj 22:40)

This combative jihad being both defensive and offensive is something which is commanded by Allah upon the Muslims. Through this command the oppressed and weak are rescued from the tyranny of the world:

"And what is the matter with you that you do not fight in the cause of Allah and for those weak, ill treated and oppressed among men, women and children whose only cry is; 'Our Lord, rescue us from this town whose people are oppressors and raise for us from you one who will protect and raise for us from you one who will help" (Surah An-Nisa 4:75)

Anyone who knows the early history of Islam will know that all those nations and empires which came under the fold of Islam were indeed previously oppressed. When the companions of the Prophet Muhammed (saws) went out for the offensive jihad against the Egyptians, the Persians and the Romans, we find that the people did not resist against them at all. Rather, they accepted Islam on such a scale, that it is inconceivable that the jihad of Islam could be anything other then a liberation for these people; a liberation from centuries of tyranny. In fact, with the Byzantine Egyptians and the people of Spain, the Muslims were even beckoned to come and liberate these lands from the oppression of their kings.

This is the glorious track record of the Muslim jihad Compare this with the brutal track record of warfare in the Western world over the centuries. From the crusades against the Muslims to the days of colonial warfare, the Western world has killed, destroyed and plundered everything which has come in its way.

Even today this merciless killing goes on by the Western nations. While claiming to be about world peace and security, Western nations are ready to bomb innocent civilians at the drop of a hat. The classic example of this is the recent bombings of Sudan and Afghanistan. Whilst claiming that Sudan and Afghanistan were havens for Islamic terrorists, the bombings of these two nations could not have come at a better time for the American president Bill Clinton. The destruction of innocent lives which were a result of these bombings clearly seem to have been an attempt by Clinton to avert attention away from his sexual misdemeanours; something which he so often gets caught up in. Without doubt this was the reason for such terror from the American military upon innocent people.

This is the same American military which claims to enter the world's trouble spots under the guise of being peace keepers. But "... when it is said to them; 'Make not mischief on the Earth', they say; 'We are only peace makers'. Indeed they are the ones who make mischief, but they perceive it not" (Surah Al-Baqarah 2:11-12)

The hypocrisy of the West is indeed astounding. By looking at the rules and regulations of this combative jihad it will be clear to any sincere person that this is indeed the religion of truth. When fighting an unjust enemy, no matter how unjust they are, it is forbidden by Islam that their retreating forces are mutilated, tortured or slaughtered. The treacherous violation of treaties and carrying out assassinations after a cease fire, are also prohibited. Allah says in the Qur'an:

"And fight in the way of Allah those who fight you. But do not transgress the limits. Truly Allah loves not the transgressors" (Surah Al-Baqarah 2:190)

Not transgressing the limits means not to kill women and children, for the Messenger of Allah (saws) "forbade the killing of women and children". Not transgressing the limits means that the elderly, the sick, monks, worshippers and hired labourers are not attacked. Not transgressing the limits means not killing animals wantonly, burning crops and vegetation, polluting waters and destroying homes, monasteries, churches and synagogues", Allah does not forbid you to deal justly and kindly with those who fought not against you on account of religion, nor drove you out of your homes. Indeed, Allah loves those who deal with equity" (Surah Al-Mumtahinah 60:8)

After reading such passages from the Qur'an and knowing about what Islam commands and prohibits in jihad, the rules of warfare are given a new meaning; a meaning of justice. How sad it is then, that whilst Islam is condemned for striking terror into the hearts of the people, the likes of the Serbs, the Indian army in Kashmir and the Israeli soldiers in Palestine are left untarnished for the atrocities they have committed in the name of warfare.

So what about suicide bombing, is this too a part of jihad in Allah's path? From what has already been stated above, it can be deduced that this is not from the religion. However, unfortunately many Muslims have taken suicide bombing as being a virtuous act by which one receives reward. This could not be further from the truth. The Prophet (saws) said, "Those who go to extremes are destroyed".

Suicide bombing is undoubtedly an extremity which has reached the ranks of the Muslims. In the rules of warfare, we find no sanction for such an act from the behaviour and words of the Prophet Muhammed (saws) and his companions. Unfortunately, today (some misguided) Muslims believe that such acts are paving the way for an Islamic revival and a return to the rule of Islam's glorious law. However, we fail to bear in mind that the Prophet (saws) said, "Do not be delighted by the action of anyone, until you see how he ends up".

So, for example what is the end of a suicide bomber in Palestine? A leg here, an arm there. Due to massive retaliation by the Israeli's in the West Bank and Gaza more

Muslims killed and persecuted. How can we be delighted with such an end? What really hammers the final nail in the coffin of this act, is that it is suicide; something which is clearly forbidden in Islam. The Messenger of Allah (saws) said: "He who kills himself with anything, Allah will torment him with that in the fire of Hell".

Some are under the misconception that by killing oneself for an Islamic cause, one commits an act which deserves Paradise. Once when a man killed himself, the Prophet (saws) said, "He is a dweller of the Fire". When the people were surprised at this, the Prophet (saws) said, "A person performs the deeds which to the people appears to be the deeds befitting the dweller of Paradise, but he is in fact one of the dwellers of the Fire."

The taking of ones life which Allah has given as a trust to the human, is a great sin. Likewise the taking of other lives (which is so often the case with suicide bombing) is also forbidden, as human life is indeed precious:"...If anyone killed a person not in retaliation for murder or to spread mischief in the land, it would be as if he killed the whole of mankind. And (likewise) if anyone saved a life, it would be as if he saved the whole of mankind." (Surah Al-Maaida 5:32)

Thus, all other types of extremities such as hostage taking, hijacking and planting bombs in public places, are clearly forbidden in Islam.

The Media

By going through the teachings of Islam, it is clear that such a religion has only come to benefit mankind - not to destroy it. So why is there so much hatred for this noble religion in the West?

The answer is simple, the media. It is the Jewish influenced media of the West which has portrayed Islam to be something that it is not. During the 70's and 80's when the PLO (Palestine Liberation Organisation) was carrying out daring highjack on the worlds airways, the media in the West portrayed it as being Islamic.

When the Shi'ite suicide bombers of the 80's were causing so much havoc in the Lebanon and in the Gulf region, the media in the West portrayed it as a part of Islam. However, it is known by the heads of the media that the likes of the PLO were not an Islamic organisation, and that according to Islam, Shi'ites are outside the fold of Islam.

Yet such facts are never portrayed by a media which seeks to cover the truth of this religion. A number of years ago, when the Oklahoma City bomb went off, a headline in one of the newspapers, 'Today', summed up this attitude. With a picture of a fire fighter holding a dead child in his arms, the headline read, "In The Name of Islam".

Time has of course proven that this bigoted assumption was incorrect, as Timothy McVeigh, a right wing radical now faces the death penalty for the crime.

Likewise the bombs which went off in the Paris metro in 1995 were also blamed on Muslim fanatics. It has now emerged that the Algerian secret service who having routinely bribed many European journalists and MPs, were actually behind it. The desire to throw a veil over Islam is immense by these people, "They intend to put out the light of Allah with their mouths, but Allah will complete His light even though the disbelievers hate (it)" (Surah As-Saff 61:8)

Whilst trying to destroy Islam through this instrument of the media, the Jews clearly try to portray an image of themselves as being the oppressed people. Every year, we are reminded as to how many Jews perished under the Nazis in World War II. We are made to feel sorry for these same people who have gone on to commit so many crimes upon the Palestinian people. Some may say that this is a racist and biased viewpoint. But we say; If this media was not run and orchestrated by the Jews and was truly neutral, then why are Menachem Begin and Yitzhak Shamir, two former Israeli prime ministers, not held aloft as being terrorists? Anyone who knows about the history of the Palestinian occupation will tell you that these two men were members of the Stern Gang and Irgun, two notorious Jewish terror groups who killed many innocent people.

If this media was truly impartial, then why does it not tell about the extent of the Israeli bombardment and illegal occupation of Southern Lebanon and its people? And if this media really had nothing against the religion of Allah, then why does it not inform the people that every day hundreds are entering the religion of Islam? Such things will never be highlighted in the Western media, simply because to do so would be against their very interests.

With such immense pressure against it, it is indeed a blessing from Allah that Islam goes from strength to strength. It continues to grow faster then any other religion in the Western world, conquering the hearts and minds of thousands. All this should not even surprise us though, for Allah has promised us that this religion will prevail, "It is He who has sent His Messenger with the guidance and the religion of truth, so that He may make it victorious over all other religions, even though the disbelievers detest it" (Surah As-Saff 61:9)

It is a must that humanity comes towards the religion of Islam. Without it, we will continue to slip down the road of inequity and darkness. With it we can establish a society of justice and peace. Religion of terror? ... No. The way forward? ... Yes.

"There is no compulsion in religion. The right path has indeed become distinct from the wrong. So whoever rejects false worship and believes in Allah, then he has grasped the most trustworthy handhold that will never break. And Allah is All Hearing, All Knowing" Surah Al-Baqarah 2:256).

The Most Enduring Terrorists

The bombings in East Africa and Northern Ireland have

drawn responses of formidable hypocrisy. The US Secretary of State, Madeleine Albright, said, "We will not be intimidated or pushed off the world stage by people who do not like what we stand for; and that is, freedom, democracy and the fight against disease, poverty and terrorism." It is now clear that the mostly African victims of the two US embassy bombs were left to suffer in appalling conditions while Albright flew home with the bodies of ten American dead to a flag-draped media event featuring a tearful Bill Clinton. Although more than 5,000 people were wounded in Nairobi and Dar es Salaam, few were given medical help by the Americans. One Boeing 707 chartered by the US government, able to carry 60 bed-bound casualties, flew from Nairobi to Pretoria with no Kenyans on board, only three Americans, one on a stretcher and two who were able to walk off the plane. In contrast, staffs at Nairobi's Kenyatta Hospital were so overwhelmed that only the seriously injured were treated; in the morgue, hundreds of bodies were piled on tables.

This is the metaphor of the "world stage" across which Madeleine Albright struts. The source of the embassy bombs was undoubtedly the Middle East, where the policies of Albright's government and its predecessors cast long shadows. In 1991 a force led by the US killed more than 200,000 Iraqis in a colonial massacre, with one side having a huge advantage in forces and weapons. US and British forces fired tens of thousands of depleted uranium shells, an illegal weapon under UN Resolution 32/84, which bans the use of "radioactive material weapons". The Americans also bombed and buried alive Iraqi conscripts who were offering no resistance or were already in retreat. Both of these actions are war crimes.

Most important, the Middle East is subjected to an American-designed "peace process". This means the opposite. It is a war and terrorism process that has corralled the Palestinians between Israeli military forces and foreign invaders, known as "settlers", who are sponsored and armed by the Israeli government and subsidised by the US. The model is apartheid South Africa. In the meantime, the Palestinians and all Arabs must put up with stereotypes about Islamic fundamentalism and violence, when, in fact, not only have Muslims been responsible for a tiny proportion of deaths caused by terrorism, but in recent years it is they who have been the greatest sufferers from state terrorism, in Palestine, Iraq, Bosnia, Chechnya and Somalia.

The omission from public debate of these truths, and of the pervasive violence of western fundamentalism as it goes about its divine work, is given respectability by western academics, journalists and think tanks and by popular western culture. Arnold Schwarzenegger, in the movie True Lies, kills 80 terrorists, all of them Arab Muslims. In Hollywood, as in the American and British media, it is apostasy to describe the democracies as terrorist states, regardless of their record.

Tony Blair said he "simply wept" for the victims of the terrorist act in Omagh. He also wept following the massacre of children at Dunblane when he vowed to "outlaw" handguns. Categories of guns were banned in Britain; but as the world's second biggest exporter of arms, the Blair government has secretly issued export licences for small arms sales to Kenya and Turkey, where members of the parliamentary opposition and journalists are routinely murdered. British-made hand-guns have also gone to the Far East, Algeria, Sri Lanka and Colombia - countries engulfed in day-to-day political and criminal violence. Rapid-firing Heckler and Koch machine guns, made by British Aerospace, equip Indonesia's militarised gestapo, Kopassus, which is responsible for the worst atrocities in East Timor.

In October, the UN Special Commission for Iraq is likely to recommend a partial lifting of the sanctions that have devastated that country since the 1991 slaughter. The US and Britain will almost certainly veto this. Protocol 1,

Article 54 of the Geneva Convention states, "Starvation of civilians as a method of warfare is prohibited." Under rules drawn up by a US-controlled committee, baby food and enriched powdered milk are banned. People are operated on without anaesthetic because vital equipment is blockaded, along with bandages, sutures, medical swabs, stethoscopes, X-ray equipment, scanners and water purifiers. Even ambulances are banned. Customs officers at Heathrow recently confiscated antibiotics from a humanitarian delegation flying to Iraq, and threatened to prosecute. Children's clothes, sanitary towels, light bulbs, schoolbooks, paper, pencils, shoelaces - all are banned.

Anyone doubting the scale of this terrorism by the governments of Britain and the US should read Geoff Simons' superb, scholarly and damningbook, The Scourging of lraq, Sanctions, law and natural justice. Eight years of sanctions have killed two million Iraqis, including one million children. That is the child population of a medium-sized British city. Robin Cook, who dreamt up the stunt of an ethical foreign policy, likes to talk about humanitarian exemptions. "Exemptions," writes Simons, "are for public relations. Sanctions are designed to kill. A doctor might as well call for the humane implementation of torture." George Bush, supported by John Major, began them. Now Clinton enforces them, backed by Blair, "the perfect peacekeeper" in the words of the UN Secretary General Kofi Annan. Generally, this holocaust has been consigned to media oblivion. A recent ITN report blamed the "inadequacies of the Iraqi medical system" and concentrated on the brilliant care given to one Iraqi refugee in Britain.

The genocidal effect of government policy was effectively airbrushed. According to the great American dissenter Richard Falk, professor of international relations at Princeton, western scholarship and journalism have simply taken the humanity out of the study of nations.

Western foreign policy, he says, "is formulated through a self-righteous, one-way moral/legal screen [with] positive images of western values and innocence portrayed as threatened, validating a campaign of unrestricted political violence." In other words, the most important terrorists are rarely identified.

Faces of Terrorism

According to sociologists and experts on terrorism, the words terrorist and terrorism were coined for the first time during the French revolution. The T-word was first used in 1795 in the context of the 'Reign of Terror' initiated by the revolutionary government in France. The agents of the Committee of Public Safety and the National Convention that enforced the policies of "The Terror" were referred to as 'terrorists'. The French revolution set an example for future states in oppressing their own people. It also prompted a reaction by royalists and other opponents of the revolution who also used terrorist tactics such as assassination and intimidation in resisting the revolutionary agents. The systematic use of terror as state policy was first recorded in England in 1798.

The words terrorism and terrorist were first used as political terms to describe atrocities of an occupying power – say colonial government.

Researches on the history of terrorism also reveal the word 'terrorist' being used in describing the tactics used by the extremist revolutionaries in Russia (1866) and in accounts of Jewish tactics against the British in Palestine (1947). During the anti-colonial struggle, what one party called terrorism was referred to as a guerrilla war or fight for freedom by the opposite party. This was so in case of the anti-British actions in India (1857), in Cyprus (1956) and the war in Rhodesia (1973). The word terrorist has also been used, at least retroactively, to describe the Marquis resistance in occupied France during World War II. The

British first used the terms 'terrorism' and 'terrorist' to describe anti-establishment forces who adopted hit-and-run tactics against British colonialism.

It is apparently not easy to define terrorism even though it is not a new phenomenon for the world. A western writer observes, "Terrorism has been described variously as both a tactic and strategy; a crime and a holy duty; a justified reaction to oppression and an inexcusable abomination." Obviously, a lot depends on whose point of view is being represented. Terrorism has often been an effective tactic used by the weaker side in a conflict. In an asymmetric conflict it confers coercive power with many of the advantages of military force at a fraction of the cost.

The popular online encyclopaedia – Wikipedia – notes, "The word 'terrorism' is politically and emotionally charged and this greatly compounds the difficulty of providing a precise definition." A 2003 study by Jeffrey Record for the US army quoted a source (Schmid and Jongman) documenting 109 definitions of terrorism incorporating a total of 22 different definitional elements. Says Record, "Terrorism expert Walter Laqueur also has counted over 100 definitions" and concludes that the "only general characteristic generally agreed upon is that terrorism involves violence and the threat of violence. Yet terrorism is hardly the only enterprise involving violence and the threat of violence. So does war, coercive diplomacy and bar-room brawls."

The lack of agreement on a definition of terrorism has been a major obstacle to meaningful international countermeasures. In India, the onslaught of the media and law enforcement agencies with their assumptions and repeated mention of Muslim names after each terror attack has entered the psyche of ordinary Indians. Thus an impression has gained currency that terrorism in the country is a Muslim monopoly. But the facts on the ground tell a different story.

In Jammu and Kashmir, the terrorists are Muslims. But they are only one of the several terrorist groups operating in the country. In Punjab, the terrorists are Sikhs. The United Liberation Front of Assam (ULFA) is a Hindu terrorist group. Tripura also has seen the rise and fall of several terrorist groups. Then we have the Bodo terrorists, Christians mostly, who in their fight for autonomy killed hundreds of Muslims in 1993. Some of its leaders are now cabinet ministers in Tarun Gogoi's government in Assam. Christian Mizos mounted an insurrection for decades. And Christian Nagas and Manipuris are still heading militant groups. They have bombed trains, assassinated hundreds of innocent men, women and children. This year they boycotted and attempted to disrupt Independence Day (August 15) celebrations in at least five of the country's seven north-eastern states.

But most lethal of all are the Maoist terrorist groups who reportedly now have a presence in no less than 150 of India's 600 districts. They have attacked police stations and killed and ransacked the property of innocent villagers who oppose them. There is nothing Muslim about these Maoist groups. On September 2, 2006 national English daily published from Mumbai had a detailed report on a few dozen 'Hindu Mujahideen' who had for years been working for the Hizb ul-Mujahideen (HM) in Jammu and Kashmir. The news report had all the necessary details – names, ages, addresses of the recruits (all from the Jammu region) and the year they joined the HM. Similarly, in some non-Muslim outfits such as ULFA in Assam, Muslim members are not barred from joining.

On February 24, 2008 bombs blasted inside the local RSS office and at the bus stand in Tenkasi in Tamil Nadu. The national media carried detailed reports on the blasts. The sangh parivar organised demonstrations in various parts of the state, demanding the arrest of "Muslim terrorists", who according to them had committed the crime. However, the Tamil Nadu police acted sensibly. A special team led by P. Kannappan, deputy inspector general of police, Tirunelveli range, made a thorough investigation and arrested three persons, S. Ravi Pandian (42), a cable TV operator, S. Kumar (28), an autorickshaw driver, both from Tenkasi, and V. Narayana Sharma (26) of Sencottai. All of them were activists of the sangh parivar. As reported by the media, the last accused had assembled 14 pipe bombs in the office of Ravi Pandian.

Urdu Times, a Mumbai daily, reported on April 18, 2008 that the Malegaon police had raided the Smith Pathology Laboratory situated in the basement of More Accident Hospital, Malegaon. One pistol, five live RDX bombs, three used RDX cases, four fake 1,000 rupee notes, a laptop, a scanner, Rs 5,000 in cash and two mobile phones were recovered during the raid, according to the newspaper report. The names of the three Hindu terrorists arrested were given as Nitish Ashire (20), Sahab Rao Sukhdev Dhevre (22) and Jitendar Kherna (25). The last one is the owner of the pathology lab.

Following the Jaipur serial blasts on May 13, 2008, the police were reportedly on the hunt for a woman who had allegedly promised Rs. 1, 00,000 to a rickshaw-puller to carry out the terror attacks. "We are looking for a woman identified as Meena who tried to lure a rickshaw-puller, Vijay, to carry out the attacks," an unidentified police officer told a national daily. The Aaj Tak TV channel telecast video clips of Vijay saying, "Stop the lady (Meena) or she will explode bombs at Katwali." By that time a bomb had already been exploded in the Katwali area. Vijay, who was detained just an hour after the Jaipur blasts, told the police that Meena lived near one of the blast sites. What happened to Meena and Vijay? What further information did the police extract from Vijay? Were they able to locate and interrogate Meena? All this remains a mystery till date.

The special issue of *Communalism Combat* (July-August 2008) carried extensive reports on the involvement of several Hindu extremist groups in several bomb blasts in the state since 2003.

In the last week of July 2008 bombs exploded in Bangalore and Ahmedabad on two consecutive days. The Ahmedabad blasts killed 42 people and injured another 200. Over the next few days a large number of unexploded bombs were found and defused in Surat. In an email sent out five minutes before the Ahmedabad blasts a little known group calling itself the 'Indian Mujahideen' claimed that it was responsible for the blasts. The police investigating the Ahmedabad blasts case traced the email to an apartment in Navi Mumbai. Interestingly, the resident of the apartment turned out to be not some "Islamist group" but an American: Kenneth Haywood (48), a Christian preacher operating under cover of a dummy IT company. In a highly curious turn of events, Haywood fled India even while the ATS had put out a lookout alert against him.

Police officials had no satisfactory explanation as to how no surveillance was maintained on a man suspected of possible involvement in a major terrorist attack. Would the ATS and the rest of the police machinery have acted in the same cavalier fashion had the laptop been in possession of a Muslim? Terrorism is a political virus. It breeds where there is greed for power, injustice or intolerance. No one in the world is immune from the direct or indirect effect of terrorism now. Whatever their stated cause, all terrorists have a common goal – generating fear through violence. To effectively counter terrorism we must all bear in mind that terrorism has no religion.

9

Spiritual Jihad against Terrorism

Our society is whirling down a spiral of violence of which terrorism is the face that is currently at the front of our minds. There is a growing exploitation by religious extremists, political extremists, nationalist extremists, etc. All of these share a "religious" element in that they are all convinced that they are God's agents to bring about and enforce their "right" belief on everyone else, and that they, and they alone - know the "right" way. This "religious" element is particularly dangerous because it is devoid of spirituality.

More innocent lives are in danger today than in any previous period of history. The entire world is in danger. We are at the beginning of a new century and a new millenium, and it is possible that we will not complete either without destroying ourselves.

We are violent, not only with each other but with the environment, and even with our spiritual selves. We are one human race but isolate ourselves from each other through fear, suspicion and selfishness. We have broken our ties with the natural order and with each other.

Our beliefs may be different but our suffering and sorrow are shared.

"Sorrow prepares you for joy. It violently sweeps everything out of your house, so that new joy can find space to enter. It shakes the yellow leaves from the bough of your heart, so that fresh, green leaves can grow in their place. It pulls up the rotten roots, so that new roots hidden beneath have room to grow. Whatever sorrow shakes from your heart, far better things will take their place. (Rumi)

Too often, we excuse "our" violence and condemn "their" violence (whether individual or state) in the name of ethnicity, culture, politics, self-defense, religion, — but, no matter the "reason" or excuse, the end result is the same, more death and destruction.

Terrorism is only one aspect of this widespread violence. Currently it is most commonly associated with "Islamic terrorism" although this is an oxymoron just as much as "Christian terrorism" or "Jewish terrorism". The truth is that TERROR HAS NO RELIGION! There are lots of reasons given for why terrorism has become so common in our times, and why in the last few years the perpetrators so often seem to be Muslims. Most commonly this is attributed to either a response to policies or an inherent flaw in Islam. This "either/or" critique is an over-simplification of a complex issue. Is there something wrong with religion, something wrong with our political policies, or is there more to the issue?

It is of course true - as Shabbir Akhtar has noted - that powerlessness can corrupt as insistently as does power. But to comprehend is not to sanction or even to empathize. To take innocent life to achieve a goal is the hallmark of the most extreme secular utilitarian ethic, and stands at the opposite pole of the absolute moral constraints required by religion. There was a time, not long ago, when the 'ultras' were few, forming only a tiny wart on the face of the worldwide attempt to revivify Islam. Sadly, we can no longer enjoy the luxury of ignoring them. The extreme has broadened, and the middle ground, giving way, is everywhere dislocated and confused. And this enfeeblement of the middle ground, was what was enjoined by the Prophetic example, is in turn accelerated by the opprobrium which the extremists bring not simply upon themselves, but upon committed Muslims everywhere.

For here, as elsewhere, the preferences of the media work firmly against us. David Koresh could broadcast his fringe Biblical message from Ranch Apocalypse without the image of Christianity, or even its Adventist wing, is being in any way besmirched. But when a fringe Islamic group bombs Swedish tourists in Cairo, the muck is instantly spread over 'militant Muslims' everywhere. ... At this critical moment in our history, the umma has only one realistic hope for survival, and that is to restore the 'middle way', defined by that sophisticated classical consensus which was worked out over painful centuries of debate and scholarship. That consensus alone has the demonstrable ability to provide a basis for unity. But it can only be retrieved when we improve the state of our hearts, and fill hem with the Islamic virtues of affection, respect, tolerance and reconciliation. This inner reform, which is the traditional competence of Sufism, is a precondition for the restoration of unity in the Islamic movement. The alternative is likely to be continued, and agonising, failure?

As an American-Muslim I feel moral repugnance towards terrorism and violence, and at the same time I feel concern and frustration for what is happening to Muslims (and others in the third world) daily. Because the legitimate grievances of some have been hijacked by criminals as a pretext for terrorism does not de-legitimize the concerns. The issues still need to be addressed. Much of the world suffers from oppression, occupation, tyranny and injustice. We cannot stop terrorism without first working to end the injustice.

"Until we can sympathise with the victims of terrorism regardless of their nationality, skin colour or religion whether they are Egyptian or British, Palestinians or Israelis, Iraqis or Americans—all of us are in store for a great deal more anguish. Our ability to empathise with "the Other", whoever he or she may be, to see the world from a different perspective, to feel other people's pain, share their grief and understand their injustice, better enables us to address the misunderstandings, as well as the practical problems, that divide us. By acknowledging the legitimacy of other peoples' grievances, their disappointments and frustrations, we demonstrate to the world that we care not only about ourselves. We also come to see the world differently and act in it accordingly. recognising our common humanity is the first step towards creating a better future for all of us, a world with less violence, less suffering and possibly even less terrorism. It might make us collectively safer. It will also make us more human."

Mainstream American Muslims are in a unique position to act as a bridge between two cultures. We are also in a very difficult position in that we are under suspicion and are marginalized in our own country for being Muslims, and also tainted by the extremists for being the "wrong" kind of Muslims.

Most of us say that we believe in one of the great faith traditions? Judaism, Christianity, Islam, Hinduism, Buddhism all of whom teach brotherhood, justice, mercy, tolerance, compassion, the highest ideals to which humanity can aspire. But, it would seem that if so many people held such beliefs and followed such teachings we would see the practical results of that belief somewhere. And, when we look around us at the condition of humanity and the planet there is no light shining from anywhere which reflects the results of establishing a real society based on actually following these teachings which we say we believe in.

The Crusades, the Inquisition, blatant Colonialism, outright slavery are in the past, and yet the mentality which brought these about is still prevalent. We still have too many people who are so strongly committed to their own beliefs that they are willing to see others die for those beliefs and too few who are so strongly committed to their beliefs that they are willing to give their own life for those beliefs!

Looking at the state of the world it would not be unreasonable to conclude that all of these belief systems are a failure. Or, we might conclude, as I have, that the failure is with us because we lack either the courage or the vision or the commitment to act on those beliefs.

Now is a good time to test those beliefs, because at the same time that we are realizing that we have economic, social and environmental problems that are global in scope. At the same time that we face these global problems, the systems we have depended on have failed us. We are witnessing the collapse, or at least the redefinition of established social, political, economic and ideological systems worldwide. Colonialism (political or spiritual), apartheid, communism, materialism, nationalism, capitalism, sexism, racism, any of the systems which saw one group of human beings versus another, or all human beings versus nature are collapsing or being challenged.

They have failed because instead of being based on a belief in God and a commitment to act and order our lives based on that belief they were based on the small dreams of small people who had made themselves small by their own definitions of themselves. There is no justification in any of these belief systems for what we have done or what we are doing. It is we who have defined ourselves as members of a particular race, tribe, and ethnic, religious, political or linguistic group to the exclusion of others who do not belong to the same groups. It is we who have defined the essential element of ourselves not as human beings but as members of these categories. It is we who have created systems that were also based on these small definitions, and these systems have failed.

We have tried every violent means as a solution to our differences, too often even in the name of religion and it has gotten us nowhere. We have walked our separate roads and when our paths crossed that meeting has been marked most often by violence, intolerance and injustice. We have now come to a point in history where it is obvious that all partial solutions have failed. We have a situation in which it is possible to imagine the total destruction of the world as we know it either through nuclear war or through continuing destruction of the environment. We rea1ly are between a rock and a hard place.

I believe that it is time for all of those who believe in GOD, who believe that there is a purpose to this life, who believe that we are responsible and accountable for our actions to see this crossroads we are at as an opportunity to take the first steps on a new road that we can walk together in peace.

In America we may have the greatest opportunity to see this possibility become a reality. We are just beginning to realize that we have become a multi-cultural, multi-ethnic, multi-racial, multi-religious society. We used to think of ourselves as a melting pot but that concept implies trying to change people, to make them all the same, to homogenize them. It won't happen, and it can't be done without damaging the human spirit. Perhaps if we discarded the idea of being a melting pot in favor of a mosaic we might be able to begin making connections. A mosaic not only accepts the fact of difference, it requires difference, it rejoices in difference, it uses difference. The different colors, textures and shapes together create something more beautiful and powerful than any single element could.

Each generation has had to make choices, but for most of the course of human history those choices were limited to a relatively small area of impact (individual families, clans, tribes or ethnic groups). This generation faces what may be the biggest challenge because the choices we make may have global impact. The choices of our generation may be the choices that will define our future as a species on this planet.

The United Nations has not accepted any definition of terrorism as being authoritative. However, the UN "academic consensus definition," written by terrorism expert A.P. Schmid and widely used by social scientists, runs, Terrorism is an anxiety-inspiring method of repeated violent action, employed by (semi-) clandestine individual, group or state actors, for idiosyncratic, criminal or political reasons, whereby? in contrast to assassination ? the direct targets of violence are not the main targets. The immediate human victims of violence are generally chosen randomly (targets of opportunity) or selectively (representative or symbolic targets) from a target population, and serve as message generators. Threat- and violence-based communication processes between terrorist (organization), (imperilled) victims, and main targets are used to manipulate the main target (audience(s)), turning it into a target of terror, a target of demands, or a target of attention, depending on whether intimidation, coercion, or propaganda is primarily sought," (Schmid, 1988).

The U.S. government's definition of terrorism—

"the unlawful use of force or violence against persons or property to intimidate or coerce a government, the civilian population or any segment thereof, in furtherance of political or social objectives"

It seems to me that we are confusing ourselves with unnecessary complications. How about working on a more simplified definition. Terrorism is any action either by an individual or government that targets civilians?, or even "Terrorism is violence committed against non-military targets for political purposes."

There are a lot of questions to be considered before coming up with a final definition, a few might be:

- Are government sponsored actions that target civilians to be included in the definition? - What about bombings in times of war that target civilians, e.g. Hiroshima, Nagasaki, Hamburg, Dresden? (Note: "The president of the U.S. Conference of Catholic Bishops said, that like terrorism today, the atomic bombs that the United States dropped on Japan to end World War II were unjustifiable because they failed to "discriminate between noncombatants and combatants.") - How much collateral damage is acceptable? - If government troops do not act to prevent a slaughter of civilians, e.g. the Dutch U.N. Peace-keepers at Srebenica, are they complicit in terrorism? - If government troops actually surround a civilian population so they cannot escape allowing another party to commit a massacre, e.g. Israeli troops at Sabra & Shatilla, are they also complicit in terrorism? - Is the use of WMD's terrorism (how about depleted uranium)? - If one government funds anothers tyrannical government, does it bear any responsibility, e.g. the Shah of Iran's torture chambers? - How about pre-emptive war, torture, sanctions, genocide, ethnic cleansing?

Whatever definition we come up with, we can agree that all violence is best avoided.

"I object to violence because when it appears to do good, the good is only temporary; the evil it does is permanent." Gandhi

"An eye for an eye will only make the whole world blind." Gandhi

"Is Eric Rudolph a "Christian terrorist"? Well, it depends on your definition. But if he's not a Christian terrorist, Osama bin Laden isn't an Islamic terrorist. His views and actions closely parallel those of Islamist

radicals who attack targets inside majority-Islamic countries with a goal of instituting Islamic states. Christians—and not just conservatives, but moderates and liberals—will say that Eric Rudolph isn't really Christian. Christianity, of course, is a religion of peace. Now, where have we heard that before? There is, of course, a long history of murder and war in the name of the Prince of Peace. It hardly stopped with the Crusades or the Thirty Years' War. Nor is it confined to Ireland. I don't believe there's any creed that can't be perverted to violence."

This is one of the difficult issues to dialogue about, but it is an issue that needs to be dealt with - What was the religious affiliation of, - Those who enslaved and murdered the Native Americans; - Those who colonized most of what is now the "Third World"; - Those who dropped the atomic bomb; - Those who developed and participated in the political systems of Naziism and Fascism; - Those who participated in torture at Abu Ghraib; - Those who carried out ethnic cleansing against the Bosnian Muslims; - Those who were responsible for the death of millions in Germany's death camps?

I know that if the answer to any of these questions had been - Islam - that the term Islamic terrorism would have been used to describe the event. I don't believe that these events represent Christianity, but I also don't believe that the terrorist acts that are referred to as Islamic terrorism represent Islam. They are deviant actions that happened in spite of the religion of the perpetrators.

There have been Christians that have defended terrorism, or at least some forms of what others would see as terrorism. A recent example is Chuck Spingola and some Christian clergy have defended slavery, KKK lynchings, and even the Nazi regime.

In 1999 Pat Robertson called the assassination of foreign leaders"practical."

Christian Coalition President Pat Robertson said it might be "practical" foreign policy to assassinate some international leaders. Speaking Aug. 9 on "The 700 Club," Robertson said, "I know it sounds somewhat Machiavellian and evil, to think that you could send a squad in to take out somebody like (terrorist) Osama bin Laden or to take out the head of North Korea. But isn't it better to do something like that, to take out (Serbian President Slobodan) Milosevic, to take out (Iraqi President) Saddam Hussein, rather than to spend billions and billions of dollars on a war that harms innocent civilians and destroys the infrastructure of a country? It would just seem so much more practical to have that flexibility."

There is a Struggle within Christianity

My sense is that history has come to a point where only one thing will save this venerable faith tradition at this critical time in Christian history, and that is a new Reformation far more radical than Christianity has ever before known and that this Reformation must deal with the very substance of that faith. This Reformation will recognize that the pre-modern concepts in which Christianity has traditionally been carried will never again speak to the post-modern world we now inhabit. This Reformation will be about the very life and death of Christianity. Because it goes to the heart of how Christianity is to be understood, it will dwarf in intensity the Reformation of the 16th century. It will not be concerned about authority, ecclesiastical polity, valid ordinations and valid sacraments. It will be rather a Reformation that will examine the very nature of the Christian faith itself. It will ask whether or not this ancient religious system can be refocused and re-articulated so as to continue living in this increasingly non-religious world.

In the case of Jewish terrorists Wikipedia includes the disclaimer; Some of these Jewish groups believe that God gave Jews the land of Israel and so they advocate ethnic cleansing of Palestinians from Israel, West Bank and Gaza. Most, if not all, however, support the transfer of Palestinians to other regions within the Middle East. And, while this entry on Religious Terrorism includes many entries for Islamic terrorism, doesn't even mention many groups affiliated with Christianity or Judaism who have resorted to terrorism.

There have been some Jews who defended terrorism; In this terrible time of crisis, we remember the words of HaRav Yitzchak Nissim, the Chief Sephardic Rabbi of Israel that said in 1968, "The Land of Israel was, with its borders, defined for us by Divine Providence. Thou shalt be, says the Almighty, and there it is. No power on earth can alter that which was created by Him. In this connection it is not a question of law or logic, neither is it a matter of human treatment or that sort of thing."

"And how can you apply the adjective life-affirming to thousands of ferociously angry settlers in Gaza determined to rip down every brick in place, cut down every tree, root up every vine, people who have been widely reported to be poisoning the land they will have to surrender? It seems to me that Israel itself represents the focus of just such a struggle going on in Judaism, the only difference between it and what we see in Islam being one of numbers."

The list of terrorist acts attributed to "Islamic" Terrorism doesn't need to be repeated here because it so widespread as to be "common knowledge — common, but not accurate. Any act committed by any criminal who happens to be a Muslim will be labelled Islamic Terrorism.

We need to question whether al-Qaeda is *"an evil ideology whose roots lie in a perverted and poisonous misinterpretation of Islam"* as Tony Blair has said, or is it a violent response to perceived injustices, twisting Islamic belief in an attempt to justify that response by misusing the Qur'an and going against 1400 years of Islamic thought.

This is a deceptive wording that gives a very different impression than the disclaimers for Christianity and Judaism.

"Terrorism, which is termed hirabah (not jihad) in Arabic, was uniformly condemned by all the classical Islamic scholars, even by those who were imprisoned by the authorities (which included all the greatest scholars in Islamic history), because it was the classic example of the fasad (or societal corruption) that destroys civilization (al hadara al islamiya). Osama bin Laden is nothing less than a Beast of the Anti-Christ (the masiah al dajal) and his terrorism against America is hirabah al shaitaniyyah, a satanic war that can only plunge all of humanity into centuries or millennia of barbarism. ... We must understand where he is coming from, but also where he is going. Our task is not merely to stop evil, which can't be done, but to promote good, which can overcome it, in sha'a Allah."

Currently, to add to this misunderstanding and mutual distrust we have:

1. Blame leveled at the entire religion — the problem is not just Muslim terrorists but an "evil" Islam. (TAM has a collection of alarming anti-Muslim quotes - many by "respectable" community and religious leaders);

"Responsibility" is a better word than "blame". We demand it, rightly, of those who carry out the atrocities; we should demand it also of ourselves and our rulers. The bombers, or rather those who control and influence them, are clear they are at war. President Bush seemed to agree when he declared a "war on terror". Is our role in this war a just one? Do we want to continue the war? If not, what will we do to stop it? Those are the questions we need to ask ourselves.

2. Demands for the Muslim community to apologize for every criminal action that is carried out by any individual who happens to be a Muslim (Many

Muslims are very frustrated by this demand for an apology for something that is not the fault of Islam). Almost daily, one Muslim leder or another is called on to engage in what amounts to calling into doubt the sanctity of Islam - falling just short of being asked to condemn their religion.

Terrorism and Islam's Exceptionalism

Modern forms of terrorism were introduced into the Middle East in the 1940s by Jewish groups in then British-occupied Palestine. It was the Irgun, the Stern gang, and the Hagana that began the practice of bombing "gathering places [and] crowded Arab areas [in an attempt to] terrorize the Arab community" (Smith, 1992: 19; 140). The Stern gang even attacked Jewish banks, resulting in "Jewish loss of life". The Irgun, as we know, "slaughtered about 250 men, women and children whose mutilated bodies were stuffed down wells" in the village of Dair Yassin. Even though many such terror tactics continued until fairly recent times, people in the U.S. did not put world Jewry on call by asking Jews to explain what Judaism has to say about killing innocent civilians. People may have denounced these terrorist groups-freedom fighters to many-but they did not call on all Jews to explain which Torah or Talmud the Jewish terrorists were reading, or ask the "real" Judaism to "stand up." Why, then, this assault on Muslims to explain what their "bible" - as that savant, Larry King, calls the Qur'an - teaches about violence? (He even badgered Hanan Ashrawi, assuming that because she's Palestinian, she's a Muslim, even though she's not.) The same people who say (like the anonymous author I quoted earlier does) that they don't give a "rat's —" about Islam nonetheless are shrieking for the "real" Islam to stand up! In an atmosphere where only Muslims are expected to keep protesting our humanity and to defend our religion, my politics dictated that I should not speak at all in any forum on Islam. But, my religion teaches the jihad of knowledge and, as a Muslim, this jihad is obligatory for me.

It is very unkind for Muslims to blame Christianity for the abominations of pagan secularists and their blind followers, especially because Muslims are victims of precisely the same sort of demonizing everywhere themselves. If Muslims want others to let them define Islam, they should let devout Christians define Christianity and devout Jews define the essence of Judaism. Confrontation through polemical denial of the other's right to self-identity is universally to be condemned as perhaps the worst possible affront to human dignity.

Verses taken out of context to "prove" that the Qur'an encourages terrorism or that the Muslim world is backwards because of the teachings of the Qur'an;

Imagine asking Christians or Jews to reconcile Christianity or Judaism in light of an out-of-context verse from the Bible, such as, "Now go and smite Amalek, and utterly destroy all that they have, and spare them not; but slay man and woman, infant and suckling, ox and sheep, camel and ass." (1 Samuel 15:3) Or this verse, "The people of Samaria must bear their guilt because they have rebelled against their God. They will fall by the sword; their little ones will be dashed to the ground, their pregnant women ripped open." (Hosea 13:16)... This is certainly not a fair or scientific way to understand neither the Bible nor the peaceful message of Christianity or Judaism. The Qur'an, like all other scriptures, cannot be understood except within its context. Taking a verse out of its theological or historical context can lead to misinterpretations, often the hallmark of extremists. Just as the Bible has been abused by fanatics to justify slavery and the holocaust, so have Muslim fanatics abused the Qur'an to further their murderous agenda.

The most recent of these blame Islam diatribes were by Thomas Friedman. On July 8, 2005 Thomas Friedman wrote "If it's A Muslim Problem, It Needs a Muslim Solution" in which he said "To this day - to this day - no major Muslim cleric or religious body has ever issued a fatwa condemning Osama bin Laden."

I use Friedman as an example throughout this paper simply because his writing so clearly exemplifies so many of the issues rose. His is the average? American point of view.

"The second false presupposition Mr. Friedman puts forward is that bin Ladenite jihadism is a Muslim problem that begs Muslim solutions. I wonder whether throughout the years that the IRA terrorized Britons in London any pundit ever called the predicament of the Irish a "Catholic problem with Catholic solutions." ... It is true that Islam, like any other religion, is understood in competing and at times contradictory ways. But each of these competing interpretations of Islam corresponds and reacts to particular situations in which Muslims find themselves. One cannot understand violent interpretations of jihad outside the violence to which Muslim majority nations have been subjected. In other words, Islam is not innately predisposed to violence; it does not breed savagery ex nihilo, thus the fallacy of terrorism as a "Muslim problem." Somehow it is easier for many western pundits to understand that rather than a "Catholic problem," violence in Northern Ireland had much to do with British Empire."

Muslims have spoken up just as loudly against terrorism as any other group. Hundreds of clerics and theologians have condemned al Qaeda's and Osama bin Laden's violence. There have been fatwas issued on every aspect of violence and terrorism and even fatwas to clarify who is qualified to issue a fatwa.

"Fatwa has entered the media's vocabulary. Fatwa, like other borrowed Arabic terms, (e.g., intifada, jihad, madrasa, sharia) carries an assumed meaning, is draped in mystery, and leads to misunderstanding. Linguistically, fatwa means "an answer to a question" ? the question may be rhetorical or actual. The answer represents only the opinion of the person who offered it. In Islamic jurisprudence, fatwa means the opinion of a scholar based on that scholar's understanding and interpretation of the intent of the sources of Islam, that scholar's knowledge of the subject in question, and the social milieu that produced the issue or question. The scholar's answer or fatwa is not a binding rule; rather, it is a recommendation. The answer (fatwa) may be opposed, criticized, accepted, or rejected. In addition, the answer (fatwa) may itself become the subject of debate or questions. ... In an egalitarian system such as Islam, a fatwa gains acceptance based on the integrity of the person who offered the fatwa (in Arabic, a mufti), that person's knowledge of Islamic sources as well as knowledge of the issue and of the social context that raised the issue. Any of the aforementioned prerequisites may be challenged and the answer (fatwa) is an opinion and that opinion may be incorrect. To consider a fatwa issued by anyone as binding on all Muslims is a dangerous contemporary trend that merely stifles Islam's rich history of debate and dissent. Moreover, it would allow individuals to claim authority over others by virtue of their supposed knowledge of God's will. The purpose of a fatwa is to offer an opinion, not to silence discourse."

TAM has a lengthy collection of references under the heading Muslim Voices against Terrorism. The fatwa recently issued by the Fiqh Council of North America (which was insulted as coming late) was simply the latest in a long list of such *fatwas*. Perhaps if we continue to issue such *fatwas* and statements enough times they will finally be heard even by the deafest of those who continue to deny that such statements have been made.

"Whether we are American, Nigerian, Indonesian, or British, we look like them, we dress like them, we speak like them, and we pray like them. We cannot identify them before they strike. They hate us because we reject their ideology. They would kill us as "infidels." We are Muslims. So are they. But they are terrorists and we are not. That is the distinction. This is where we must make our stand. ... As troubling as it is for Muslims to be identified as potential terrorists, the truth is that the terrorists conducting such barbaric acts in today's society are Muslims. That is not to say that they are the only or the biggest terrorists, but they are the most mindless, unpredictable, and deliberately merciless. Driven by motives or grievances that they may legitimately share with countless other Muslims, they have devised their own demonic modus operandi that almost all others abhor and are repulsed by. In an open society they bear no distinctive traits. ... While the recent terror acts have been committed by Muslims, there is nothing "Islamic" about them. They are totally antithetical to the fundamental principles of Islam and represent a heretical deviation of the religion. When the 9/11 Commission went out of its way to define terrorism as not just any generic terrorism, but specifically as "Islamist," this pejorative label, despite the banal niceties of "Islam being a religion of peace," sent a chilling message to Muslims worldwide that terrorism is a hallmark or prerogative of Islam, or that when committed by other groups it is in some way mitigated by intrinsic extenuating circumstances. The leap from deviant Muslims perpetrating atrocities to a religion being impugned for the sins of its supposed adherents is breath-taking in its audacity. This distinction has become critical ever since the "showdown with Saddam" transmuted into the "war on terror." With the daily mind-numbing imagery of maniacal Muslim "insurgents" savaging troops and civilians alike, a transformation rapidly took place, The problem was just not Muslim terrorists but an "evil" Islam itself. This is a theme broadcast with malevolent glee by talk shows on a daily basis thereby intensifying suspicion, fear, contempt, and hatred of Islam. Demonizing Islam makes it the enemy in the "war on terror." ... Ironically, it is us Muslims who have the greatest vested interest in eradicating terrorism. We need to do this to salvage our religion and our self-respect. As long as we are marginalized by the West and taunted by the extremists, we are made to feel as if we were part of the problem rather than of the solution, and our commitment becomes ambivalent. If the so-called war on terrorism has any chance of being won, there needs to be an immediate redefinition of the enemy."

To say that recent terrorist acts are specifically a Muslim problem is to remove them from the historical context.

"The terrorist acts of a few Muslims are terrible tragedies, but do they have a history behind them? Is there a history of Western provocations in the Muslim world? Does the Western world at any point enter the historical chain of causation that now drives a few sane Muslims to acts of terrorism? The only history that Friedman will acknowledge is one of Western innocence. There is no blowback, hence, no Western responsibility, no Western guilt. ... Mr. Friedman speaks on this authoritatively and with clarity. The Muslim world has produced a "jihadist death cult in its midst." "If it does not fight that death cult, that cancer, within its own body politic, it is going to infect Muslim-Western relations everywhere." His two-fold verdict is clear. Inexplicably, the Muslims have produced a death cult, a religious frenzy that is driving those infected by it to kill innocent Westerners without provocation. Equally bad, the Muslims have done nothing to condemn, to root out this death cult they have spawned. ... There is not even a hint of history in these words. The historical amnesia is truly astounding. Does Mr. Friedman know any history? Of course, he does; but the history he knows is better forgotten if he is to succeed in demonizing the Muslim world. The oppressors choose to forget the history of their depredations, or substitute a civilizing mission for their history of brutalities, bombings, massacres, ethnic cleansings and expropriations. It is the oppressed peoples who know the history of their oppression, they know it because they have endured it. Its history is seared into their memory, their individual and collective memory. Indeed, they can liberate themselves only by memorializing this history."

"Two weeks ago, we saw how a group of young Muslims swallowed the bait of fiery rhetoric riddled with out-of-context verses spun in order to serve a nihilistic ideology of anger and despair offered to them disguised as Islam. Within a short period of time, these young men fell prey to the hate-filled dogma and were transformed into beings capable of blowing themselves up, taking with them innocent lives whom God has also blown in them from his spirit and "conferred dignity on the children of Adam" (Quran 7:70) which cuts through barriers of race, gender and creed...As they commit the crime against themselves and others, they drag with them the reputation and image of the religion they claim to venerate. They not only violate its basic teachings, but disfigure the message of "mercy to the worlds" into a justification for cruel, cowardly and repulsive behaviour. In this way, hearts that were supposed to be opened to the word of God got closed and minds that were hoped to have been opened to the light of guidance are shut."

To remove the discussion of terrorism from the historical context makes it easy to turn this in to us and them struggle that has no other solution but violence.

The triumph of the West, or the resurgence of an Islam interpreted by bestselling Pentecostal authors as a chastisement and a demonic challenge, signals the end of a growing worry about the religious meaninglessness of late modernity. Tragically, however, neither protagonist seems validly linked to the remnants of established religion, or shows any sign of awareness of how to connect with history. Fundamentalist disjuncture is placing us in a kind of metahistorical parenthesis, an end-time excitement in which, as for St Paul, old rules are irrelevant, and Christ and Antichrist are the only significant gladiators on the stage. Fundamentalists, as well as mystics, can insist that the moment is all that is real. ... In such a world of pseudo-religious reaction against the postmodern erosion of identity, it follows that if you are not with us you are with the devil. Or, when this has to be reformulated for the benefit of the blue-collar godless, you are a cheese-eating surrender monkey. Where religion exists to supply an identity, the world is Augustinian, if not quite Manichean. The West's ancient trope of itself as a free space, perhaps a white space, holding out against Persian or Semitic intruders, is being coupled powerfully, but hardly for the first time, with Pauline and patristic understandings of the New Israel as unique vessel of truth and salvation, threatened in the discharge of its redemptive project by the Oriental, Semitic, Ishmaelitic other. In the West, at least, the religious resources for this dualism are abundant and easily abused.

"No doubt, Muslims are facing a deep spiritual crisis. Islam has been hijacked and turned into an ideology in pursuit of worldly success instead of a religion meant to purify the soul and focus one's life on Almighty God. ... I don't deny that there are "Muslim terrorists" out there. Rather, like many people, I'm rather cynical about the conduct of what so far has been a rather selective war on terrorism. Indeed, a blind-eye is being turned to other great atrocities in the world and problems that cost far more human lives are being ignored. In the hands of ideologues who seemingly believe that military force can solve many of the world's complex problems, the "War on Terror" has been expanded to include not only countries that are seemingly uninvolved, but carried out in gross violation of the very international laws that the terrorists are guilty of violating. Unfortunately, we live in an age where well-intentioned criticism is often considered un-patriotic especially when coming from a Muslim. Being a good citizenship these days seems to mean shutting up and climbing on the bandwagon. Critical thinking and moral courage seem to be in short supply. Finding a semblance of them is as tough as finding an honest man in Congress.

We only hope that our attempts to understand the motives for a crime are never understood to be endorsements of it. In order to develop reasonable, coherent and viable solutions to the plague of ignorance and extremism that we're facing, we need to study the sources, context and motives behind the crimes. Simple solutions are bogus solutions, and most of the tough problems facing the human race can't be solved by using military force. ... As a God-fearing and morally upright community, we've got to join together and bring our resources to bear in order to refute with a vengeance these extremist "Protestant Muslims" and their flaky "Do-It-Yourself" religion that has cast aside over 1,400 years of peerless scholarly tradition. In this undertaking, it's crucial that we stay balanced, moderate and true to our blessed tradition. ...We need to explain the high moral standards of our faith; that it is a religion that primarily emphasizes not only the infinite mercy of God but encourages mercy between all human beings. Indeed, Islam condemns terrorism, murder, hijacking, kidnaping, and taking the law into your own hands and so on. None of this is compromised by the fact that we also have a "Just War" theory which is extremely similar to the ones advocated not only by various churches, but by international law as well. Our beloved Prophet was sent as a mercy to the worlds (Qur'an 21:107), so we have to save Islam from the reckless few that have made a large part of humanity feel that it's a scourge rather than a blessing."

We are in the midst of wars between the different families of Abraham, Jews, Christians, and Muslims. ? Some of the family members actually define these wars as religiously required. ... Even worse, there are groups within the Muslim, Christian, and Jewish communities that are trying to incite and create an all-out war between Islam and "the West." Such a war would bring misery upon the peoples of all nations.

Spiritual Jihad against Terrorism

Put simply, there are three possible views of war that a religion might adopt. The pacifist view, all violence and killing is wrong. Belief in 'a Just War', some wars, at least, are right because they are perceived to be in the interests of justice - and should therefore be fought according to just rules. Belief in 'Holy War', the God of a religion is perceived to ask, or command, its followers to make war on those who do not believe in that religion and who pose a threat to those who do.

Like many other religious terms jihad, often mistranslated as "holy war", is a deeply nuanced concept that has been relined and relined many times throughout more than fourteen centuries of Islamic history. As Bruce Lawrence, a noted American Islamicist, recently pointed out, jihad historically has had as much to do with political ideology as with religion proper, since "all proponents of jihad, whether writers or actors, intellectuals or politicians, are ideologues. ... Despite this rather obvious but often overlooked fact (which is equally true when applied to the concept of "holy war" in Christianity), it should not be forgotten that within Islam the relationship between religion and ideology is inherently reciprocal; consequently, any ideologue who calls for jihad must come up with sound scriptural and legal justification for doing so. The resulting medley of religious, political, and moral discourses in numerous parts of the world and over many centuries has made jihad into an extremely complex concept ? so much so, in fact, that a completely thorough discussion of the term can only be conducted on a case-by-case basis.

What limits does the just war doctrine impose?

"The moral issue here is not merely whether suicide bombing can be justified, because only those who have lost even the rudiments of civilized values can possibly think that it is. A larger issue is whether the terrorist's actions can be categorized as war. If

> so, what limits does the just war doctrine impose as recognized universally by the classical scholars in all the worlds religious traditions. ... The larger challenge to global civilization in the twenty-first century is how does one manage conflict with hate-filled extremists who are immune to all tactics of conflict resolution? Can such extremists be marginalized by marshaling spiritual and intellectual powers against which they have no defenses? If so, is there a grand strategy to do so?"

The attempt to discuss the just war concept (as well as the concept of jihad) has never been more important.

> "These are difficult times in relations between the West and the Islamic world. Wars and rumors of war abound, and terrorism (although rarely its context) dominates the headlines. A shooting war continues between the United States and al Qaeda in Afghanistan, and war evidently impends between the United States and the United Kingdom on the one hand and Iraq on the other. Fundamentalisms—Muslim, Jewish, and Christian— metastasize. Atop all else, violence reigns unchecked in Israel and the Occupied Territories, and makes effective responses to assorted other challenges enormously more difficult. With polarities unprecedented in modern times between the West and the Islamic world, and seething anger among Muslims worldwide against the United States, it is difficult indeed to discuss objectively concepts with such emotive resonance as terrorism and Jihad. But the attempt to do so has never been more important. ... It is unfortunate that in the West a putative validation of terrorism has come to be understood as incarnated in the Arabic word Jihad. And in the Islamic world, far too many today understand Jihad as justifying, indeed demanding, the taking of the lives of

innocent civilians in countries or cultures against which Arabs and Muslims may have very real and painful grievances. Misperceptions, and rampant ignorance, reign almost everywhere. Especially in the United States and the Arab world, there is today an enormous need for an intellectual and spiritual Jihad, or effort, to readdress soberly the whole issue of terrorism, and the significance of the concept of Jihad over the entire span of Islamic history."

The Tao Te Ching, the ancient Chinese manual on the art of living, reads, "Weapons are the tools of fear... a decent person will avoid them except in the direst necessity and, if compelled, will use them only with the utmost restraint ....Our enemies are not demons but human beings like us. The decent person doesn't wish them personal harm. Nor do they rejoice in victory. How could we rejoice in victory and delight in the slaughter of people? Enter a battle gravely, with sorrow and with great compassion, as if attending a funeral." (c. 550 B.C.E.)

The Just war theory that has found its way into International law is based on the Christian teaching of just war first promulgated by the Catholic Church. Here is the Catholic Just War Doctrine:

Just War (2307-17) "All citizens and all governments are obliged to work for the avoidance of war. Despite this admonition of the Church, it sometimes becomes necessary to use force to obtain the end of justice. This is the right, and the duty, of those who have responsibilities for others, such as civil leaders and police forces. While individuals may renounce all violence those who must preserve justice may not do so, though it should be the last resort, "once all peace efforts have failed." [Cf. Vatican II, Gaudium et spes 79, 4]

As with all moral acts the use of force to obtain justice must comply with three conditions to be morally good. First, the act must be good in itself. The use of force to obtain justice is morally licit in itself. Second, it must be done with a good intention, which as noted earlier must be to correct vice, to restore justice or to restrain evil, and not to inflict evil for its own sake. Thirdly, it must be appropriate in the circumstances. An act which may otherwise be good and well motivated can be sinful by reason of imprudent judgment and execution.

In this regard Just War doctrine gives certain conditions for the legitimate exercise of force, all of which must be met:

"1. The damage inflicted by the aggressor on the nation or community of nations must be lasting, grave, and certain; 2. All other means of putting an end to it must have been shown to be impractical or ineffective; 3. There must be serious prospects of success; 4. The use of arms must not produce evils and disorders graver than the evil to be eliminated. The power of modern means of destruction weighs very heavily in evaluating this condition".

The responsibility for determining whether these conditions are met belongs to "the prudential judgment of those who have responsibility for the common good." The Church's role consists in enunciating clearly the principles, in forming the consciences of men and in insisting on the moral exercise of just war.

The Church greatly respects those who have dedicated their lives to the defense of their nation. "If they carry out their duty honorably, they truly contribute to the common good of the nation and the maintenance of peace. [Cf. Gaudium et spes 79, 5]" However, she cautions combatants that not everything is licit in war. Actions which are forbidden, and which constitute morally unlawful orders that may not be followed, include:

Attacks against, and mistreatment of, non-combatants, wounded soldiers, and prisoners; - genocide, whether of a people, nation or ethnic minorities; - indiscriminate destruction of whole cities or vast areas with their inhabitants.

Given the modern means of warfare, especially nuclear, biological and chemical, these crimes against humanity must be especially guarded against.

In the end it is not enough to wage war to achieve justice without treating the underlying causes. "Injustice, excessive economic or social inequalities, envy, distrust, and pride raging among men and nations constantly threaten peace and cause wars. Everything done to overcome these disorders contributes to building up peace and avoiding war". The Church has no illusions that true justice and peace can be attained before the Coming of the Lord. It is the duty of men of good will to work towards it, nonetheless. In the words of the spiritual dictum, we should work as if everything depended upon our efforts, and pray as if everything depended upon God.

Islamic Views of Just War

Some of the Qur'anic verses which lay out the purpose and nature of war include the following:

To stop oppression, "To those against whom war is made, permission is given to fight, because they are oppressed. Verily, God is Capable of aiding them. They are those who have been expelled from their homes in defiance of what is just, for no other reason than that they say, "Our Lord is God." Had God not restrained one set of people by means of another, monasteries, churches, synagogues, temples and mosques wherein God's name if oft-mentioned would have been destroyed. God will certainly aid those who aid His cause. (Qur'an, Chapter 22:39-40). Notice the mention of all houses of worship.

In self-defense, "Fight in the cause of God against those who fight you, but do not transgress limits by aggressing; surely God does not love transgressors." (Qur'an, Chapter 2:190.) Notice that permission is given to fight in self-defense, but not to transgress.

Peace is a desired state, "If they incline toward peace, then seek you peace also. And place your trust in God, for God hears and knows all things." (Qur'an, Chapter 8:61).

In the Hadith, the Prophet Muhammad is quoted as saying: "Do not kill women or children or non-combatants and do not kill old people or religious people (he also mentioned priests, nuns and rabbis). Do not cut down fruit-bearing trees and do not poison the wells of your enemies." ... The Prophet also said, "Whoever unjustly harms a Christian or a Jew will not even smell the scent of paradise."

Muslim extremists get their textual interpretations by taking verses in the Qur'an out of their social-historical context, not considering the time, place, and specific circumstances in which these verses were revealed. The commonly quoted verse that follows must be understood in its proper context, namely during the struggle of the early Muslims against the specific group of Makkans who fought, persecuted and killed them first in Makkah, and then after they established a state in Medina, where early Muslims fought back for the first time. These verses can neither be used to justify killing non-Muslims, nor targeting innocent civilians.

"Fight and slay the pagans wherever you find them, and seize them and beleaguer them and lie in wait for them in every stratagem of war. But if they repent, and establish regular prayers, and practice regular charity, then open the way for them, for God is Oft-forgiving, Most Merciful. If any among them asks for asylum, grant it to him so that he may hear the word of God. Then escort him to his place of security. This is because they are without knowledge."

Jewish Views of Just War

"They shall beat their swords into ploughshares and their spears into pruning hooks, nation shall not lift up sword against nation, neither shall they learn war any more." (The Old Testament: Isaiah 2:4)

Peace is the central teaching of rabbinical Judaism (teachings based on the writings of early Jewish scholars). However, Judaism is not a pacifist religion. The idea of Holy War occurs in the Hebrew Bible, but it was not about making others Jewish, but about survival. ... The idea of 'Just War' is clearly expressed both in the Old Testament and in the later rabbinical tradition. So while revenge and unprovoked aggression are condemned, self defence is justified. Jews have been victims of dreadful persecution, usually at the hands of Christians, for nearly two thousand years, culminating in the Holocaust during the Second World War (1939-1945). On the other hand, defending modern Israel and dealing justly with the Palestinians places thoughtful Jews in difficult dilemmas.

I'm trying to organize support for a constitutional amendment to deny voting rights to Christians. I feel if your citizenship is in the Bible? Like a Christian? Is? You should give up your citizenship. [Garrison Keillor]

This is our land. This is our world. This is our heritage, and with God's help, we shall claim this nation for Islam. And no power on earth can stop us. [D. James Kennedy]

As an American Muslim who read these quotes in their original version, I can tell you how it feels, it hurts! And, it raises fear, especially when so many of the people making such statements are government officials and well known religious and media figures.

Extremists on both sides would like to see a clash of religiously defined civilizations. And the more extremists define conflict in those terms, the more it will turn out to become a true clash of civilizations. There is thus a real danger of this being a self-fulfilling prophecy, a danger that the rest of us must fight against.

Is there such a thing as Christian terrorism, Jewish terrorism, Islamic terrorism, Hindu terrorism, Buddhist terrorism, etc.? What is Christian, Jewish, Muslim, Hindu or Buddhist terrorism? What could distinguish this from any criminal act committed by an individual or group of individuals who happen to be members (no matter how nominally) of any particular religious community? How can we stop terrorism?

What elements need to be present in order for a particular act of terrorism to be defined as Christian terrorism, Jewish Terrorism, or Muslim terrorism? Is it enough that, the individual or group is a member of a particular religious group; the individual or group claims the act in the name of their religion; the individual or group defines themselves in their name as belonging to a particular religion; does the individual need to be a practicing member of the religious group?

Is there within the Abrahamic faiths a context in which the politically alienated can be radicalised? Are there fanatics because of some legitimate interpretation of religion or are they fanatics in spite of their religion?

When an interviewer for the Britain-based Independent asked celebrity journalist Christopher Hitchens what he considered the real axis of evil, he replied

"Christianity, Judaism and Islam, the three leading monotheisms."

The question arises in Western civilization, including Islam, what happens when one abolishes belief in the transcendent, whether de jure as in post-modern thought, or only de facto in the politicalsation of Islam as a cover for alienated individuals to express their hatred through nihilistic violence. In Western culture one is left with belief that utopia on earth can come now. It will not come at the behest of God but through the free will of man embodied in a leader who claims to know the laws of history or promises to create them through his own unlimited power. The purpose of man in the new secular dispensation is to conquer the world through man's rational intellect in order to bring forth heaven on earth. ... This is the ultimate polytheism, because it amounts to the worship not only of oneself but of the human species as God.

Possibly when we mix religion and political power (church and state) we are in danger of losing the spiritual dimension.

Despite our secularism, the United States has rarely been so publicly and politically "Christian" as it is today. Or perhaps it is because of our secularism. We can no longer tell good theology from bad. We, mainline denominations, need to take our share of the blame, For decades we took it for granted that Christianity and citizenship were inextricably linked, that American power was the natural outgrowth of American righteousness. For too long we, too, preached American triumphalism. We did not remind people of the overarching guidance God gives all people in search of redemption, the necessity of the examined life. Ironically, our triumphalism may have fueled America's secularism. With God on our side, there didn't seem to be much need for self-examination and humility. ... It is clear now that a sectarian Christian view of history, a dualism that views war as a kind of redemptive purgative, is having at least some influence on the administration's rhetoric. It is characterized by a stark refusal to acknowledge accountability, because to suggest accountability is to question American purity, which would undermine the secular theology of "good versus evil" inherent in present U.S. policy. ... The dominance of the religious right in political affairs makes it appear that a Christian worldview dominates American politics. But if, as I believe, this worldview is really American triumphalism, Christianity has taken a backseat to joyous secularism. Within Christianity and Judaism in this country, there are denominations and branches with the philosophical and institutional power and authority to challenge that triumphalism, but bold stands such as the NCC's are still the exception. ... With the political emergence of joyous secularism, the churches are challenged to preach an alternative message, grace, hope and redemption—the truth of Biblical faith. This is both our pastoral and our political responsibility. In a nuclear age, American triumphalism is not only spiritually bereft; it is, quite possibly, apocalyptic in its implications.

No matter what supposed religious justification anyone attempts to put forward for violence - it is a lie!

"We condemn the abuse of religion by fanatics whose sole purpose is to rouse hate and beget further violence. Nothing is as antithetical to all religion and especially to Islam, as the wanton violence. ... We cry out against such violence, and seek to console those who have suffered from it. ... We declare that all religions have the same relative value with respect to the high goals we seek to reach as humans, and the same lack of value of when they fail to call forth the unity of God. ... We pray for a future that is replete with peace and love for all of humanity across the world and for a future that is far, far different from the tumultuous, hateful times that we live in now..." Imam Feisal Abdul Rauf.

10

Source of Terrorism and Violence

Since Cain, the son of Adam, killed his brother, Abel, human beings have struggled to understand evil. If God created humans in His likeness, why do we see so much evil in the world? Through the Qur'an, Allah has made clear three principal reasons, and the third is the greatest of them all. First, individual persons are evil because they have the free will to do and be whatever they want. Otherwise they could not choose well, in awareness that this is the Will of Allah. Also there would be no merit in doing well if they could not choose it's opposite. But why does God permit people to choose evil? Why did he permit fanatics on September 11th to kill thousands of innocent people in cold blood, and to do it in the name of Islam? The second explanation revealed in the Qur'an for the existence of evil is that we are here to be tested. Allah tells us, I will test you by means of each other, that is, the greatest tests will be by other human beings. During Ramadhan, which in sha'a Allah starts this evening, we are to strengthen ourselves so that we can withstand these tests, and so that we can help ourselves and others to be better people. And there is a third, still greater reason for what we perceive as evil. This can be understood perhaps best by the analogy of the ant slowly creeping across the beautiful Persian carpet. The carpet is decorated with elaborate designs and symbols of Allah's attributes, a beautiful work of art. But, the ant knows nothing about all this. The vision of the carpet's creator is beyond the ant's comprehension.

There are many claims to understanding this terrible phenomena - and they may all contain a seed of truth, but the 'truth' is far more complex than any single explanation. We need to search impartially and understand the underlying causes before we can begin to find a solution. There are two primary schools of thought. One school links terror directly to the war on Iraq, another believes that terror groups are ideologically, rather than politically motivated, thus reinforcing the "clash of civilizations" argument.

"Not only do these arguments fail to candidly inspect a variety of other factors that might have contributed to the spread of terrorism, but they imprudently encourage measures that will most probably give terrorists more fuel to carry on with their mission of violence, cajoling additional recruits and resources."

A recent study by Robert Pape dismissed many of the commonly held illusions about terrorism.

"While Friedman may be concerned with "shutting people up", he's much less concerned with the real origins of terror. His own paper the New York Times ran a very scholarly article just 3 weeks ago by Robert Pape, "Al Qaeda's Smart Bombs" (7-9-05) that dismissed many of the commonly held illusions about terrorism. Pape, who documented every case of suicide bombing between 1980 and 2004, says that the "core motivating factor behind suicide terrorism" is "a nationalistic response to occupation"; "The root cause of terrorism is occupation, not Islam." ... Wow. ... Pape's "fact-based" analysis directly challenges Friedman's "hate-mongering" theory of terror. The distinction between the two hypotheses is colossal. If Friedman is correct than the West is justified in invading

Muslim countries to rid them of, what Tony Blair called, "an evil ideology whose roots lie in a perverted and poisonous misinterpretation of Islam". This is the rationale that supports the US occupation of Iraq; presenting the conflict as "the central battlefield in the war on terror". ... However, if Pape's analysis is right then the real catalyst for terrorism is the American occupation itself; a permanent recruiting sergeant for Muslim extremists and jihadis. If that is the case, the only reasonable solution would be a quick transfer of power and a complete withdrawal of American forces. ... This is not a debate that Friedman or his colleagues in the corporate establishment can afford to lose. Pape threatens to derail the Iraqi master plan by simply presenting the facts of his investigation and changing the hearts and minds of the American public. That explains why every media bullhorn is feverishly broadcasting some variant of Friedman's "hate mongering" theory; trying to keep alive the fading belief that America is fighting "Islamo-fascism" in an apocalyptic battle between good and evil. It is a storyline that grows more threadbare by the day."

We are all held captive by a fanatical, criminal minority.

"There are several reasons for the continuation of violence. The first and foremost reason is the notion promoted by a tiny minority that claims to speak in the name of religion that justice is secured through the barrel of a gun. This minority tends to justify its actions by using religious scriptures and interpreting them to suit its interests. ... The second reason is the inability of activists to control their anger in adverse situations. When they read or see an anti-Islamic incident, the first response that comes to the mind of these angry people is to resort to violence against those responsible for the action. They are also often provoked by leaders who use others to settle their scores with the power elites. ... The third reason is the manipulation of innocent individuals in the name of religion by those who are working for various intelligence and spying agencies. Such groups have already established religious groups with their own religious leaders to recruit young Muslims to carry on attacks in the name of religion. Their main purpose is to create chaos and turmoil and destabilize societies. ... The fourth reason is the prevalence of extreme inequalities where the powerless find themselves chained in the bonds of poverty and inequality almost on a daily a basis. For such people, life has lost any meaning. They find no hope to overcome their own sufferings; hence they lose confidence in their ability to change their conditions unless those whom they perceive responsible for their plight are avenged. ... The fifth reason is the presence of large scale mercenaries who are willing to kill anyone if the price is right. They come from all ethnic and religious groups and make a living from taking others' lives to sustain themselves. ... The most effective voice to control violence is the voice of forgiveness. It is a voice that can make a definite change in the lives of people if it is raised from the pulpits of religious institutions. The religious leadership must raise this voice if it truly wants to serve God. "

The real cause, the real taproot of terrorism is the bankruptcy of materialist ideologies which may pay lip service to religion but are devoid of spirituality.

The real causes of terrorism are not poverty and oppression per se, but rather the bankruptcy of materialist ideologies, like Neo-Conservatism, which promise much but deliver little. ... They fail to comprehend the need for a paradigm of justice and therefore are blind to what concerns most of the people in the world. This failure is the taproot of terrorism. ... Terrorism has arisen as the new threat to civilization because the terrorists know that all the dominant paradigms of the twentieth century are bankrupt. In their hopeless rage they will not consider even the possibility of anything else, other than their own blind rampage of destruction. What they do not know is that they are creatures of this bankruptcy. They are part of the problem, not of the solution. Terrorists are products of Western cultural disintegration, even though they will die for the illusion that they are not.

Religion is a powerful tool. Correctly used, it has led to the vision of God. But when usurped by violent men, religion has proven extremely effective in rousing the masses to violence and aggression. For those souls who have sought and found union in the vision of God, religions are but a diversity of creeds and practices that are merely ways to the One Goal, the vision of God. We who have grasped this truth recognize that everything is a veil hiding the Essential, and therefore seek to peel away those veils that hide the knowledge of the sole true Reality. We recognize that all religions have the same relative value with respect to the high goal to be reached, and the same lack of value if they fail to call forth the love of God. This alone is the uniform standard of value in the assessment of religions. Our voices, raised together to proclaim the recognition of the unity of God, serve to bring mankind together, while those voices that focus on the differences of our laws cause division and loss. The great 13th century mystic poet Jalal ud-Din Rumi (1207-1273) expressed this when he wrote in one of his poems, the lovers of ritual are one group, and those whose hearts and souls are aglow with love of God are another.

Sadly, one of the things we have in common is that the Abrahamic religions (as well as other religions) have the capability of producing extremists of the most brutal kind - terrorists. Christianity, Judaism, Islam, and other faiths have all been used as a justification for violence and terrorist acts.

It is possible to use verses amputated, distorted, perverted, or misrepresented from religious texts (the Torah, New Testament, Qur'an) to justify terrorism and individuals and groups have done this throughout history. There are verses in all of these texts that can be easily abused either through purposeful or malicious manipulation of meaning or through ignorance of even the fundamentals of scriptural analysis.

There have been many crimes committed and millions of people killed by individuals, groups and governments in the name of one religion or another - justifying their actions by some perversion of the revealed texts. The victims come from every race, ethnicity, and religious group. At the current moment, although many of the perpetrators are Muslims, the primary victims are also Muslims. All of us are targets.

And worse, this could not have happened or continue to happen if most of us were not complicit in our silence. There is self righteousness on both sides - Osama bin Laden exploits powerless people to fight for him by making them believe they are morally superior people - and governments exploit their citizens to fight by making them believe that they are morally superior.

Mainstream Muslims, Christians and Jews regularly condemn terrorism and consider such acts to be an egregious violation of their religious beliefs. And, yet the violence continues to escalate and spread. We have to live together. If we are to survive we must find ways to live together in peace. There are no more options left except the option of peace. Peace between man and nature and between men and other men. Let us focus on what we have in common. Let us take the first step of getting to know one another.

The Qur'an gives us a mandate to do just this.

Unto every one of you have we appointed a different law and way of life? And if God had so willed, He could surely have made you all one single community: but He willed it otherwise in order to test you by means of what He has revealed to you. Compete then with one another in doing good works! Unto God you all must return and then

He will make you truly understand all that on which you were wont to differ.

True piety (or righteousness) does not consist in turning your faces towards the east or west but truly pious is he who believes in God and the last day and the angels and revelation, and the prophets; and spends his substance upon his near of kin, and the orphans, and the needy, and the wayfarer, and the beggar, and for the freeing of human beings from bondage; and is constant in prayer, and renders the purifying dues; and truly pious are they who keep their promises whenever they promise, and are patient in misfortune and hardship and in time of peril, it is they that have proved themselves true, and it is they, they who are conscious of God. 2: 177.

The Qur'an is appealing to us, both Muslims and non Muslims to acknowledge that we do have different religious practices, but not to allow those differences to stop us from doing what needs to be done, and in fact to compete in doing good deeds. And, the Qur'an is telling us clearly that what is essential to our faith is simply how we treat one another. We need to take this advice to heart. To realize that we are brothers and sisters we are in this together. Hopefully, through coming to know each other we will be able to discover our similarities and to find ways of resolving our differences and solving our problems.

Diana Eck of Harvard has asserted,

One world cannot be built on the foundation of competition and polarization between the superpowers. One world cannot be built on the foundation of science, technology and the media. One world cannot be built on Christian, Muslim, Jewish or Sikh triumphalism. One world cannot be built on the foundation of mutual fear and suspicion. Laying the foundations for one world is the most important task of our time. These foundations are not negotiated statements and agreements. These foundations are, rather, in the stockpiling of trust through dialogue and the creation of relationships that can sustain both agreements and disagreements. Moving forward in dialogue with those other faiths we will create the foundational relationship of One World. Moving forward alone, we will not.

There is a struggle going on within all the religious groups, not only for the soul of Christianity, Judaism and Islam, but beyond that, all of us together for the soul of humanity. Some individuals have experienced a profound spiritual event and named it "the dark night of the soul". Civilizations have experienced the same phenomena. For example, Western Civilization went through such a period and named it "the Dark Ages". Today, humanity is experiencing a dark night of its collective soul, a historical event as yet unnamed, which could lead us further into darkness, or provides an opportunity to do good works and be a source of light in the darkness. More than ever before in history it is becoming clear that all the races, all the species, all the nations, all the religions, are in this together.

All of us are at a crossroads. All of us are living in an epidemic of violence for which we must find a solution. We have had a lot of experience with violence. We are surrounded by it now and have been surrounded by it through our history. And yet we still don't always recognize its many faces and we don't seem to know what to do about it. We still haven't learned how to settle differences peaceably between friends, between family members, between nations, between races or between religions.

The imperative need for a more inclusive, universal, values based approach to religion is underscored by the increasing influence of the exclusive, sectarian, ritual oriented interpretation of religion in the contemporary world. This is one of the most formidable challenges confronting almost every religion. In Hinduism for instance the narrow Hindutva ideologues with their chauvinistic articulation of the religion are seeking to repudiate the inherent universalism of the Vedas and the Bhagavad Gita. In Buddhism, a small segment of the clergy is now attempting to present the religion in dogmatic terms thus betraying the all-embracing enlightenment of its founder. Within the Jewish community there are Rabbis who have adopted a bellicose stance towards the 'infidels' without any regard for some of the universal notions of justice contained in Judaism. Some Christian evangelists today are trapped in a distorted, perverted understanding of the religion which negates Jesus' central message of love and mercy for the whole of humanity. Likewise, among Muslims, as we have seen, there are bigoted elements who are trying to hijack a religion whose very name is linked to peace and which describes God as 'The Compassionate and The Merciful' in every Chapter of the Quran. ... It is only too apparent that there is a struggle of singular significance unfolding within each and every religion. It is a struggle that has serious implications for inter-religious encounters. For those who subscribe to an exclusive view of religion have very little interest in communicating with the religious 'other' let alone establishing empathy with her. Those who espouse an inclusive approach to religion, on the other hand, are willing to transcend religious boundaries and embrace the whole of humanity—especially in their quest for universal justice and dignity." Hegemony and Civilizational Interaction, Chandra Muzaffar.

Our beliefs may be different, but our suffering is shared. The murderous acts of a few, whether Muslims or others, should not shake our eternal faith that we, as human beings or believers in God, can live in harmony.

The Cherokee tell a story about this being a battle between two wolves. One wolf is EVIL - it is anger, envy, jealousy, greed, arrogance, self-pity, guilt, resentment, inferiority, lies, false pride, superiority, and ego. One wolf is GOOD - it is joy, peace, love, hope, serenity, humility, kindness, benevolence, empathy, generosity, truth, compassion, and faith. The wolf that wins the battle is the wolf that you feed!!

I pray that we begin to feed the good wolf.

PRAYER OF ST. FRANCIS OF ASSISSI

"O Lord, make me an instrument of Thy Peace!

Where there is hatred, let me sow love;

Where there is injury, pardon;

Where there is discord, harmony;

Where there is doubt, faith;

Where there is despair, hope;

Where there is darkness, light, and

Where there is sorrow, joy.

Oh Divine Master, grant that I may not

so much seek to be consoled as to console;

to be understood as to understand; to be loved

as to love; for it is in giving that we receive;

It is in pardoning that we are pardoned;

and it is in dying that we are born to Eternal Life."

"There was a time when I took it amiss in my companion if his religion was not near to mine; But now my heart takes on every form; it is a pasture for gazelles, a monastery for monks, A temple of idols and a Ka`ba for pilgrims, the tables of the Torah and the holy book of the Qur'an. Love is my religion, and whichever way its riding beasts turn, that way lies my religion and belief." Muhyi'd-Din Ibn al`Arabi.

The common desire to prevent WWIII and bring peace to the world requires that we first come to a common understanding of religious terminology and beliefs, and of political and social terminology. Without this we are talking at each other, but not with each other. For example if I say we need a jihad against terror that will be heard differently by mainstream Muslims than it will be heard by Christians or Jews who will probably only hear the loaded term jihad which will trigger an emotional reaction, effectively blocking real communication.

Catholicism is a language. Judaism is a language. Islam is a language. They have to be respected. They bring something unique and important, but they have to meet in a way in which they can converse with each other as if there was a kind of a spiritual Esperanto. And I can speak to my peers and speak a common language, at the same time recognizing that the particular language has to be respected. So I have to overcome the either/or notion and speak in term of the both/and notion. Rabbi Harold Schulweis.

It would seem that we are allowing our personal loyalties to our religious, ethnic and national identities and prejudices to get in the way of fairness and justice. We are currently substituting profit for justice, occupation for liberty, exclusiveness for inclusiveness, sectarian for universal causes, self-existence for pro-existence, destruction for change, violence for dialogue, bullets for words, and ritual oriented for values based religion.

We need to regain our consciousness to be aware of our connection to each other to care about not only what happens to US but what happens to THEM. We need to recognize violence in all its forms. We recognize war and murder as violence. We need to recognize poverty, hunger, homelessness, racism, prejudice and all forms of intolerance, bigotry and injustice against any people anywhere as acts of violence which damage the human spirit, and to understand that we cannot have peace as long as these acts of violence continue.

As we try to find our way out of present circumstances to the next level (inshaa a-Llaah) of human development, we must not shirk our personal or community responsibility, our national or our moral and ethical foundation, our duty to look critically at the tracks in the sand before they disappear, to see from whence we came, and to look ahead to the horizon, towards where we are headed. Let us go forward with our hands extended in sisterhood and brotherhood to all as peacemakers, reconcilers, seekers after knowledge, and givers of hope. Other people may define us with their words; let us define ourselves with our actions and contributions. Allah (subhaanahu wa ta'aalaa) alone is the best Guide and the best Friend. Fundamentals and Fundamentalism, Shaykh Ahmed Abdur Rashid.

"For me, then the question, How to Stop Terrorism is easy. We stop terrorism first of all by stopping our own terrorism! We cannot fight terrorism by becoming terrorists. We cannot end terrorism by using the methods of terrorism to bomb and kill Iraqis, to occupy Iraq, to support the terrorist occupation of the Palestinians, and to hold the world hostage with our nuclear weapons. We must bring the troops home from Iraq, fund nonviolent democratic peacemakers in Iraq, send food and medicine to Iraq, and support United Nations? nonviolent peacemaking solutions, end world hunger immediately, cut all U.S. military aid everywhere, dismantle every one of our nuclear weapons, fund jobs, education and healthcare at home and abroad, clean up the environment and teach nonviolence to everyone around the world, beginning at home in every U.S. classroom. ... As I watch the TV news reporters and commentators, I am amazed at their lack of understanding. Half the world considers the United States the leading terrorist in the world, by our public spokespeople remain clueless about what's really going on. We are seen as terrorists by many around the world because we bombed and killed 100,000 people in Iraq in 2003, and because we have over

20,000 weapons of mass destruction, (many of them in my neighborhood in New Mexico), which we are willing to use on any nation that does not support U.S. interests. Our wars and bombing raids and hostility toward the world's poor are turning the world against us. We are breeding thousands of new terrorists, desperate poor people who have nothing, whose backs are up against the wall, and who have learned from our total violence to adopt the lunacy of violence, even suicidal violence, to strike back, blow up trains and buses, and spend their lives spreading fear. ... Violence in response to violence can only lead to further violence. Jesus taught us that as the soldiers were dragging him away to his death when he said, Those who live by the sword, will die by the sword. Gandhi taught us that when he said, an eye for an eye only makes the whole world blind. ... Violence cannot stop violence. We have to break the cycle of violence, renounce violence, start practicing creative active nonviolence on a level that the world has never seen, and reach out and embrace the world's poor by meeting their every need. Then, we will win over the world, and no one will ever want to hurt a Westerner again. On that new day, we will sow the seeds of love and peace and discover what a world without terrorism, war, poverty, and fear is like. ... I do not understand our love of violence. If you want other people to be nonviolent, you first have to be nonviolent. If you want to remove the speck from someone else's eye, you have to remove the two by four from your own head. If you want other nations to hold you in high regard, you first have to hold other nations in high regard, and treat every human being on the planet as a sister and brother. As someone once said, do unto others as you would have them do unto you. That is the answer to the nightmare of terrorism. How do we stop terrorism? Renounce every trace of violence in your heart and your life. Adopt the wisdom and practice of active nonviolence, as Gandhi and Dr. King taught. Beg the God of peace for the gift of peace. Join your local peace and justice group. Stand up publicly for an end to war. Let your life be disrupted, and take a new, nonviolent risk for disarmament. Create new cells of active nonviolence. Embrace the religious roots of nonviolence. Study and teach the wisdom of nonviolence. Resist your local military and government violence. Stop business as usual, government as usual, media as usual, war as usual and demand peace, justice, and disarmament for the whole world, now. Announce the vision of a new nonviolent world, a disarmed world, a world without war, poverty, injustice or nuclear weapons. Explain how such a world is possible if we give our lives for it, demand it, insist on it, work for it, and begin to live it." How to Stop Terrorism- Rev. John Dear.

In an age when, in the words of Frithjof Schuon, "the outward and readily exaggerated incompatibility of the different religions greatly discredits, in the minds of most of our contemporaries, all religion",93 a "call to God" which is based on universal inclusively rather than dogmatic exclusivity is much more likely to be heeded. The Quranic discourse explicitly refers to the fragility and illogicality of confessional or denominational exclusivity, and affirms truths of a universal nature, doing so, moreover, with an insistence and in a manner that is unparalleled among world scriptures. It is therefore uniquely situated, in intellectual terms, to assist in the resolution of the contemporary crisis precipitated by mutually exclusive religious claims. ... Wisdom is explicitly called for in the verse we have cited above; and wisdom, by definition, is not something that can be laid down in advance of all the concrete and unique situations in which wisdom needs to be applied, as if it were a formal rule or a blue-print. On the contrary, it is, on the one hand, a Divine bestowal, and on the other, a quality that can be developed and cultivated only through intellectual, moral, and spiritual effort. In the Quran, wisdom is described as a gift from God, "He giveth wisdom to whom He will; and he to whom wisdom is given hath been granted great good" (2:269). But it is also a quality which can be cultivated, acquired, or learned, and this is implied in the following verse, where the Prophet is described as one who teaches and imparts not just the formal message, but the wisdom required to understand and creatively apply that message, "He it is Who hath sent among the unlettered ones a Messenger of their own, to recite unto them His revelations and to make them grow [in purity], and to teach them the Scripture and wisdom" (62:2). ... One of the most important aspects of wisdom taught by the scripture of the Quran and the conduct of the Prophet is tolerance of those with belief-systems different from one's own, a tolerance grounded in a consciousness of the Reality which transcends all systems of belief, one's own included, but which is also mysteriously present in the depths of each human soul. Authentic dialogue emerges in the measure that this presence of God in all human beings is respected. For Muslims living at a time when the alternative to dialogue is not just diatribe but violent clash, the imperative of highlighting that which unites the different religions, of upholding and promoting the common spiritual patrimony of mankind, is of the utmost urgency. As we have seen, there is ample evidence in the Quranic text itself, and in the compelling commentaries on these verses by those most steeped in the spiritual tradition of Islam, to demonstrate that the Quran not only provides us with a universal vision of religion, and thus with the means to contemplate all revealed religions as "signs" of God, but also opens up paths of creative, con-structive dialogue between the faithful of all the different religious communities, despite their divergent belief-systems. It provides us with the basis for dialogue and mutual enrichment on aspects of religious life and thought that go beyond the outward forms of belief, yielding fruit in the fertile fields of metaphysical insight, immutable values, contemplative inspiration, and spiritual realization. The Metaphysics of Interfaith Dialogue, Reza Shah-Kazemi.

We might consider acting upon one or more of the following important documents that have already been developed; A Universal Declaration of a Global Ethic; the U.N. Universal Declaration of Human Rights; the Cairo Declaration on Human Rights.

It would seem to me that the real issue is that 'terrorism'is a problem no matter who carries it out, and that is a problem we all face and need to work towards solving. Our voice needs to be louder - but it cannot be just a Muslim voice - it must be a combined voice of all people of faith who unite for the sake of peace and justice.

Terrorism like any other criminal behaviour, is the sole responsibility of those committing the acts, not of the religion or the people with which they happen to be associated. However, since the terrorists are using religion as an excuse, all of us who hold our faiths dear become obligated to counter their false claims with the truth.

We need to be certain that the expression of justice and compassion is for all victims of violence - and that the same standards are applied to all. We must expose the roots of violence and hatred and reject exclusivist ideologies that privilege one group over another.

Jews, Muslims, and Christians agree that God is one - Creator of the Universe. We have much in common and on which we agree - and much that we disagree about - and that causes us too often to look at each other with suspicion and mistrust. Abraham - the friend of God - is spiritually the shared ancestor of half the people alive today - Jews, Christians and Muslims. Abraham is a defining figure - our common patriarch, - a source of inspiration, - and sadly through much of our shared history a source of argument, bloodshed, persecution and suffering. In the story of Abraham we can find justification for continued suspicion and mistrust, or we can find in Abraham the point of contact, the cornerstone for a new relationship.

Abraham is discussed in the Torah, in the New Testament and in the Qur'an, but the stories often disagree even on basic points - we have what may be seen as competing traditions. The story of Abraham offering his son to God is remembered on Rosh Hoshonah, at Easter and on Id al-Adha - one of the two holiest days of the year for Muslims. Abraham was one man - but our varied understandings of the man and his story and the fact that each of us has maintained that Abraham is ours alone has led to tragic family fights on a grand scale - over the inheritance of Abraham.

The Torah tells us that Abrahams legacy is that through his descendants God will bless the nations of the world.

The New Testament tells us in John 8:39 that if we were Abraham's children we would do the works of Abraham.

The Qur'an tells us in chapter 11:118 that if our Lord had so pleased, He would have made humanity one community. And further in 2:147-148 that "The truth is from your Lord, so do not be one of the doubters. Each community has a direction to which it turns, so compete with one another in doing good works. Wherever you may be, God will bring you all together, for God has power over all things."

We have forgotten the legacy of Abraham - forgotten that to be blessed and to be a blessing we must be like Abraham and compete only in doing good and we have not been much of a blessing to the world. From the time of Isaac and Ishmael until today we have fought over Abraham and his heritage. Perhaps we can find a way through dialogue and building relationships to bring reconciliation - even Isaac and Ishmael reconciled and came together to bury Abraham. Perhaps we – Abraham's unruly children can do the same.

We are all witnesses to the faith of Abraham in our own communities - and as in a court of law - no two witnesses agree on all the details - we can agree to disagree.

Pope John Paul II visited Jerusalem in 2000 and left a prayer written on a piece of paper in a crack in the Western Wall:

God of our fathers, you chose Abraham and his descendants to bring your name to the nations. We are deeply saddened by the behaviour of those who in the course of history have caused these children of yours to suffer. And asking your forgiveness, we wish to commit ourselves to genuine brotherhood with the people of the covenant.

If the children of Abraham would compete in doing good and struggling against injustice and misery we could truly be a blessing for this world - and regain our shared legacy from Abraham.

Let us pray to God to enlighten and guide us.

"We do not have to look far to see the need for interfaith dialogue. Perhaps first we must look at our interfaith relations before we can even have dialogue. ... The modern world is pushing us out of our normal isolated and separated lives into contact with others who do not think as we do. Nowhere is this more pronounced than in the religious realm. The attack on the World Trade Center by people who claimed to be acting with a religious purpose has forced religion to the center of discussion. ... However, religion usually is not in the news for the purpose of quiet discussion about God, but rather the background matter for political statements and corresponding actions. ... The whole world has to look at the religious thought and standards by which we act. Self identity and nationalism are easily manipulated by political and religious leaders in order to move people in the directions they want. The present situation is so excitable that it does not even need further agitation to cause problems. ..." Saying "Amen", Rev. Emmett Barnes.

When we close our hearts to others, our eyes are closed to see the beauty of God in them. The message of Islam, Judaism, Christianity and all other religions is one of love and service to others. ... If God decides to care and love and feed even those who deny his existence, then who are we to deprive someone else of our love just because he is of different color or speaks a different language or is born in a different country or prays to the same God but in a different direction, using different words? We must try to transcend the barriers among humans so that we break the barriers between humans and God. We must see ourselves in others and we must see God in each of us. We must love others in order to be loved by God, and we must enter into surrender peacefully, willingly and wholeheartedly. We Must Love Others to Be Loved By God, Dr. Shahid Athar.

Rabbi Jonathan Sacks, Chief Rabbi of the United Hebrew Congregations of the British Commonwealth, has stated,

Nothing has proved harder in civilization than seeing God or good or dignity in those unlike ourselves. There are surely many ways of arriving at that generosity of spirit, and each faith may need to find its own way. I propose that the truth at the heart of monotheism is that God is greater than religion, that God is only partially comprehended by any one faith? What would such a faith be like? It would be like being secure in my own home and yet moved by the beauty of a foreign place knowing that while it is not my home, it is still part of the glory of the world that is ours. It would be knowing that we are sentences in the story of our people but that there are other stories, each written by God out of the letters of lives bound together in community. Those who are confident of their faith are not threatened but enlarged by the different faiths of others. In the midst of our multiple insecurities, we need now the confidence to recognize the irreducible, glorious dignity of difference. Clash of Civilizations or Opportunity for Dialogue? David Smock.

"Reality is the only thing we have that can possibly nourish hope. Hope is not based on the ability to fabricate a better future; it is grounded in the ability to remember with new understanding an equally difficult past either our own or someone else's. The fact is that our memories are the seedbed of our hope. They are the only things we have that prove to us that whatever it was we ever before thought would crush us to the grave, would trample our spirits into perpetual dust, would fell us in our tracks, had actually been survived. And if that is true, then whatever we are wrestling with now can also be surmounted. ... Hope lies in the memory of God's previous goodness to us in a world that is both bountiful and harsh. The God who created this world loves it and us in it, but at the price of our own effort, at the cost of our own craving for more of the vision, more of the depth, more of the truth of the life. The God who made this world has blessed it with good things, yes but all of them take working at, coconuts need to be cracked, soil needs to be tilled, mountains need to be climbed, water needs to be conserved. God does not do this for us. God simply companions us as we go. God has given us in this unfinished world a glimpse of eternity and walks with us through here to there, giving us possibility, giving us hope. ... The proofs of eternal rebirth are everywhere. Spring comes every year. Dawn comes every morning. Love happens out of hate. Birth absorbs the pain of death. And people everywhere look to Nirvana, to enlightenment, to reincarnation, to resurrection in the hope of eternal renewal. To the Christian, both the crucifixion and the resurrection of Jesus we see as proof of God's will for the world, and in the Paschal Mystery the demonstration of the cycle of struggle." Hope is a Choice, Joan Chittister, and O.S.B.

And, in the process of getting real we need to focus on the only dimension that has a chance of helping us regain our equilibrium - the spiritual dimension.

Somehow we need to find a way of coalescing our mutual desire to do better so that together we can give voice to our need to, bring light to our hearts instead of vengeance; pray instead of beating war drums, ad to send love into the world to fill it with healing, caring, and kindness, rather than the current anger that will only continue to increase the darkness and Godless, soulless actions. If we were all to focus the enormous energy of our shared sorrow about our current predicament into building a better world, we could accomplish something......... We keep making the same mistakes over and over, and one of the most dangerous of these mistakes has been to define the problem by its manifestations rather than its causes. The root cause is a spiritual void.

"A movement toward a progressive politics of meaning has clearly begun. It is a movement that does not require a specific belief in God, much less a belief in the orthodox versions of the major religions. It does, however, rest upon the conviction that a satisfactory human life requires more than the accumulation of material goods, especially when those goods are held by a tiny minority of the human population. As Rabbi Lerner expressed it, "The deepest human desires, the desires for loving connection for transcendent meaning to life, and for peace and justice, not for ourselves but for others are rooted in what we call a spiritual conception of the world." This same notion is expressed very well in the Quranic verse, And the word of your Lord is fulfilled and perfected in Truth and Justice. [Surah Al An'am 6:115]A Review of the NSP Conference on Spiritual Activism, Shakh Kabir Helminski.

Instead of a violent World War III, I would hope to see a Spiritual battle, a battle for hearts and minds. This would be the greatest jihad a spiritual war the war within. In this counter vision of war, the goals would be to see, compassion wins the war over anger; forgiveness wins the war over revenge; intelligence wins the war over passive acceptance; truth wins the war over lies; love wins the war over hatred; creativity wins the war over continuing on a well worn and tired path of endless violence. The only way this can happen is if there is a real coming together of our spiritual brothers and sisters across the globe from heart to heart and spirit to spirit and mind to mind to end the madness of fighting and create a different world of higher vibration, values, hopes and reality.

"What we need today is more positive models and less conflict-ridden ones. We need healing, justice and forgiveness, both globally and at home. We need to put forth restorative concepts of justice. Restorative justice aims at healing the victim, the family of the victim and the community at large. It requires, for example, reparation and participation. It does not focus only on the offender or on retribution. It is this kind of justice that our faiths advocate. (3) Unfortunately, we have fallen short of this kind of justice and consequently ended up with a world full of conflict. So, we need to change." Islam and Global Conflict, Azizah al-Hibri.

"Most people want to live in a different world, but most are very skeptical that such a world is possible. They have been so deeply indoctrinated into a depressive belief that no one else will ever respond to the vision of the good to which they themselves resonate, they have become so deeply committed to the alleged truth that everyone else is either too stupid or too evil to ever transcend the materialism and selfishness that governs this society, that they effectively remain cheerleaders for the very cynical realism that they simultaneously despise. It is this duality in people, the desire for spiritual transcendence and the despair about its possibility in the case of the Other, which presents the central challenge for a Politics of Meaning. Undermining that depressive resignation will take incredible levels of creativity, psychological sensitivity, spiritual awareness, and political courage. Why America Needs a Spiritual Left, Rabbi Michael Lerner.

In response, many of us are struggling to create new forms of community—renewing Christianity, Judaism, Islam, Buddhism, etc. to see each other and all life-forms as part of our community. The project of renewal means digesting some transformative aspects of Modernity (the equality of women and men, democracy, full respect for other life-giving cultures and traditions) and integrating them into the older traditions. The result will be, is already becoming, something new—yet bearing deep identity with each of the older traditions. The Dance of God in Our Theology and Action, Rabbi Arthur Waskow.

Dr. Aslam Adullah's words bear repeating "The most effective voice to control violence is the voice of forgiveness. It is a voice that can make a definite change in the lives of people if it is raised from the pulpits of religious institutions. The religious leadership must raise this voice if it truly wants to serve God." as do Dr. Robert Crane's words, "Our task is not merely to stop evil, which can't be done, but to promote good, which can over some it, if God is willing."

We need heroes to lead the way. But, if we think about who are really our heroes and heroines, who are the people we would really like to trade places with. This may tell us something about ourselves. How many of our real heroes represent something worthwhile? ... We do give a sort of false honor to a few worthwhile individuals who obviously embody in their actions those qualities and beliefs we say we value. But it is an honor that doesn't demand that we see them as role models for our own behaviour. We see them as so far above and different from "normal" people that we don't feel we need to try to be like them. This actually degrades and dishonors their purpose because a hero is meant to be an inspiration for us, an example of possibilities. The whole point is that they are normal people, no better or worse than any of us. When we see them as somehow innately superior, paranormal, as if there is a certain percentage of humanity who are born with a gene for heroism, we take away their heroism. After all, what would be heroic about doing what comes naturally?

Heroism must be an effort, a struggle, and an act of courage, of overcoming limitations, of "doing" in spite of these human limitations. ... In fact, if we are being really honest we would have to admit that if someone in our own family were to consider leading such a life or following their example, we would at the very least try to talk them out of their "idealism". In normal life the real world, the trait of idealism, the person of the idealist, has become the object of insults and suspicion. Idealism has come to be seen as the opposite of realism. We do like to have a few idealists around as token "good guys" to make us feel better about ourselves. But not too many of them are demanding that we change. We are willing to support them in their personal sacrifice and efforts, even send money, as long as they are the ones making the sacrifices. But when they begin to demand that we change, they are almost certain to become martyrs. Can We Get Along, Sheila Musaji.

Individual commitment, idealism, if you will, is a powerful force. We can make a difference. Individuals don't have to be merely pawns. Most individuals may be merely carried along by the forces of history—but the forces that shape history are also the product of individuals. Whatever reforms are made, however our systems are redefined, whichever ideology will dominate and shape the future, whatever movements develop will be started by individuals.

We may choose not to make a stand to play it safe but that choice at this moment in history will only mean that we will be carried along with whatever movements and systems are now developed or redefined to fill the current vacuum. And, that vacuum will be filled. Because some individual or collection of individuals will step forward to guide and lead society in one direction or another from this crossroads. Whether or not that force will be for good or for evil depends on who steps forward and what they stand for.

If you think that this can't apply to you because you are not important enough or rich enough or intelligent enough, or any other limitation or excuse you can come up with remember what Martin Luther King said:

"Everybody can be great because anybody can serve. You don't have to have a college degree to serve. You don't have to make your subject and your verb agree to serve. You don't have to know Einstein's Theory of Relativity to serve. You don't have to know the second theory of thermodynamics in physics to serve. You only need a heart full of grace. A soul generated by love."

Look inside yourself to see what it is that you do best, what is your God given talent. Then look outside yourself to see where that talent can best be put to use.

Our various paths have led us to the crossroads where we now stand and where we now have to face our future together. Whether or not you participate, or watch from the sidelines, you will be affected by the direction history moves from this crossroads.

We should begin now to make contacts, to join with others and to work together to find positive solutions to injustices rather than to continue condemning the injustices that come from all sides in the present breakdown of civilization. (Dr. Robert D. Crane).

We need to work together on some projects that can help to bring us through this crisis.

The globalization of Spirit requires that we overcome the false dichotomy between changing our selves and changing societal structures. At times we may be inclined to say, "I need to work on my own head first, then later I'll try to change society." But this strategy can be the beginning of a slippery slope toward narcissistic self-absorption, just as the "I'll change society first and then worry about inner life" strategy can be a slippery slope to the insensitivity and spiritual obtuseness of most contemporary political movements. Emancipators spirituality encourages a living synthesis of individual and social transformation. ... No amount of social change can replace attention to one's inner life. The fruits of social change won't last if they're implemented by people who are out of touch with their own spiritual dimension—and the change won't ever be achieved, because most people eventually drop out of social change movements before they've achieved their goals because they are so lacking in nourishment for the soul. At the same time, no amount of inner enlightenment can adequately nourish a spiritual life if one's day is drenched in soul-destroying social realities. ... So where do we start? Both places with spiritual practice in our own lives and with attempts to transform the world of work and other aspects of our political, economic and social institutions.

Because peace as both the absence of violence and the presence of justice for all humans is the necessary condition for the complete development of the full humanity of all humans, individually and communally, all individuals and communities should strive constantly to further the growth of peace on all levels, personal, interpersonal, local, regional, national and international, granting that; a) the necessary basis of peace is justice for all concerned; b) violence is to be vigorously avoided, being resorted to only when its absence would cause a greater evil; c) when peace is ruptured, all efforts should be bent to its rapid restoration—on the necessary basis of justice for all. At the same time, it should be recognized that peace, like liberty, is a positive value which should be constantly cultivated, and therefore all individuals and communities should make the necessary prior efforts not only to avoid its break-down but also to strengthen its steady development and growth. From a Universal Declaration of a Global Ethic.

For example, putting together an interfaith statement—a Declaration of Interdependence — that suicide bombing as well as all other forms of terrorism are completely unlawful in ALL circumstances. No matter what the provocation, terrorism is not the solution and no matter what supposed religious justification is offered, it is unacceptable. There are transcendent religious values and they honor no exceptions to cover what are criminal acts, and all such criminal acts will be labeled what they are no matter who they are carried out by or where they originate. Hirabah and terrorism require universal condemnation.

We need to declare our intolerance for all political violence - we cannot win a "war" on terrorism no matter how much the "experts" recommend more bombing and to turn away from the current "solutions."

"These experts perhaps mean well. They want to do something to make America safe, instead of giving sermons to evil perpetrators. But they ignore the laws of motion, especially Sir Isaac Newton's law of reciprocal actions. The law states: Whenever one body exerts force upon a second body, the second body exerts an equal and opposite force upon the first body. In popular vernacular, this law is also known as "for every action there is an equal and opposite reaction." Osama bin Laden has translated Newton's law into his own words, "If you bomb our cities, we will bomb yours." Morality, Terrorism and the Laws of Motion, By Liaquat Ali Khan.

If your heart has turned away from something, eventually your face also will turn away. This existence is one unified field. Eventually, the body's electromagnetic field will physicalize into a movement of muscles and limbs away from what is futile. When Musa, 'alayhi-s-salam, came to the pharonic state and found the people taken in by despotism aided by magic, he could not accept it. He advocated instead the worship of the one and only Reality. He then moved away from the oppression, taking his people with him. The Prophet 'Isa, 'alayhi-s-salam, came to revive what Musa had brought, and he also turned away, revolting against the dominant values. ... Man wants longevity and has invested in cultural habits and traditions, which oppose the imposition of the prophetic message. The message is bound to be opposed. ... Revolution is an essential meaning of qalb. If, however, we do not leave the state of foolishness and indiscrimination, we will equate revolution with an outer havoc not based upon an inner reality. If the revolution is a real one, it will not cause outer havoc. The revolutions of the Prophets and the awliya (friends of Allah) were the most peaceful revolutions. Muhammad, salla-ilahu 'alayhi wa alihi wa sallam, did not wage war, he only defended himself as a last resort. Qalaba; The Turning of the Heart, Shaikh Fadhlallah Haeri.

Interfaith initiatives will not be successful unless toleration and religious liberty are explicitly recognized as fundamental human rights. We need to speak out against all expressions of religious bigotry whether by Muslims, Christians, or Jews.

Religious leaders must do more than condemn injustice and violence; they must stress in their sermons how we can turn moral indignation into a positive force to change the world without resorting to violence.

The Cordoba Initiative is a multi-faith organization whose objective is to heal the relationship between the Islamic World and America. Working through civil dialogue, policy initiatives, education, and cultural programs, the Initiative focuses on Thought, Action and Outcomes. ... For hundreds of years during the middle Ages, Cordoba was the capital of Muslim Spain. During its "golden age" from the 8th to 12th centuries, the Cordoba Caliphate witnessed a great flowering of culture, art, and philosophical inquiry amid a remarkable climate of religious tolerance. Religious freedom, although not perfect, was sufficient that many Jewish and Christian intellectuals were attracted to Cordoba, where they lived, wrote and flourished side by side with their Muslim counterparts in a strikingly pluralistic society. The largest of Cordoba's 70 libraries was believed to contain 400,000 volumes, making it vastly larger than anything else in Europe at the time.

"Somewhere, in all of these stirrings, I see the seeds of a wisdom-based, Earth-honoring, pro-democracy movement—one that affirms and applauds religious and spiritual impulses, while opposing fundamentalism, chauvinism and theocracy. Over time, this kind of progressive movement has the potential to win—and win big—in the United States. To be honest; it is probably the only type of progressive movement that stands a chance in a country as religious as ours. ... Such a movement is within reach. But progressives must abandon the old pattern of reducing the Great Faiths to their worst elements, constituents and crimes—and then dismissing all other facts and features. It is not just stupid political strategy. At a moral level, it is a form of blindness and bigotry that is beneath all of us." The Religious Left Fights Back, By Van Jones.

"Rabbi Lerner invites American Muslims to join with him in creating the Network of Spiritual Progressives, an organization which seeks to challenge the misuse of God and the Bible by the Christian Right, the hostility toward religion and spirituality by some sections of the liberal and progressive culture of the Left, and the materialism and selfishness of consumer culture in America. 1,200 people attended the first of two founding conferences, and Rabbi Lerner wishes to increase the percentage of Muslim participation in the founding of this enterprise.

Ramadan Meets Rosh Hashanah and Assisi, Oct 3, 2005 - In October of 2005, the Muslim holy month of Ramadan and the Jewish holy month of Tishrei (which begins with Rosh Hashanah) will coincide. ... This confluence offers us an extraordinary moment for interweaving our celebrations in these three traditions - Judaism, Christianity, and Islam - the families of Abraham. ... We are tottering on the precipice of religious and civilizational war. God has given us a special gift to help us step away from the cliff; The gift of the time and time to help us walk hand-in-hand, listening to the Spirit alongside each other.

We are members of the families of Abraham - Muslims, Christians, and Jews. Our traditions teach us to have compassion, seek justice, and pursue peace for all peoples. We bear especially deep concern for the region where

Abraham learned and taught, journeyed and flourished. Today that region is known as the greater Middle East - from Iraq, where Abraham grew up, to Israel and Palestine, where he sojourned. Today our hearts are broken by the violence poured out upon the peoples of that region. That violence has included the occupation of Palestinian lands by Israel and of Iraq by the United States; terrorist attacks on Americans, Israelis, Iraqis, and others by various Palestinian and Iraqi groups and by Al Qaeda; the torture of prisoners by several different police forces, military forces, and governments in the region. ... From our heartbreak at these destructive actions, we intend to open our hearts more fully to each other and to the suffering of all peoples. In the name of the One God Whom we all serve and celebrate, we condemn all these forms of violence. To end the present wars and to take serious steps toward the peace that all our traditions demand of us, we call on governments and on the leaders of all religious and cultural communities to act. We urge the US government to set a firm and speedy date, preferably no later than December 1, 2004, for completing the safe return home from Iraq of all Americans under military control or contract so that Hanukkah, Christmas, and Eid el Adha can actually be celebrated as festivals of peace. We urge the UN to work directly with Iraqi political groupings to transfer power in Iraq to an elected government.

We urge the UN, the US, the European Union, and Russia to convene a comprehensive peace conference through which the governments of Israel, the Palestinian Authority, Iran, and all Arab states conclude a full diplomatic, economic, and cultural peace with Israel and Palestine, defined approximately on the 1967 boundaries, with small mutual adjustments. We urge the international community to work out lawful and effective means to deal with the dangers of international terrorism, the spread of nuclear and similar weapons, and conflicts over the control of oil and water. We ourselves will act to create transnational and interfaith networks of Jews, Christians, and Muslims who will covenant together - to insist that governments take these steps, to undertake whatever nonviolent actions are necessary to prevent more violence and achieve a just peace throughout the region, and to grow grass-roots relationships that bind together those who have been enemies into a Compassionate Coalition. According to tradition, Abraham kept his tent open in all four directions, the more easily to share his food and water with travelers from anywhere. In that spirit, we welcome all those who thirst and hunger for justice, peace, and dignity."

O mankind, truly We have created you male and female, and have made you nations and tribes that ye may know one another. Truly the most noble of you, in the sight of God, is the most God-conscious (49:13). For every community (of faith) We have appointed ways of worship, which they aught to observe. Hence, do not let those (who follow other ways) draw you into dispute on this score, but summon them to their Sustainer: for you are on the right way. And if they argue with you, say, God knows best what you are doing (22:67).

Truly those who believe, and the Jews, and the Christians, and the Sabaeans whoever believes in God and the Last Day and performs virtuous deeds surely their reward is with their Sustainer, and no fear shall come upon them, neither shall they grieve (2:62).

It was we who revealed the Torah; therein was guidance and light. By its standard the Jewish people have been judged by the Prophets who surrendered to God's will, as well as by the Rabbis and the doctors of Law, for to them the protection of God's book was entrusted: If any do fail to judge by what God has revealed (including the Torah), they are (no better than) unbelievers (5:44). We ordained for the Children of Israel that if anyone slew a person unless it be for murder or for spreading mischief in the land, it would be as if he slew all of humanity; and if anyone saved a life it would be as if he saved the life of all of humanity (5:32). We ordained therein for them; "A life for a life, an eye for an eye, a nose for a nose, an ear for an ear, a tooth for a tooth and equivalence in harm done." But if anyone by way of charity foregoes that retaliation, it is an act of atonement for him. And if any fail to judge by what God has revealed they are wrongdoers (5:45).

And in their footsteps We sent Jesus, the son of Mary, confirming the law that had come before him; We sent him the Gospel: and therein was guidance and light and confirmation of the law that had come before him; a guidance and an admonition to those who are conscious of God (5:45-46). To Jesus, the son of Mary, We gave clear signs and strengthened him with the Holy Spirit (2:253).

O you who keep the faith! When you go abroad in the way of God, be clear and circumspect and say not to anyone who offers you a greeting of peace: "You are not a believer!" (4:94). Tsso each community among you, we have prescribed a Law and a way of life. If God had so willed, He would have made you a single people, but His plan is to test you in what He has given you, so strive as in a race in all virtues. The goal of you all is to God; it is He that will show you the truth of the matters in which you differ (5:48).

And do not argue with the followers of earlier revelations except in the gentlest manner (29:46). Goodness and Evil cannot be equal. Repel Evil with something better, then the one who hated you will become your friend and intimate! And no one will be granted such goodness except those who exercise patience and self-restraint, none but persons of the greatest good fortune. And when the Evil One incites discord, seek refuge in God. He is the One Who hears and knows all things (41:34). And the servants of the Infinitely Compassionate are those who walk on the earth in humility and when the ignorant accost them, they only reply "Peace." (25:65).

Let there be no compulsion in religion. Truth stands out clearly from error; whoever rejects evil and has faith in God has grasped the most trustworthy, unfailing handhold. And God hears and knows all things. God is the Protector of those who have faith, from the depths of darkness. He will lead them forth into light (2:256-257).

And, I would add:

"But if they incline to peace, you also incline to it, and (put your) trust in God. Verily, He is the All-Hearer, the All-Knower" Qur'an 8:61

In the absence of the voices of hope, moderation and forgiveness, the voices of division are left to howl for the blood of our children. We need to speak out loudly and clearly and turn us away from the precipice. I call on our Muslim, Christian and Jewish religious leaders to come together, join with groups such as Rabbi Lerner's Network of Spiritual Progressives, and work to make your voices heard not only in our local communities but in the greater community of man.

Bibliography

Abraham, A. J. *Islamic Fundamentalism and the Doctrine of Jihad*. Lima, OH: Wyndham Hall Press, 2002.

AbuKhalil, As'ad. *Bin Laden, Islam, and America's New 'War on Terrorism'*. Open Media Pamphlet Series. New York: Seven Stories Press, 2002.

Ahmed, Nafeez Mosaddwq. *The War on Truth: 9/11, Disinformation and the Anatomy of Terrorism*. Northampton, MA: Olive Branch Press, 2005.

Aho, James. *Politics of Righteousness: Idaho Christian Patriotism*. Seattle, WA: University of Washington Press, 1995.

Alexander, Yonah. *European Terrorism Today & Tomorrow*. Brassey's Terrorism Library. Washington, DC: Brassey's, 1992.

Alexander, Yonah. *Middle East Terrorism: Current Threats and Future Prospects*. International Library of Terrorism; 5. New York: G.K. Hall & Co., 1994.

Alexander, Yonah. *Middle East Terrorism: Selected Group Profiles*. Washington, DC: Jewish Institute for National Security Affairs, 1994.

Alexander, Yonah. *Palestinian Religious Terrorism: Hamas and Islamic Jihad*. New York: Transnational, 2002.

Alexander, Yonah. *Palestinian Secular Terrorism: Profiles of Fatah, Popular Front for the Liberation of Palestine, Popular Front for the Liberation of Palestine-General Command, and Democratic Front for the Liberation of Palestine*. New York: Transnational, 2003.

Alexander, Yonah. *Terrorism in Europe*. New York: St. Martin's Press, 1982.

Alexander, Yonah. *Usama bin Laden's al-Qaida: Profile of a Terrorist Network*. Ardsley, NY: Transnational Publishers, 2001.

Alexander, Yonah; Latter, Richard, editors, *Terrorism and the Media: Dilemmas for Government, Journalists and the Public*. Washington, DC: Brassey's, 1990.

Al-Khattar, Aref M. *Religion and Terrorism: An Interfaith Perspective*. Westport, CT: Praeger, 2003.

Anderson, Chris. *The Billy Boy: The Life and Death of LVF Leader Billy Wright*. Edinburgh: Mainstream, 2002.

Anderson, Sean. *Terrorism: Assassins to Zealots*. Lanham, MD: Scarecrow Press, 2003.

Anti-Defamation League, *Extremism in the Name of Religion: The Violent Record of the Kahane Movement and Its Offshoots*. New York: ADL, 1995.

Anti-Defamation League, *Extremism in the Name of Religion: The Violent Legacy of Meir Kahane and Its Offshoots*. Update. New York: ADL, 1995.

Anti-Defamation League, *Extremism on the Right: A Handbook*. New York: Anti-Defamation League, 1988.

Appleby, R. Scott. *Ambivalence of the Sacred: Religion, Violence, and Reconciliation*. Lanham, MD: Rowman & Littlefield Publishers, 2000.

Arostegui, Martin C. *Twilight Warriors: Inside the World's Special Forces*. London: Bloomsbury Publishing, 1995.

Ateneo Center for Asian Studies, *Before and After September 11, 2001: An Asian Perspective*. Quezon City: Ateneo de Manila University Press, 2005.

Avruch, Kevin. *Culture and Conflict Resolution*. Washington, DC: United States Institute of Peace, 1998.

Bar, Shmuel. *Warrant for Terror: Fatwas of Radical Islam and the Duty of Jihad*. Hoover Studies in Politics, Economics, and Society. Lanham, MD: Rowman & Littlefield, 2006.

Bartholomeusz, Tessa J. *Buddhist Fundamentalism and Minority Identities in Sri Lanka*. New York: State University of New York Press, 1998.

Barton, Greg. *Indonesia's Struggle: Jemaah Islamiyah and the Soul of Islam*. Sydney, Australia: University of New South Wales Press, 2004.

Cateura, Linda Brandi. *Voices of American Muslims: 23 Profiles*. New York: Hippocrene Books, 2005.

Catholic Institute for International Relations, *Guatemala, Never Again*. Maryknoll, NY: Orbis Books, 1999.

Davies, Barry. *Terrorism: Inside a World Phenomenon*. London: Virgin Books, 2003.

Devji, Faisal. *Landscapes of the Jihad: Militancy, Morality, Modernity*. Ithaca, NY: Cornell University Press, 2005.

Devji, Mantoshe Singh. *The Mad Messiah: Osama bin Laden and the Seeds of Terror*. Scottsdale, AZ: Inkwell Productions, 2002. Emerson, Steven. *American Jihad: The Terrorists Living Among Us*. New York: Free Press, 2002.

Emerson, Steven. *Worldwide Jihad Movement: Militant Islam's Target the West*. Jerusalem, Israel: Institute of the World Jewish Congress, 1995.

Eriksson, Tore. *11th March 2004 Madrid Terrorist Attacks: Observation Report*. Karlstad, Sweden: Swedish Rescue Services Agency, 2006.

Ernst, Carl W. *Following Muhammad: Rethinking Islam in the Contemporary World*. Chapel Hill, NC: University of North Carolina Press, 2003.

Esposito, John L. *Islam: The Straight Path*. 3rd edition. New York: Oxford University Press, 1998.

Esposito, John L. *The Islamic Threat: Myth or Reality?*. New York: Oxford University Press, 1992.

Esposito, John L. *The Oxford Dictionary of Islam*. New York: Oxford University Press, 2003.

Esposito, John L. *Unholy War: Terror in the Name of Islam*. New York: Oxford University Press, 2002.

Etzioni, Amitai. *How Patriotic is the Patriot Act? Freedom Versus Security in the Age of Terrorism*. New York: Routledge, 2004.

Fandy, Mamoun. *Saudi Arabia and the Politics of Dissent*. New York: Palgrave, 2001.

Farah, Douglas. *Blood From Stones: The Secret Financial Network of Terror*. New York: Broadway Books, 2004.

Gardell, Mattias. *Gods of the Blood: The Pagan Revival and White Separatism*. Durham, NC: Duke University Press, 2003.

Gerges, Fawaz A. *The Far Enemy: Why Jihad Went Global*. New York: Cambridge University Press, 2005.

Habeck, Mary R. *Knowing the Enemy: Jihadist Ideology and the War on Terror*. New Haven, NY: Yale University Press, 2006.

Han, Henry H., editor. *Terrorism & Political Violence: Limits & Possibilities of Legal Control*. Terrorism (Oceana Publications, inc.) ; 2nd series. New York: Oceana, 1993.

Hiro, Dilip. *War Without End: The Rise of Islamist Terrorism and Global Response*. New York: Routledge, 2002.

Hoffman, Bruce. *Holy terror: The Implications of Terrorism Motivated by a Religious Imperative*. Santa Monica, CA: RAND, 1993.

Howard, Russell D. *Defeating Terrorism: Shaping the New Security Environment*. Guilford, CT: McGraw-Hill, 2004.

Huband, Mark. *Warriors of the Prophet: the Struggle for Islam*. Boulder, CO: Westview Press, 1999.

Hudson, Rex A. *Who Becomes a Terrorist and Why: The 1999 Government Report on Profiling Terrorists*. Guilford, CT: Lyon Press, 2002.

Jaber, Hala. *Hezbollah: Born with a Vengeance*. New York: Columbia University Press, 1997.

Jacquard, Roland. *In the Name of Osama bin Laden: Global Terrorism & the bin Laden Brotherhood*. Durham, NC: Duke University Press, 2002.

Jaimoukha, Amjad M. *The Chechens: A Handbook*. New York: Routledge Curzon, 2005.

Karawan, Ibrahim. *Islamic Impasse*. New York: Oxford University Press, 1997.

MacArthur, John. *Terrorism, Jihad, and the Bible: A Response to the Terrorist Attacks*. Nashville, TN: W Publishing Group, 2001.

Lutz, James M. *Global Terrorism*. New York: Routledge, 2004.

Maley, William. *Fundamentalism Reborn?: Afghanistan and the Taliban*. New York: New York University Press, 2001.

Miniter, Richard. *Losing Bin Laden: How Bill Clinton's Failures Unleashed Global Terror*. Washington, DC: Regnery, 2003.

Mishal, Shaul. *The Palestinian Hamas: Vision, Violence, and Coexistence*. New York: Columbia University Press, 2000.

Napoleoni, Loretta. *Modern Jihad: Tracing the Dollars Behind the Terror Networks*. Sterling, VA: Pluto Press, 2003.

Noorani, A. G. *Islam & Jihad: Prejudice versus Reality*. New York: Zed Books, 2002.

Nusse, Andrea. *Muslim Palestine: The Ideology of Hamas*. Amsterdam: Harwood Academic Publishers, 1998.

O'Ballance, Edgar. *Islamic Fundamentalist Terrorism, 1979-95: The Iranian Connection*. Washington Square, NY: New York University Press, 1997.

O'Ballance, Edgar. *Islamic Fundamentalist Terrorism: 1979-95*. Basingstoke: Macmillan, 1997.

Ojeda, Auriana. *Islamic Fundamentalism*. San Diego, CA: Greenhaven Press, 2003.

O'Kane, Rosemary. *Revolutionary Reign of Terror: the Role of Violence in Political Change*. Brookfield, VT: Elgar, 1991.

Rana, Muhammad Amir. *A to Z of Jehadi Organizations in Pakistan*. Lahore: Mashal Books, 2004.

Randal, Jonathan C. *Osama: The Making of a Terrorist*. New York: Knopf, 2004.

Rapoport, David C. *The Rationalization of Terrorism*. Frederick, MD: University Publications of America, 1982.

Scheuer, Michael. *Through Our Enemies Eyes: Osama bin Laden, Radical Islam, and the Future of America*. Rev. ed., 2nd ed. Washington, DC: Potomac Books, 2006.

Taheri, Amir. *Holy Terror: Inside the World of Islamic Terrorism*. Bethesda, MD: Adler & Adler, 1987.

Venske, Ben. *The al-Qaeda Threat: An Analytical Guide to al-Qaeda's Tactics & Targets*. Alexandria, VA: Tempest Publishing, 2003.

Waardenburg, Jacques. *Muslims and Others: Relations in Context*. New York: Walter de Gruyter, 2003.

Wiktorowicz, Quintan. *Global Jihad: Understanding September 11*. Falls Church, VA: 2002.

Zacharias, Ravi K. *Light in the Shadow of Jihad*. Sisters, OR: Multnomah Publishers, 2002.

Index

A

Abominations, 240
Al-qaeda, 135
Agents provocateurs, 50
Apocalyptic terrorist groups, 141
Apologetics, 148

B

Bible, 162, 165, 168, 171, 188, 239, 240, 254, 287
Bombings, 62, 74, 113, 135, 137, 155, 157, 159, 213, 217, 234, 244

C

Cellular structure, 126, 132
Clash of civilizations, 260
Compassionate coalition, 289
Criminal organizations, 38
Cordoba, 286

D

Dark web terror, 83
Darul Uloom, 21, 22
Deadly scenario, 84
Decapitation, 146, 147, 148, 149, 150, 151, 152, 155, 156
Denominations, 256, 257

E

Enduring terrorists, 217
Ethnic conflicts, 65

F

Faces of terrorism, 221
False bands, 51
Futuwwa, 205
Fundraising, 115

G

Globalization, 36, 38, 283
Golden age, 286
Great unifier, 12

H

Hate mongering, 261
Healing touch, 6
Hindu mujahideen, 223

I

Islamic roots, 144
Ideological cause, 32
Internal enemy, 142
Islamic terrorism, 39, 60, 228, 235, 237, 255
Islamic theology, 146, 147, 148

J

Jihad, 10, 11, 16, 22, 89, 90, 95, 97, 98, 102, 135, 136, 137, 138, 139, 140, 141, 142, 143, 144, 145, 146, 148, 152, 156, 157, 175, 176, 197, 210, 211, 212, 213, 214, 227, 229, 231, 233
Jihadists, 97, 137, 140, 141, 144
Jyllands-posten, 143
Jahiliyya, 189

M

Mitigating factors, 96
Madarasas, 21
Money laundering, 123
Mullah borjan, 55
Muslim jurisprudence, 137

N

National security, 31

O

Organized crime, 35, 36, 37, 38
Old Europe, 77

P

Paramilitaries, 110, 119, 126, 129, 130, 131
Protestant, 107, 110, 126, 129, 130, 131, 198, 247
Political conspiracy, 1
Post-cold war, 62
Pseudo-secularism, 1

R

Religion of peace, 2, 156, 235, 243

S

Samson terrorists, 183
Separatists, 34
Soviet islamists, 50, 64

T

Transnational, 37, 110, 171, 288
Triumphalism, 256, 257, 265
Transitional phase, 173

U

Utilitarian, 150, 183, 194, 228

V

Violence, 2, 3, 7, 8, 9, 22, 27, 106, 107, 108, 111, 113, 114, 144, 156, 175, 180, 204, 227, 228, 229, 230, 232

W

Westernisation, 177, 180, 183
Wisdom, 3, 9, 53, 83, 161, 168, 176, 190, 204, 271, 272, 273, 286
Westernisation of islam, 177
Worst enemies, 202, 203

Y

Yellow press, 80

Z

Zaiter, 37
Zallaqa, 151
Zealots, 29, 170, 181, 184, 199, 204
Zionist ideologue, 189